|| श्री गणेशाय नमः ||

An Astrology Book Beginner's To Advanced Complete Guide

All Rights Reserved By

Shivnath © Shinde

Dedication :

This book is dedicated to my beloved mother, Laxmi Shatrughna Shinde. Her unwavering support, love, and encouragement have been the guiding force behind my journey as an astrologer. Her wisdom, strength, and grace have inspired me to delve deeper into the mysteries of the cosmos and to share my knowledge with the world.

Mom, you have been my guiding star, illuminating my path with your unconditional love and belief in my abilities. Your unwavering faith in me has been a constant source of motivation and inspiration. This book is a tribute to your profound influence in my life and a token of gratitude for all the sacrifices you have made.

Your unwavering dedication, nurturing spirit, and innate wisdom have shaped not only my understanding of astrology but also my character as an individual. It is through your teachings and guidance that I have come to appreciate the intricate connections between celestial bodies and human existence.

Thank you, Mom, for instilling in me a passion for astrology and for being my pillar of strength throughout my journey. This book is a testament to your love and support, and it is my hope that it will serve as a source of knowledge and inspiration for others who seek to explore the depths of astrology.

With love and gratitude,

Shivnath Shatrughna Shinde

Table Of Content:

| || श्री गणेशाय नमः || 0
| All Rights Reserved By 1
| Shivnath Shinde 1
| Dedication : 2
| Table Of Content: 4
| Associations Between Planets and Various Factors: 59
| Author : 62
| About me 63
| Preface: 64
| Introduction 66
| 1. The Cosmic Symphony: Understanding the Language of the Stars 69
| Unveiling the Hidden Lagna: Correcting Birth Time Mistakes : 69
| Predicting Life Events: Vimsottari and Antara Dashas 72
| Addressing Doubts 73
| Influence of Planets from the Houses of Occupation: 73
| Planets as Lords of the Twelve Signs: 74
| Friendship and Enmity among Planets: 75
| Exaltation and Debilitation of Planets: 76
| The degrees of planets : 78
| 2. The Zodiac Tapestry: Exploring the Twelve Signs 81

The 12 houses in astrology:...............................81
The first house Description : 83
The second house Description : 85
The third house Description : 87
The fourth house Description:...........................88
The fifth house Description : 90
The sixth house Description : 92
The seventh house Description : 94
The eighth house Description : 95
The ninth house Description : 97
The tenth house Description : 99
The eleventh house Description : 100
The twelfth house Description : 102

3. Predictions of the Planets with Reference to Arise Ascendant 105
   1. Sun in Aries 105
      Sun in the 1st House (Aries):..........................105
      Sun in the 2nd House (Taurus):......................105
      Sun in the 3rd House (Gemini): 106
      Sun in the 4th House (Cancer): 106
      Sun in the 5th House (Leo):............................107
      Sun in the 6th House (Virgo): 107
      Sun in the 7th House (Libra):........................107
      Sun in the 8th House (Scorpio):.....................108
      Sun in the 9th House (Sagittarius): 108
      Sun in the 10th House (Capricorn): 108
      Sun in the 11th House (Aquarius):.................109
      Sun in the 12th House (Pisces): 109
   2. Moon in Aries..109

Moon in the 1st House (Aries): 110
Moon in the 2nd House (Taurus): 110
Moon in the 3rd House (Gemini):.....................110
Moon in the 4th House (Cancer):.....................111
Moon in the 5th House (Leo): 111
Moon in the 6th House (Virgo): 111
Moon in the 7th House (Libra): 112
Moon in the 8th House (Scorpio): 112
Moon in the 9th House (Sagittarius): 112
Moon in the 10th House (Capricorn):...............113
Moon in the 11th House (Aquarius): 113
Moon in the 12th House (Pisces):....................113
3. Mars in Aries..113
Mars in the 1st House (Aries): 114
Mars in the 2nd House (Taurus): 114
Mars in the 3rd House (Gemini):.....................114
Mars in the 4th House (Cancer):.....................115
Mars in the 5th House (Leo): 115
Mars in the 6th House (Virgo): 115
Mars in the 7th House (Libra): 115
Mars in the 8th House (Scorpio): 116
Mars in the 9th House (Sagittarius): 116
Mars in the 10th House (Capricorn):...............117
Mars in the 11th House (Aquarius): 117
Mars in the 12th House (Pisces):....................117
4. Mercury in Aries..118
Mercury in the 1st House (Aries): 118
Mercury in the 2nd House (Taurus): 118
Mercury in the 3rd House (Gemini):................119

Mercury in the 4th House (Cancer): 119
Mercury in the 5th House (Leo): 119
Mercury in the 6th House (Virgo): 120
Mercury in the 7th House (Libra): 120
Mercury in the 8th House (Scorpio): 120
Mercury in the 9th House (Sagittarius): 120
Mercury in the 10th House (Capricorn): 121
Mercury in the 11th House (Aquarius): 121
Mercury in the 12th House (Pisces): 121
5. Jupiter in Aries 122
Jupiter in the 1st House (Aries): 122
Jupiter in the 2nd House (Taurus): 122
Jupiter in the 3rd House (Gemini): 122
Jupiter in the 4th House (Cancer): 123
Jupiter in the 5th House (Leo): 123
Jupiter in the 6th House (Virgo): 123
Jupiter in the 7th House (Libra): 123
Jupiter in the 8th House (Scorpio): 124
Jupiter in the 9th House (Sagittarius): 124
Jupiter in the 10th House (Capricorn): 124
Jupiter in the 11th House (Aquarius): 124
Jupiter in the 12th House (Pisces): 125
6 . Venus in Aries 125
Venus in the 1st House (Aries): 125
Venus in the 2nd House (Taurus): 125
Venus in the 3rd House (Gemini): 126
Venus in the 4th House (Cancer): 126
Venus in the 5th House (Leo): 126
Venus in the 6th House (Virgo): 126

Venus in the 7th House (Libra): 127
Venus in the 8th House (Scorpio): 127
Venus in the 9th House (Sagittarius): 127
Venus in the 10th House (Capricorn): 127
Venus in the 11th House (Aquarius): 128
Venus in the 12th House (Pisces): 128
7. Saturn in Aries 128
Saturn in the 1st House (Aries): 128
Saturn in the 2nd House (Taurus): 128
Saturn in the 3rd House (Gemini): 129
Saturn in the 4th House (Cancer): 129
Saturn in the 5th House (Leo): 129
Saturn in the 6th House (Virgo): 130
Saturn in the 7th House (Libra): 130
Saturn in the 8th House (Scorpio): 131
Saturn in the 9th House (Sagittarius): 131
Saturn in the 10th House (Capricorn): 131
Saturn in the 11th House (Aquarius): 132
Saturn in the 12th House (Pisces): 132
8. Rahu in Aries 132
Rahu in the 1st House (Aries): 132
Rahu in the 2nd House (Taurus): 133
Rahu in the 3rd House (Gemini): 133
Rahu in the 4th House (Cancer): 133
Rahu in the 5th House (Leo): 134
Rahu in the 6th House (Virgo): 134
Rahu in the 7th House (Libra): 134
Rahu in the 8th House (Scorpio): 134
Rahu in the 9th House (Sagittarius): 135

Rahu in the 10th House (Capricorn): 135
Rahu in the 11th House (Aquarius): 135
Rahu in the 12th House (Pisces): 136
9. Ketu in Aries 136
Ketu in the 1st House (Aries): 136
Ketu in the 2nd House (Taurus): 136
Ketu in the 3rd House (Gemini): 137
Ketu in the 4th House (Cancer): 137
Ketu in the 5th House (Leo): 137
Ketu in the 6th House (Virgo): 137
Ketu in the 7th House (Libra): 138
Ketu in the 8th House (Scorpio): 138
Ketu in the 9th House (Sagittarius): 138
Ketu in the 10th House (Capricorn): 139
Ketu in the 11th House (Aquarius):..................139
Ketu in the 12th House (Pisces): 139

4. Predictions of the Planets with Reference to Taurus Ascendant 139
1.Sun in Taurus 139
Sun in the 1st House (Taurus): 139
Sun in the 2nd House (Gemini): 140
Sun in the 3rd House (Cancer): 140
Sun in the 4th House (Leo): 140
Sun in the 5th House (Virgo): 141
Sun in the 6th House (Libra): 141
Sun in the 7th House (Scorpio):.......................141
Sun in the 8th House (Sagittarius): 141
Sun in the 9th House (Capricorn): 142
Sun in the 10th House (Aquarius):...................142

Sun in the 11th House (Pisces): 142
Sun in the 12th House (Aries): 142
2. Moon 143
Moon in the 1st House (Taurus): 143
Moon in the 2nd House (Gemini): 143
Moon in the 3rd House (Cancer): 143
Moon in the 4th House (Leo): 144
Moon in the 5th House (Virgo): 144
Moon in the 6th House (Libra): 144
Moon in the 7th House (Scorpio): 144
Moon in the 8th House (Sagittarius): 144
Moon in the 9th House (Capricorn): 145
Moon in the 10th House (Aquarius): 145
Moon in the 11th House (Pisces): 145
Moon in the 12th House (Aries): 145
3. Mars 146
Mars in the 1st House (Taurus): 146
Mars in the 2nd House (Gemini): 146
Mars in the 3rd House (Cancer): 146
Mars in the 4th House (Leo): 147
Mars in the 5th House (Virgo): 147
Mars in the 6th House (Libra): 147
Mars in the 7th House (Scorpio): 148
Mars in the 8th House (Sagittarius): 148
Mars in the 9th House (Capricorn): 148
Mars in the 10th House (Aquarius): 148
Mars in the 11th House (Pisces): 149
Mars in the 12th House (Aries): 149
4. Mercury 149

Mercury in the 1st House (Taurus): 149
Mercury in the 2nd House (Gemini): 150
Mercury in the 3rd House (Cancer): 150
Mercury in the 4th House (Leo): 150
Mercury in the 5th House (Virgo): 151
Mercury in the 6th House (Libra): 151
Mercury in the 7th House (Scorpio): 151
Mercury in the 8th House (Sagittarius): 151
Mercury in the 9th House (Capricorn): 152
Mercury in the 10th House (Aquarius): 152
Mercury in the 11th House (Pisces): 152
Mercury in the 12th House (Aries): 152
5. Jupiter 153
   Jupiter in the 1st House (Taurus): 153
   Jupiter in the 2nd House (Gemini) : 153
   Jupiter in the 3rd House (Cancer): 153
   Jupiter in the 4th House (Leo): 154
   Jupiter in the 5th House (Virgo): 154
   Jupiter in the 6th House (Libra): 154
   Jupiter in the 7th House (Scorpio): 155
   Jupiter in the 8th House (Sagittarius): 155
   Jupiter in the 9th House (Capricorn): 155
   Jupiter in the 10th House (Aquarius): 156
   Jupiter in the 11th House (Pisces): 156
   Jupiter in the 12th House (Aries): 157
6. Venus 157
   Venus in the 1st House (Taurus): 157
   Venus in the 2nd House (Gemini): 157
   Venus in the 3rd House (Cancer): 158

Venus in the 4th House (Leo): 158
Venus in the 5th House (Virgo): 158
Venus in the 6th House (Libra): 159
Venus in the 7th House (Scorpio): 159
Venus in the 8th House (Sagittarius): 159
Venus in the 9th House (Capricorn): 160
Venus in the 10th House (Aquarius): 160
Venus in the 11th House (Pisces): 160
Venus in the 12th House (Aries): 161
7. Saturn 161
Saturn in the 1st House (Taurus): 161
Saturn in the 2nd House (Gemini): 161
Saturn in the 3rd House (Cancer): 162
Saturn in the 4th House (Leo): 162
Saturn in the 5th House (Virgo): 163
Saturn in the 6th House (Libra): 163
Saturn in the 7th House (Scorpio): 163
Saturn in the 8th House (Sagittarius): 164
Saturn in the 9th House (Capricorn): 164
Saturn in the 10th House (Aquarius): 164
Saturn in the 11th House (Pisces): 165
Saturn in the 12th House (Aries): 165
8. Rahu 165
Rahu in the 1st House (Taurus): 165
Rahu in the 2nd House (Gemini): 166
Rahu in the 3rd House (Cancer): 166
Rahu in the 4th House (Leo): 166
Rahu in the 5th House (Virgo): 167
Rahu in the 6th House (Libra): 167

Rahu in the 7th House (Scorpio): 168
Rahu in the 8th House (Sagittarius): 168
Rahu in the 9th House (Capricorn): 168
Rahu in the 10th House (Aquarius): 169
Rahu in the 11th House (Pisces): 169
Rahu in the 12th House (Aries): 169

9. Ketu 170
Ketu in the 1st house (Taurus): 170
Ketu in the 2nd house (Gemini): 170
Ketu in the 3rd house (Cancer): 170
Ketu in the 4th house (Leo): 170
Ketu in the 5th house (Virgo): 171
Ketu in the 6th house (Libra): 171
Ketu in the 7th house (Scorpio): 171
Ketu in the 8th house (Sagittarius): 171
Ketu in the 9th house (Capricorn): 172
Ketu in the 10th house (Aquarius): 172
Ketu in the 11th house (Pisces): 172
Ketu in the 12th house (Aries): 173

5. Gemini Ascendant Predictions for Sun in Gemini Ascendant: 174
1. Sun 174
Sun in the 1st House (Gemini): 174
Sun in the 2nd House (Cancer): 174
Sun in the 3rd House (Leo): 174
Sun in the 4th House (Virgo): 175
Sun in the 5th House (Virgo) for Gemini sign: 175
Sun in the 6th House (Scorpio): 176
Sun in the 7th House (Sagittarius): 176

Sun in the 8th House (Capricorn): 176
Sun in the 9th House (Aquarius):.....................176
Sun in the 10th House (Pisces): 177
Sun in the 11th House (Aries):.......................177
Sun in the 12th House (Taurus):......................178
2.Moon..178
Moon in the 1st H2use (Gemini): 178
Moon in the 2nd House (Cancer):.....................178
Moon in the 3rd House (Leo): 179
Moon in the 4th House (Virgo): 179
Moon in the 5th House (Libra): 179
Moon in the 6th House (Scorpio): 179
Moon in the 7th House (Sagittarius): 180
Moon in the 8th House (Capricorn):................180
Moon in the 9th House (Aquarius): 180
Moon in the 10th House (Pisces):....................180
Moon in the 11th House (Aries): 180
Moon in the 12th House (Taurus): 181
3.Mars..181
Mars in the 1st House (Gemini): 181
Mars in the 2nd House (Cancer):....................182
Mars in the 3rd House (Leo): 182
Mars in the 4th House (Virgo): 182
Mars in the 5th House (Libra): 183
Mars in the 6th House (Scorpio): 183
Mars in the 8th House (Capricorn):.................184
Mars in the 9th House (Aquarius): 184
Mars in the 10th House (Pisces):.....................184
Mars in the 11th House (Aries): 184

Mars in the 12th House (Taurus): 185
4. Mercury 185
    Mercury in the 1st House (Gemini): 185
    Mercury in the 2nd House (Cancer): 185
    Mercury in the 3rd House (Leo): 186
    Mercury in the 4th House (Virgo): 186
    Mercury in the 5th House (Libra): 186
    Mercury in the 6th House (Scorpio): 187
    Mercury in the 7th House (Sagittarius): 187
    Mercury in the 8th House (Capricorn): 187
    Mercury in the 9th House (Aquarius): 188
    Mercury in the 10th House (Pisces): 188
    Mercury in the 11th House (Aries): 188
    Mercury in the 12th House (Taurus): 189
5. Jupiter 189
    Jupiter in the 1st House (Gemini): 189
    Jupiter in the 2nd House (Cancer): 189
    Jupiter in the 3rd House (Leo): 190
    Jupiter in the 4th House (Virgo): 190
    Jupiter in the 5th House (Libra): 190
    Jupiter in the 6th House (Scorpio): 191
    Jupiter in the 7th House (Sagittarius): 191
    Jupiter in the 8th House (Capricorn): 191
    Jupiter in the 9th House (Aquarius): 192
    Jupiter in the 10th House (Pisces): 192
    Jupiter in the 11th House (Aries): 192
    Jupiter in the 12th House (Taurus): 192
6. Venus 193
    Venus in the 1st House (Gemini): 193

Venus in the 2nd House (Cancer): 193
Venus in the 3rd House (Leo): 194
Venus in the 4th House (Virgo): 194
Venus in the 5th House (Libra): 194
Venus in the 6th House (Scorpio): 194
Venus in the 7th House (Sagittarius): 195
Venus in the 8th House (Capricorn): 195
Venus in the 9th House (Aquarius): 195
Venus in the 10th House (Pisces): 196
Venus in the 11th House (Aries): 196
Venus in the 12th House (Taurus): 196

7. Saturn 197
   Saturn in the 1st House (Gemini): 197
   Saturn in the 2nd House (Cancer): 197
   Saturn in the 3rd House (Leo): 198
   Saturn in the 4th House (Virgo): 198
   Saturn in the 5th House (Libra): 198
   Saturn in the 6th House (Scorpio): 198
   Saturn in the 7th House (Sagittarius): 199
   Saturn in the 8th House (Capricorn): 199
   Saturn in the 9th House (Aquarius): 199
   Saturn in the 10th House (Pisces): 200
   Saturn in the 11th House (Aries): 200
   Saturn in the 12th House (Taurus): 200

8. Rahu 201
   Rahu in the 1st House (Gemini): 201
   Rahu in the 2nd House (Cancer): 201
   Rahu in the 3rd House (Leo): 201
   Rahu in the 4th House (Virgo): 202

Rahu in the 5th House (Libra): 202
Rahu in the 6th House (Scorpio): 202
Rahu in the 7th House (Sagittarius): 202
Rahu in the 8th House (Capricorn): 203
Rahu in the 9th House (Aquarius): 203
Rahu in the 10th House (Pisces): 203
Rahu in the 11th House (Aries): 203
Rahu in the 12th House (Taurus): 203
9.Ketu 204
Ketu in the 1st House (Gemini): 204
Ketu in the 2nd House (Cancer): 204
Ketu in the 3rd House (Leo): 205
Ketu in the 4th House (Virgo): 205
Ketu in the 5th House (Libra): 205
Ketu in the 6th House (Scorpio): 205
Ketu in the 7th House (Sagittarius): 205
Ketu in the 8th House (Capricorn): 206
Ketu in the 9th House (Aquarius): 206
Ketu in the 10th House (Pisces): 206
Ketu in the 11th House (Aries): 206
Ketu in the 12th House (Taurus): 207

6.Cancer Ascendant Predictions for Sun in Cancer Ascendant: 207
1.Sun 207
Sun in the 1st House (Cancer) 207
Sun in the 2nd House (Leo): 208
Sun in the 3rd House (Virgo): 208
Sun in the 4th House (Libra): 208
Sun in the 5th House (Scorpio): 209

Sun in the 6th House (Sagittarius): 209
Sun in the 7th House (Capricorn): 209
Sun in the 8th House (Aquarius): 210
Sun in the 10th House (Aries): 210
Sun in the 11th House (Taurus): 210
Sun in the 12th House (Gemini): 211
2.Moon 211
Moon in the 1st House (Cancer): 211
Moon in the 2nd House (Leo): 211
Moon in the 3rd House (Virgo): 212
Moon in the 4th House (Libra): 212
Moon in the 5th House (Scorpio): 212
Moon in the 6th House (Sagittarius): 213
Moon in the 7th House (Capricorn): 213
Moon in the 8th House (Aquarius): 213
Moon in the 10th House (Aries): 214
Moon in the 11th House (Taurus): 214
Moon in the 12th House (Gemini): 214
3.Mars 215
Mars in the 1st House (Cancer) 215
Mars in the 2nd House (Leo) 215
Mars in the 3rd House (Virgo) 215
Mars in the 4th House (Libra) 216
Mars in the 5th House (Scorpio) 216
Mars in the 6th House (Sagittarius) 217
Mars in the 7th House (Capricorn) 217
Mars in the 8th House (Aquarius) 217
Mars in the 9th House (Pisces) 218
Mars in the 10th House (Aries) 218

Mars in the 11th House (Taurus) 218
Mars in the 12th House (Gemini) 219
4. Mercury 219
Mercury in the 1st House (Cancer) 219
Mercury in the 2nd House (Leo) 220
Mercury in the 3rd House (Virgo) 220
Mercury in the 4th House (Libra) 221
Mercury in the 5th House (Scorpio) 221
Mercury in the 6th House (Sagittarius) 221
Mercury in the 7th House (Capricorn) 221
Mercury in the 8th House (Aquarius) 222
Mercury in the 9th House (Pisces) 222
Mercury in the 10th House (Aries) 222
Mercury in the 11th House (Taurus) 223
Mercury in the 12th House (Gemini) 223
5. Jupiter 223
Jupiter in the 1st House (Cancer) 223
Jupiter in the 2nd House (Leo) 224
Jupiter in the 3rd House (Virgo) 224
Jupiter in the 4th House (Libra) 225
Jupiter in the 5th House (Scorpio) 225
Jupiter in the 6th House (Sagittarius) 225
Jupiter in the 7th House (Capricorn) 226
Jupiter in the 8th House (Aquarius) 226
Jupiter in the 9th House (Pisces) 226
Jupiter in the 10th House (Aries) 227
Jupiter in the 11th House (Taurus) 227
Jupiter in the 12th House (Gemini) 227
6. Venus 227

Venus in the 1st House (Cancer)....................228
Venus in the 2nd House (Leo).......................228
Venus in the 3rd House (Virgo) 229
Venus in the 4th House (Libra) 229
Venus in the 5th House (Scorpio)...................229
Venus in the 6th House (Sagittarius)..............229
Venus in the 7th House (Capricorn) 230
Venus in the 8th House (Aquarius).................230
Venus in the 9th House (Pisces) 230
Venus in the 10th House (Aries).....................231
Venus in the 11th House (Taurus)..................231
Venus in the 12th House (Gemini).................231

8. Saturn 232
Saturn in the 1st House (Cancer) 232
Saturn in the 2nd House (Leo).......................232
Saturn in the 3rd House (Virgo) 233
Saturn in the 4th House (Libra)......................233
Saturn in the 5th House (Scorpio) 233
Saturn in the 6th House (Sagittarius).............234
Saturn in the 7th House (Capricorn)...............234
Saturn in the 8th House (Aquarius) 234
Saturn in the 9th House (Pisces) 235
Saturn in the 10th House (Aries) 235
Saturn in the 11th House (Taurus) 235
Saturn in the 12th House (Gemini) 236

8. Rahu 236
Rahu in the 1st House (Cancer) 236
Rahu in the 2nd House (Leo).........................237
Rahu in the 3rd House (Virgo) 237

Rahu in the 4th House (Libra).........................237
Rahu in the 5th House (Scorpio) 238
Rahu in the 6th House (Sagittarius)................238
Rahu in the 7th House (Capricorn).................238
Rahu in the 8th House (Aquarius) 239
Rahu in the 9th House (Pisces)......................239
Rahu in the 10th House (Aries) 239
Rahu in the 11th House (Taurus) 240
Rahu in the 12th House (Gemini) 240
9.Ketu 240
Ketu in the 1st House (Cancer) 241
Ketu in the 2nd House (Leo)..........................241
Ketu in the 3rd House (Virgo) 241
Ketu in the 4th House (Libra)..........................242
Ketu in the 5th House (Scorpio).....................242
Ketu in the 6th House (Sagittarius)................242
Ketu in the 7th House (Capricorn) 242
Ketu in the 8th House (Aquarius)...................243
Ketu in the 9th House (Pisces) 243
Ketu in the 10th House (Aries).......................243
Ketu in the 11th House (Taurus)....................244
Ketu in the 12th House (Gemini) 244

7.Leo Ascendant Planetary Predictions with Reference to Leo Ascendant...................................244
1.Sun 244
Sun in the 1st House (Leo): 244
Sun in the 2nd House (Virgo): 245
Sun in the 3rd House (Libra):.........................245
Sun in the 4th House (Scorpio):.....................246

Sun in the 5th House (Sagittarius): 246
Sun in the 6th House (Capricorn): 246
Sun in the 7th House (Aquarius): 247
Sun in the 8th House (Pisces): 247
Sun in the 9th House (Aries): 247
Sun in the 11th House (Gemini): 248
Sun in the 12th House (Cancer): 248
2. Moon 248
Moon in the 1st House (Leo) 248
Moon in the 2nd House (Virgo) 249
Moon in the 3rd House (Libra) 249
Moon in the 4th House (Scorpio) 249
Moon in the 5th House (Sagittarius) 250
Moon in the 6th House (Capricorn) 250
Moon in the 7th House (Aquarius) 250
Moon in the 8th House (Pisces) 251
Moon in the 9th House (Aries) 251
Moon in the 10th House (Taurus) 251
Moon in the 11th House (Gemini) 251
Moon in the 12th House (Cancer) 252
3. Mars 252
Mars in the 1st House (Leo): 252
Mars in the 2nd House (Virgo): 253
Mars in the 3rd House (Libra): 253
Mars in the 4th House (Scorpio): 253
Mars in the 5th House (Sagittarius): 254
Mars in the 6th House (Capricorn): 254
Mars in the 7th House (Aquarius): 255
Mars in the 8th House (Pisces): 255

- Mars in the 9th House (Aries): 255
- Mars in the 10th House (Taurus): 256
- Mars in the 11th House (Gemini): 256
- Mars in the 12th House (Cancer): 256

4. Mercury 257
- Mercury in the 1st House (Leo): 257
- Mercury in the 2nd House (Virgo): 257
- Mercury in the 3rd House (Libra): 257
- Mercury in the 4th House (Scorpio): 258
- Mercury in the 5th House (Sagittarius): 258
- Mercury in the 6th House (Capricorn): 258
- Mercury in the 7th House (Aquarius): 259
- Mercury in the 8th House (Pisces): 259
- Mercury in the 9th House (Aries): 259
- Mercury in the 10th House (Taurus): 259
- Mercury in the 11th House (Gemini): 260
- Mercury in the 12th House (Cancer): 260

5. Jupiter 260
- Jupiter in the 1st House (Leo): 260
- Jupiter in the 2nd House (Virgo): 261
- Jupiter in the 3rd House (Libra): 261
- Jupiter in the 4th House (Scorpio): 262
- Jupiter in the 5th House (Sagittarius): 262
- Jupiter in the 6th House (Capricorn): 262
- Jupiter in the 7th House (Aquarius): 262
- Jupiter in the 8th House (Pisces): 263
- Jupiter in the 9th House (Aries): 263
- Jupiter in the 10th House (Taurus): 263
- Jupiter in the 11th House (Gemini): 264

Jupiter in the 12th House (Cancer): 264
6. Venus 264
  Venus in the 1st House (Leo): 264
  Venus in the 2nd House (Virgo): 265
  Venus in the 3rd House (Libra): 265
  Venus in the 4th House (Scorpio): 265
  Venus in the 5th House (Sagittarius): 265
  Venus in the 6th House (Capricorn): 266
  Venus in the 7th House (Aquarius): 266
  Venus in the 8th House (Pisces): 266
  Venus in the 9th House (Aries): 267
  Venus in the 10th House (Taurus): 267
  Venus in the 11th House (Gemini): 267
  Venus in the 12th House (Cancer): 268
7. Saturn 268
  Saturn in the 1st House (Leo) 268
  Saturn in the 2nd House (Virgo) 269
  Saturn in the 3rd House (Libra) 269
  Saturn in the 4th House (Scorpio) 269
  Saturn in the 5th House (Sagittarius) 270
  Saturn in the 6th House (Capricorn) 270
  Saturn in the 7th House (Aquarius) 270
  Saturn in the 8th House (Pisces) 271
  Saturn in the 9th House (Aries) 271
  Saturn in the 10th House (Taurus) 272
  Saturn in the 11th House (Gemini) 272
  Saturn in the 12th House (Cancer) 272
8. Rahu 272
  Rahu in the 1st House (Leo): 272

Rahu in the 2nd House (Virgo): 273
Rahu in the 3rd House (Libra): 273
Rahu in the 5th House (Scorpio): 273
Rahu in the 6th House (Capricorn): 274
Rahu in the 7th House (Aquarius): 274
Rahu in the 8th House (Pisces): 274
Rahu in the 9th House (Aries): 274
Rahu in the 10th House (Taurus): 275
Rahu in the 11th House (Gemini): 275
Rahu in the 12th House (Cancer): 275
9. Ketu 275
Ketu in the 1st House (Leo) 275
Ketu in the 2nd House (Virgo) 276
Ketu in the 3rd House (Libra) 276
Ketu in the 4th House (Scorpio) 276
Ketu in the 5th House (Sagittarius) 277
Ketu in the 6th House (Capricorn) 277
Ketu in the 7th House (Aquarius) 277
Ketu in the 8th House (Pisces) 278
Ketu in the 9th House (Aries) 278
Ketu in the 10th House (Taurus) 278
Ketu in the 11th House (Gemini) 278
Ketu in the 12th House (Cancer) 279

8. Virgo Ascendant Predictions for Sun in Virgo Ascendant: 279
1. Sun 279
Sun in the 1st House (Virgo): 279
Sun in the 2nd House (Libra): 280
Sun in the 3rd House (Scorpio): 280

Sun in the 4th House (Sagittarius): 281
Sun in the 5th House (Capricorn): 281
Sun in the 6th House (Aquarius): 281
Sun in the 7th House (Pisces): 281
Sun in the 8th House (Aries): 282
Sun in the 9th House (Taurus): 282
Sun in the 10th House (Gemini): 282
Sun in the 11th House (Cancer): 282
Sun in the 12th House (Leo): 282
2. Moon 283
Moon in the 1st House (Virgo) 283
Moon in the 2nd House (Libra) 283
Moon in the 3rd House (Scorpio) 284
Moon in the 4th House (Sagittarius) 284
Moon in the 5th House (Capricorn) 284
Moon in the 6th House (Aquarius) 285
Moon in the 7th House (Pisces) 285
Moon in the 8th House (Aries) 285
Moon in the 9th House (Taurus) 285
Moon in the 10th House (Gemini) 286
Moon in the 11th House (Cancer) 286
Moon in the 12th House (Leo) 287
3. Mars 287
Mars in the 1st House (Virgo): 287
Mars in the 2nd House (Libra): 287
Mars in the 3rd House (Scorpio): 288
Mars in the 4th House (Sagittarius): 288
Mars in the 5th House (Capricorn): 288
Mars in the 6th House (Aquarius): 288

Mars in the 7th House (Pisces): 289
Mars in the 8th House (Aries): 289
Mars in the 9th House (Taurus): 289
Mars in the 10th House (Gemini): 289
Mars in the 11th House (Cancer): 289
Mars in the 12th House (Leo): 290

4. Mercury 290
Mercury in the 1st House (Virgo) 290
Mercury in the 2nd House (Libra) 290
Mercury in the 3rd House (Scorpio) 291
Mercury in the 4th House (Sagittarius) 291
Mercury in the 5th House (Capricorn) 291
Mercury in the 6th House (Aquarius) 291
Mercury in the 7th House (Pisces) 292
Mercury in the 8th House (Aries) 292
Mercury in the 9th House (Taurus) 292
Mercury in the 10th House (Gemini) 293
Mercury in the 11th House (Cancer) 293
Mercury in the 12th House (Leo) 293

5. Jupiter 294
Jupiter in the 1st House (Virgo): 294
Jupiter in the 2nd House (Libra): 294
Jupiter in the 3rd House (Scorpio): 295
Jupiter in the 4th House (Sagittarius): 295
Jupiter in the 5th House (Capricorn): 295
Jupiter in the 6th House (Aquarius): 296
Jupiter in the 7th House (Pisces): 296
Jupiter in the 8th House (Aries): 296
Jupiter in the 9th House (Taurus): 297

Jupiter in the 10th House (Gemini): 297
Jupiter in the 11th House (Cancer): 297
Jupiter in the 12th House (Leo): 298
6. Venus 298
Venus in the 1st House (Virgo) 298
Venus in the 2nd House (Libra) 299
Venus in the 3rd House (Scorpio) 299
Venus in the 4th House (Sagittarius) 299
Venus in the 5th House (Capricorn) 300
Venus in the 6th House (Aquarius) 300
Venus in the 7th House (Pisces) 301
Venus in the 8th House (Aries) 301
Venus in the 9th House (Taurus) 301
Venus in the 10th House (Gemini) 302
Venus in the 11th House (Cancer) 302
Venus in the 12th House (Leo) 302
7. Saturn 303
Saturn in the 1st House (Virgo): 303
Saturn in the 2nd House (Libra): 303
Saturn in the 3rd House (Scorpio): 304
Saturn in the 4th House (Sagittarius): 304
Saturn in the 5th House (Capricorn): 304
Saturn in the 6th House (Aquarius): 304
Saturn in the 7th House (Pisces): 305
Saturn in the 8th House (Aries): 305
Saturn in the 9th House (Taurus): 305
Saturn in the 10th House (Gemini): 305
Saturn in the 11th House (Cancer): 306
Saturn in the 12th House (Leo): 306

8. Rahu 306
    Rahu in the 1st House (Virgo): 306
    Rahu in the 2nd House (Libra): 307
    Rahu in the 3rd House (Scorpio): 307
    Rahu in the 4th House (Sagittarius): 307
    Rahu in the 5th House (Capricorn): 308
    Rahu in the 6th House (Aquarius): 308
    Rahu in the 7th House (Pisces): 308
    Rahu in the 8th House (Aries): 309
    Rahu in the 9th House (Taurus): 309
    Rahu in the 10th House (Gemini): 309
    Rahu in the 11th House (Cancer): 309
    Rahu in the 12th House (Leo): 310
9. Ketu 310
    Ketu in the 1st House (Virgo): 310
    Ketu in the 2nd House (Libra): 310
    Ketu in the 3rd House (Scorpio): 311
    Ketu in the 5th House (Sagittarius): 311
    Ketu in the 6th House (Capricorn): 311
    Ketu in the 6th House (Aquarius): 311
    Ketu in the 7th House (Pisces): 312
    Ketu in the 8th House (Aries): 312
    Ketu in the 9th House (Taurus): 312
    Ketu in the 10th House (Gemini): 313
    Ketu in the 11th House (Cancer): 313
    Ketu in the 12th House (Leo): 313

9. Libra Ascendant: Planetary Predictions with Reference to Libra Ascendant 314
    1. Sun 314

Sun in the 1st House (Libra) 314
Sun in the 2nd House (Scorpio) 314
Sun in the 3rd House (Sagittarius) 315
Sun in the 4th House (Capricorn) 315
Sun in the 5th House (Aquarius) 315
Sun in the 6th House (Pisces) 316
Sun in the 7th House (Aries) 316
Sun in the 8th House (Taurus) 316
Sun in the 9th House (Gemini) 316
Sun in the 10th House (Cancer) 317
Sun in the 11th House (Leo) 317
Sun in the 12th House (Virgo) 317

2. Moon 318
Moon in the 1st House (Libra): 318
Moon in the 2nd House (Scorpio): 318
Moon in the 3rd House (Sagittarius): 318
Moon in the 5th House (Capricorn): 318
Moon in the 6th House (Aquarius): 319
Moon in the 6th House (Pisces): 319
Moon in the 7th House (Aries): 319
Moon in the 8th House (Taurus): 319
Moon in the 9th House (Gemini): 320
Moon in the 10th House (Cancer): 320
Moon in the 11th House (Leo): 320
Moon in the 12th House (Virgo): 320

3. Mars 321
Mars in the 1st House (Libra) 321
Mars in the 2nd House (Scorpio) 321
Mars in the 3rd House (Sagittarius) 321

Mars in the 4th House (Capricorn)..................322
Mars in the 5th House (Aquarius)..................322
Mars in the 6th House (Pisces)......................323
Mars in the 7th House (Aries).........................323
Mars in the 8th House (Taurus).....................323
Mars in the 9th House (Gemini)....................323
Mars in the 10th House (Cancer)...................324
Mars in the 11th House (Leo).........................324
Mars in the 12th House (Leo).........................325
4. Mercury..325
 Mercury in the 1st House (Libra): 325
 Mercury in the 2nd House (Scorpio): 325
 Mercury in the 3rd House (Sagittarius): 326
 Mercury in the 4th House (Capricorn):............326
 Mercury in the 5th House (Aquarius): 326
 Mercury in the 6th House (Pisces):..................326
 Mercury in the 7th House (Aries): 327
 Mercury in the 8th House (Taurus): 327
 Mercury in the 9th House (Gemini):................327
 Mercury in the 10th House (Cancer):...............328
 Mercury in the 11th House (Leo): 328
 Mercury in the 12th House (Virgo): 328
5. Jupiter..328
 Jupiter in the 1st House (Libra).......................328
 Jupiter in the 2nd House (Scorpio) 329
 Jupiter in the 3rd House (Sagittarius) 329
 Jupiter in the 4th House (Capricorn)...............329
 Jupiter in the 5th House (Aquarius) 330
 Jupiter in the 6th House (Pisces)....................330

Jupiter in the 7th House (Aries) 330
Jupiter in the 8th House (Taurus) 331
Jupiter in the 9th House (Gemini) 331
Jupiter in the 10th House (Cancer) 331
Jupiter in the 11th House (Leo) 332
Jupiter in the 12th House (Virgo) 332
6. Venus 332
   Venus in the 1st House (Libra): 332
   Venus in the 2nd House (Scorpio): 333
   Venus in the 3rd House (Sagittarius): 333
   Venus in the 4th House (Capricorn): 333
   Venus in the 5th House (Aquarius): 333
   Venus in the 6th House (Pisces): 334
   Venus in the 7th House (Aries): 334
   Venus in the 8th House (Taurus): 334
   Venus in the 9th House (Gemini): 335
   Venus in the 10th House (Cancer): 335
   Venus in the 11th House (Leo): 335
   Venus in the 12th House (Virgo): 335
7. Saturn 335
   Saturn in the 1st House (Libra): 336
   Saturn in the 2nd House (Scorpio): 336
   Saturn in the 3rd House (Sagittarius): 336
   Saturn in the 5th House (Aquarius): 337
   Saturn in the 6th House (Pisces): 337
   Saturn in the 8th House (Aries): 337
   Saturn in the 8th House (Taurus): 338
   Saturn in the 9th House (Gemini): 338
   Saturn in the 10th House (Cancer): 338

  Saturn in the 11th House (Leo): 338
  Saturn in the 12th House (Virgo): 339
 8.Rahu 339
  Rahu in the 1st House (Libra): 339
  Rahu in the 2nd House (Scorpio): 340
  Rahu in the 3rd House (Sagittarius): 340
  Rahu in the 4th House (Capricorn): 340
  Rahu in the 5th House (Aquarius): 340
  Rahu in the 6th House (Pisces): 340
  Rahu in the 7th House (Aries): 341
  Rahu in the 8th House (Taurus): 341
  Rahu in the 9th House (Gemini): 341
  Rahu in the 10th House (Cancer): 342
  Rahu in the 11th House (Leo): 342
  Rahu in the 12th House (Virgo): 342
 9.Ketu 342
  Ketu in the 1st House (Libra): 342
  Ketu in the 2nd House (Scorpio): 342
  Ketu in the 3rd House (Sagittarius): 343
  Ketu in the 4th House (Capricorn): 343
  Ketu in the 5th House (Aquarius): 343
  Ketu in the 6th House (Pisces): 343
  Ketu in the 7th House (Aries): 344
  Ketu in the 8th House (Taurus): 344
  Ketu in the 9th House (Gemini): 344
  Ketu in the 10th House (Cancer): 344
  Ketu in the 11th House (Leo): 344
  Ketu in the 12th House (Virgo): 345

10.Scorpio Ascendant Predictions: Planetary

Influences on Scorpio Rising 346
    1.Sun 346
        Sun in the 1st House (Scorpio): 346
        Sun in the 2nd House (Sagittarius): 346
        Sun in the 3rd House (Capricorn) : 347
        Sun in the 4th House (Aquarius): 347
        Sun in the 5th House (Pisces): 348
        Sun in the 6th House (Aries): 348
        Sun in the 7th House (Taurus): 349
        Sun in the 8th House (Gemini): 349
        Sun in the 9th House (Cancer): 349
        Sun in the 10th House (Leo): 350
        Sun in the 11th House (Virgo): 350
        Sun in the 12th House(Venus): 351
    2.Moon 351
        Moon in the 1st House (Scorpio): 351
        Moon in the 2nd House (Sagittarius): 352
        Moon in the 3rd House (Capricorn): 352
        Moon in the 4th House (Aquarius): 352
        Moon in the 5th House (Pisces): 353
        Moon in the 6th House (Aries): 353
        Moon in the 7th House (Taurus): 354
        Moon in the 8th House (Gemini): 354
        Moon in the 10th House (Cancer): 354
        Moon in the 11th House (Virgo): 354
        Moon in the 12th House (Libra): 355
    3.Mars 355
        1st House (Scorpio): 355
        2nd House (Sagittarius): 355

    3rd House (Capricorn): 356
    4th House (Aquarius): 356
    5th House (Pisces): 356
    6th House (Aries): 357
    7th House (Taurus): 357
    8th House (Gemini): 357
    9th House (Cancer): 357
    10th House (Leo): 358
    11th House (Virgo): 358
    12th House (Libra): 358
4. Mercury 359
    Mercury in the 1st House (Scorpio): 359
    Mercury in the 2nd House (Sagittarius): 359
    Mercury in the 3rd House (Capricorn): 359
    Mercury in the 4th House (Aquarius): 360
    Mercury in the 5th House (Pisces): 360
    Mercury in the 6th House (Aries): 360
    Mercury in the 7th House (Taurus): 361
    Mercury in the 8th House (Gemini): 361
    Mercury in the 9th House (Cancer): 361
    Mercury in the 10th House (Leo): 361
    Mercury in the 11th House (Virgo): 362
    Mercury in the 12th House (Libra): 362
5. Jupiter 362
    Jupiter in the 1st House: 362
    Jupiter in the 2nd House: 362
    Jupiter in the 3rd House: 363
    Jupiter in the 4th House: 363
    Jupiter in the 5th House: 363

Jupiter in the 6th House: 363
Jupiter in the 7th House: 364
Jupiter in the 8th House: 364
Jupiter in the 9th House: 364
Jupiter in the 10th House: 365
Jupiter in the 11th House: 365
Jupiter in the 12th House: 365
6. Venus 365
Venus in the 1st House: 365
Venus in the 2nd House: 366
Venus in the 3rd House: 366
Venus in the 4th House: 366
Venus in the 5th House: 367
Venus in the 6th House: 367
Venus in the 7th House: 367
Venus in the 8th House: 368
Venus in the 9th House in Cancer 368
Venus in the 10th House: 368
Venus in the 11th House: 369
Venus in the 12th House: 369
7. Saturn 369
Saturn in the 1st House: 370
Saturn in the 2nd House: 370
Saturn in the 3rd House: 370
Saturn in the 4th House: 370
Saturn in the 5th House: 371
Saturn in the 6th House: 371
Saturn in the 7th House: 371
Saturn in the 8th House: 372

    Saturn in the 9th House in (Cancer): 372
    Saturn in the 10th House: 372
    Saturn in the 11th House: 373
    Saturn in the 12th House: 373
8.Rahu 373
    Rahu in the 1st House: 374
    Rahu in the 2nd House: 374
    Rahu in the 3rd House: 374
    Rahu in the 4th House: 374
    Rahu in the 5th House: 375
    Rahu in the 6th House: 375
    Rahu in the 7th House: 375
    Rahu in the 8th House: 375
    Rahu in the 9th House: 376
    Rahu in the 10th House: 376
    Rahu in the 11th House: 376
    Rahu in the 12th House: 376
9.Ketu 377
    Ketu in the 1st House: 377
    Ketu in the 2nd House: 377
    Ketu in the 3rd House: 377
    Ketu in the 4th House: 378
    Ketu in the 5th House: 378
    Ketu in the 6th House: 378
    Ketu in the 7th House: 378
    Ketu in the 8th House: 379
    Ketu in the 9th House: 379
    Ketu in the 10th House: 379
    Ketu in the 11th House: 379

Ketu in the 12th House: 380
11. Predictions of the Planets with Reference to Sagittarius Ascendant..381
  1. Sun 381
    Sun in the 1st House: 381
    Sun in the 2nd House: 381
    Sun in the 3rd House: 381
    Sun in the 5th House: 382
    Sun in the 6th House: 382
    Sun in the 7th House: 382
    Sun in the 8th House: 383
    Sun in the 9th House: 383
    Sun in the 10th House: 383
    Sun in the 11th House: 383
    Sun in the 12th House: 384
  2. Moon..384
    Moon in the 1st House (Sagittarius): 384
    Moon in the 2nd House (Capricorn):..............384
    Moon in the 3rd House (Aquarius): 384
    Moon in the 4th House (Pisces):....................385
    Moon in the 5th House (Aries): 385
    Moon in the 6th House (Taurus): 386
    Moon in the 7th House (Gemini): 386
    Moon in the 8th House (Cancer):..................386
    Moon in the 9th House (Leo): 387
    Moon in the 10th House (Virgo): 387
    Moon in the 11th House (Libra): 387
    Moon in the 12th House (Scorpio): 387
  3. Mars 388

Mars in the 1st House (Sagittarius): 388
Mars in the 2nd House (Capricorn):................388
Mars in the 3rd House (Aquarius): 389
Mars in the 4th House (Pisces):......................389
Mars in the 5th House in Aries......................389
Mars in the 6th House in Taurus....................390
Mars in the 7th House (Gemini): 390
Mars in the 8th House (Cancer):....................391
Mars in the 9th House in Leo.........................391
Mars in the 10th House (Leo): 392
Mars in the 11th House (Libra): 392
Mars in the 12th House (Scorpio): 393
4. Mercury..393
    Mercury in the 1st House (Sagittarius): 393
    Mercury in the 2nd House (Capricorn):...........393
    Mercury in the 3rd House (Aquarius):.............394
    Mercury in the 4th House (Pisces):................394
    Mercury in the 5th House (Aries): 395
    Mercury in the 6th House (Taurus): 395
    Mercury in the 7th House (Gemini): 395
    Mercury in the 8th House (Cancer):................395
    Mercury in the 9th House in Leo.....................396
    Mercury in the 10th House (Leo): 396
    Mercury in the 11th House (Libra): 397
    Mercury in the 12th House (Scorpio): 397
5. Jupiter..397
    Jupiter in the 1st House (Sagittarius):............397
    Jupiter in the 2nd House (Capricorn):.............398
    Jupiter in the 3rd House (Aquarius): 398

Jupiter in the 4th House in (Pisces) 398
Jupiter in the 5th House (Arise): 399
Jupiter in the 6th House (Taurus): 399
Jupiter in the 7th House (Gemini): 400
Jupiter in the 8th House (Cancer): 400
Jupiter in the 9th House (Leo): 400
Jupiter in the 10th House (Virgo): 400
Jupiter in the 11th House (Libra): 401
Jupiter in the 12th House (Scorpio): 401
6. Venus 401
Venus in the 1st House (Sagittarius): 401
Venus in the 2nd House (Capricorn): 402
Venus in the 3rd House (Aquarius): 402
Venus in the 4th House (Pisces): 402
Venus in the 5th House (Aries): 403
Venus in the 6th House (Taurus): 403
Venus in the 7th House (Gemini): 403
Venus in the 8th House (Cancer): 403
Venus in the 9th House (Leo): 404
Venus in the 10th House (Virgo): 404
Venus in the 11th House (Libra): 404
Venus in the 12th House (Scorpio): 404
7. Saturn 405
Saturn in the 1st House (Sagittarius): 405
Saturn in the 2nd House (Capricorn): 405
Saturn in the 3rd House (Aquarius): 405
Saturn in the 4th House (Pisces): 406
Saturn in the 5th House (Aries): 406
Saturn in the 6th House (Taurus): 406

Saturn in the 7th House (Gemini): 407
Saturn in the 8th House (Cancer): 407
Saturn in the 9th House (Leo):......................407
Saturn in the 10th House (Virgo): 407
Saturn in the 11th House (Libra):...................407
Saturn in the 12th House (Scorpio): 408

8. Rahu 408
Rahu in the 1st House (Sagittarius): 408
Rahu in the 2nd House (Capricorn): 408
Rahu in the 3rd House (Aquarius): 409
Rahu in the 4th House (Pisces): 409
Rahu in the 5th House (Aries): 409
Rahu in the 6th House (Taurus): 409
Rahu in the 7th House (Gemini): 410
Rahu in the 8th House (Cancer): 410
Rahu in the 9th House (Leo):.......................410
Rahu in the 10th House (Virgo): 410
Rahu in the 11th House (Libra):....................411
Rahu in the 12th House (Scorpio): 411

9. Ketu 411
Ketu in the 1st House (Sagittarius): 411
Ketu in the 2nd House (Capricorn): 411
Ketu in the 3rd House (Aquarius): 412
Ketu in the 4th House (Pisces): 412
Ketu in the 5th House (Aries):......................412
Ketu in the 6th House (Taurus):....................413
Ketu in the 7th House (Gemini): 413
Ketu in the 8th House (Cancer): 413
Ketu in the 9th House (Leo): 413

Ketu in the 10th House (Virgo): 413
Ketu in the 11th House (Libra): 414
Ketu in the 12th House (Scorpio): 414

12. Predictions of the Planets with Reference to Capricorn Ascendant: 415

   1. sun 415

     Sun in the 1st House (Capricorn): 415
     Sun in the 2nd House (Aquarius): 415
     Sun in the 3rd House (Pisces): 415
     Sun in the 4th House (Aries): 416
     Sun in the 5th House (Taurus): 416
     Sun in the 6th House (Gemini): 416
     Sun in the 7th House (Cancer): 416
     Sun in the 8th House (Leo): 417
     Sun in the 9th House (Virgo): 417
     Sun in the 10th House (Libra): 417
     Sun in the 11th House (Scorpio): 418
     Sun in the 12th House (Sagittarius): 418

   2. Moon 418

     Moon in the 1st House (Capricorn): 418
     Moon in the 2nd House (Aquarius): 419
     Moon in the 3rd House (Pisces): 419
     Moon in the 4th House (Aries): 419
     Moon in the 5th House (Taurus): 419
     Moon in the 6th House (Gemini): 420
     Moon in the 7th House (Cancer): 420
     Moon in the 8th House (Leo): 420
     Moon in the 9th House (Virgo): 421
     Moon in the 10th House (Libra): 421

Moon in the 11th House (Scorpio): 421
Moon in the 12th House (Sagittarius): 421
3. Mars 422
   Mars in the 1st House (Capricorn): 422
   Mars in the 2nd House (Aquarius): 422
   Mars in the 3rd House (Pisces): 423
   Mars in the 4th House (Aries): 423
   Mars in the 5th House (Taurus): 423
   Mars in the 6th House (Gemini): 424
   Mars in the 7th House (Cancer): 424
   Mars in the 8th House (Leo): 424
   Mars in the 9th House (Virgo): 424
   Mars in the 10th House (Libra): 424
   Mars in the 11th House (Scorpio): 425
   Mars in the 12th House (Sagittarius): 425
4. Mercury 425
   Mercury in the 1st House (Capricorn): 425
   Mercury in the 2nd House (Aquarius): 426
   Mercury in the 3rd House (Pisces): 426
   Mercury in the 4th House (Aries): 426
   Mercury in the 5th House (Taurus): 427
   Mercury in the 6th House (Gemini): 427
   Mercury in the 7th House (Cancer): 427
   Mercury in the 8th House (Leo): 427
   Mercury in the 9th House (Virgo): 428
   Mercury in the 10th House (Libra): 428
   Mercury in the 11th House (Scorpio): 428
   Mercury in the 12th House (Sagittarius): 428
5. Jupiter 428

Jupiter in the 1st House (Capricorn): 428
Jupiter in the 2nd House (Aquarius): 429
Jupiter in the 3rd House (Pisces): 429
Jupiter in the 4th House (Aries): 429
Jupiter in the 5th House (Taurus): 429
Jupiter in the 6th House (Gemini): 430
Jupiter in the 7th House (Cancer): 430
Jupiter in the 8th House (Leo): 430
Jupiter in the 9th House (Virgo): 431
Jupiter in the 10th House (Libra): 431
Jupiter in the 11th House (Scorpio): 431
Jupiter in the 12th House (Sagittarius): 431
6.Venus 432
Venus in the 1st House (Capricorn): 432
Venus in the 2nd House (Aquarius): 432
Venus in the 3rd House (Pisces): 432
Venus in the 4th House (Aries): 433
Venus in the 5th House (Taurus): 433
Venus in the 6th House (Gemini): 433
Venus in the 7th House (Cancer): 434
Venus in the 8th House (Leo): 434
Venus in the 9th House (Virgo): 434
Venus in the 10th House (Libra): 434
Venus in the 11th House (Scorpio): 435
Venus in the 12th House (Sagittarius): 435
7.Saturn 435
Saturn in the 1st House (Capricorn) 435
Saturn in the 2nd House (Aquarius) 436
Saturn in the 3rd House (Pisces) 436

    Saturn in the 4th House (Aries) 436
    Saturn in the 5th House (Taurus) 437
    Saturn in the 6th House (Gemini) 437
    Saturn in the 7th House (Cancer) 437
    Saturn in the 8th House (Leo).........................438
    In the 9th House (Virgo),................................438
    Saturn in the 10th House (Libra)....................438
    In the 11th House (Scorpio),..........................439
    Saturn in the 12th House (Sagittarius)...........439
8. Rahu 439
    Rahu in the 1st House (Capricorn) 439
    In the 2nd House (Aquarius),.........................440
    Rahu in the 3rd House (Pisces)......................440
    Rahu in the 4th House (Aries) 440
    Rahu in the 5th House (Taurus) 441
    Rahu in the 6th House (Gemini) 441
    Rahu in the 7th House (Cancer)....................441
    Rahu in the 8th House (Leo)...........................441
    Rahu in the 9th House (Virgo) 442
    Rahu in the 10th House (Libra)......................442
    Rahu in the 11th House (Scorpio) 442
    Rahu in the 12th House (Sagittarius)..............443
9. Ketu 443
    Ketu in the 1st House (Capricorn) 443
    In the 2nd House (Aquarius),.........................443
    Ketu in the 3rd House (Pisces) 443
    Ketu in the 4th House (Aries).........................443
    Ketu in the 5th House (Taurus)......................444
    Ketu in the 6th House (Gemini) 444

Ketu in the 7th House (Cancer) 444
Ketu in the 8th House (Leo) 444
Ketu in the 9th House (Virgo) 445
Ketu in the 10th House (Libra) 445
Ketu in the 11th House (Scorpio) 445
Ketu in the 12th House (Sagittarius) 445

13.Predictions of the Planets with Reference to Aquarius Ascendant 447

  1.Sun 447
    Sun in the 1st House (Aquarius) 447
    Sun in the 2nd House (Pisces) 447
    Sun in the 3rd House (Aries) 447
    Sun in the 4th House (Taurus) 448
    Sun in the 5th House (Gemini) 448
    Sun in the 6th House (Cancer) 448
    Sun in the 7th House (Leo) 448
    Sun in the 8th House (Virgo) 449
    Sun in the 9th House (Libra) 449
    Sun in the 10th House (Scorpio) 449
    Sun in the 11th House (Sagittarius) 449
    Sun in the 12th House (Capricorn) 450
  2. Moon 450
    Moon in the 1st House (Aquarius) 450
    Moon in the 2nd House (Pisces) 450
    Moon in the 3rd House (Aries) 451
    Moon in the 4th House (Taurus) 451
    Moon in the 5th House (Gemini) 451
    Moon in the 6th House (Cancer) 452
    Moon in the 7th House (Leo) 452

Moon in the 8th House (Virgo) 452
Moon in the 9th House (Libra) 452
Moon in the 10th House (Scorpio) 452
Moon in the 11th House (Sagittarius) 453
Moon in the 12th House (Capricorn)...............453
3. Mars..453
Mars in the 1st House (Aquarius) 453
Mars in the 2nd House (Pisces).....................454
Mars in the 3rd House (Aries).......................454
Mars in the 4th House (Taurus) 455
Mars in the 5th House (Gemini).....................455
Mars in the 6th House (Cancer).....................455
Mars in the 7th House (Leo) 455
Mars in the 8th House (Virgo) 456
Mars in the 9th House (Libra) 456
Mars in the 10th House (Scorpio) 456
Mars in the 11th House (Sagittarius) 456
Mars in the 12th House (Capricorn)...............457
4. Mercury...457
Mercury in the 1st House (Aquarius) 457
Mercury in the 2nd House (Pisces)................457
Mercury in the 3rd House (Aries)...................458
Mercury in the 4th House (Taurus) 458
Mercury in the 5th House (Gemini)................458
Mercury in the 6th House (Cancer)................459
Mercury in the 7th House (Leo) 459
Mercury in the 8th House (Virgo)...................459
Mercury in the 9th House (Libra) 460
Mercury in the 10th House (Scorpio).............460

Mercury in the 11th House (Sagittarius).........460
Mercury in the 12th House (Capricorn)...........461
5.Jupiter...461
Jupiter in the 1st House (Aquarius) 461
Jupiter in the 2nd House (Pisces)...................461
Jupiter in the 3rd House (Aries) 461
Jupiter in the 4th House (Taurus) 462
Jupiter in the 5th House (Gemini)..................462
Jupiter in the 6th House (Cancer)..................462
Jupiter in the 7th House (Leo) 463
Jupiter in the 9th House (Libra) 463
Jupiter in the 10th House (Scorpio) 464
Jupiter in the 11th House (Sagittarius) 464
Jupiter in the 12th House (Capricorn).............464
6.Venus...464
Venus in the 1st House (Aquarius) 464
Venus in the 2nd House (Pisces) 465
Venus in the 3rd House (Aries)......................465
Venus in the 4th House (Taurus)....................465
Venus in the 5th House (Gemini)...................466
Venus in the 6th House (Cancer) 466
Venus in the 7th House (Leo) 466
Venus in the 8th House (Virgo)......................467
Venus in the 9th House (Libra) 467
Venus in the 10th House (Scorpio).................467
Venus in the 11th House (Sagittarius) 467
Venus in the 12th House (Capricorn) 468
7.Saturn 468
Saturn in the 1st House (Aquarius).................468

Saturn in the 2nd House (Pisces)..................468
Saturn in the 3rd House (Aries).....................469
Saturn in the 4th House (Taurus)..................469
Saturn in the 5th House (Gemini)..................469
Saturn in the 6th House (Cancer)..................470
Saturn in the 7th House (Leo)........................470
Saturn in the 8th House (Virgo)....................470
Saturn in the 9th House (Libra).....................471
Saturn in the 10th House (Scorpio)...............471
Saturn in the 11th House (Sagittarius)...........471
Saturn in the 12th House (Capricorn)............472

8. Rahu..472
Rahu in the 1st House (Aquarius)..................472
Rahu in the 2nd House (Pisces)....................472
Rahu in the 3rd House (Aries).......................473
Rahu in the 4th House (Taurus)....................473
Rahu in the 5th House (Gemini)....................473
Rahu in the 6th House (Cancer)....................473
Rahu in the 7th House (Leo).........................473
Rahu in the 8th House (Virgo).......................474
Rahu in the 9th House (Libra).......................474
Rahu in the 10th House (Scorpio).................474
Rahu in the 11th House (Sagittarius).............474
Rahu in the 12th House (Capricorn)..............475

9. Ketu..475
Ketu in the 1st House (Aquarius)..................475
Ketu in the 2nd House (Pisces)....................476
Ketu in the 3rd House (Aries).......................476
Ketu in the 4th House (Taurus).....................476

Ketu in the 5th House (Gemini) 476
Ketu in the 6th House (Cancer) 476
Ketu in the 7th House (Leo)............................477
Ketu in the 8th House (Virgo) 477
Ketu in the 9th House (Libra).........................477
Ketu in the 10th House (Scorpio)....................477
Ketu in the 11th House (Sagittarius)...............478
Ketu in the 12th House (Capricorn) 478

14.Predictions for the placement of the Sun in Pisces Ascendant are as follows: 479

1 . Sun 479
Sun in the 1st House (Pisces): 479
Sun in the 2nd House (Aries):........................479
Sun in the 3rd House (Taurus): 479
Sun in the 4th House (Gemini): 480
Sun in the 5th House (Cancer): 480
Sun in the 6th House (Leo):............................480
Sun in the 7th House (Virgo): 480
Sun in the 8th House (Libra):..........................480
Sun in the 9th House (Scorpio):......................481
Sun in the 10th House (Sagittarius): 481
Sun in the 11th House (Capricorn): 481
Sun in the 12th House (Aquarius):..................482

2.Moon..482
Moon in the 1st House (Pisces):.....................482
Moon in the 2nd House (Aries): 482
Moon in the 3rd House (Taurus): 483
Moon in the 4th House (Gemini): 483
Moon in the 5th House (Cancer):....................483

Moon in the 6th House (Leo): 484
Moon in the 7th House (Virgo): 484
Moon in the 8th House (Libra): 484
Moon in the 9th House (Scorpio): 484
Moon in the 10th House (Sagittarius): 484
Moon in the 11th House (Capricorn): 485
Moon in the 12th House (Aquarius): 485
3. Mars 485
Mars in the 1st House (Pisces): 485
Mars in the 2nd House (Aries): 486
Mars in the 3rd House (Taurus): 486
Mars in the 4th House (Gemini): 486
Mars in the 5th House (Cancer): 487
Mars in the 6th House (Leo): 487
Mars in the 7th House (Virgo): 487
Mars in the 8th House (Libra): 487
Mars in the 9th House (Scorpio): 488
Mars in the 10th House (Sagittarius): 488
Mars in the 11th House (Capricorn): 488
Mars in the 12th House (Aquarius): 489
4. Mercury 489
Mercury in the 1st House (Pisces): 489
Mercury in the 2nd House (Aries): 490
Mercury in the 3rd House (Taurus): 490
Mercury in the 4th House (Gemini): 490
Mercury in the 5th House (Cancer): 490
Mercury in the 6th House (Leo): 491
Mercury in the 7th House (Virgo): 491
Mercury in the 8th House (Libra): 491

Mercury in the 9th House (Scorpio): 491
Mercury in the 10th House (Sagittarius): 492
Mercury in the 11th House (Capricorn): 492
Mercury in the 12th House (Aquarius): 492
5. Jupiter 492
Jupiter in the 1st House (Pisces): 492
Jupiter in the 2nd House (Aries): 493
Jupiter in the 3rd House (Taurus): 493
Jupiter in the 4th House (Gemini): 494
Jupiter in the 5th House (Cancer): 494
Jupiter in the 6th House (Leo): 494
Jupiter in the 7th House (Virgo): 495
Jupiter in the 8th House (Libra): 495
Jupiter in the 9th House (Scorpio): 495
Jupiter in the 10th House (Sagittarius): 495
Jupiter in the 11th House (Capricorn): 496
Jupiter in the 12th House (Aquarius): 496
6. Venus 496
Venus in the 1st House (Pisces): 496
Venus in the 2nd House (Aries): 497
Venus in the 3rd House (Taurus): 497
Venus in the 4th House (Gemini): 497
Venus in the 5th House (Cancer): 498
Venus in the 6th House (Leo): 498
Venus in the 7th House (Virgo): 498
Venus in the 8th House (Libra): 498
Venus in the 9th House (Scorpio): 499
Venus in the 10th House (Sagittarius): 499
Venus in the 11th House (Capricorn): 499

Venus in the 12th House (Aquarius): 500
7. Saturn 500
   Saturn in the 1st House (Pisces): 500
   Saturn in the 2nd House (Aries): 500
   Saturn in the 3rd House (Taurus): 501
   Saturn in the 4th House (Gemini): 501
   Saturn in the 5th House (Cancer): 501
   Saturn in the 6th House (Leo): 502
   Saturn in the 7th House (Virgo): 502
   Saturn in the 8th House (Libra): 502
   Saturn in the 9th House (Scorpio): 502
   Saturn in the 10th House (Sagittarius): 503
   Saturn in the 11th House (Capricorn): 503
   Saturn in the 12th House (Aquarius): 503
8. Rahu 504
   Rahu in the 1st House (Pisces): 504
   Rahu in the 2nd House (Aries): 504
   Rahu in the 3rd House (Taurus): 504
   Rahu in the 4th House (Gemini): 504
   Rahu in the 5th House (Cancer): 505
   Rahu in the 6th House (Leo): 505
   Rahu in the 7th House (Virgo): 505
   Rahu in the 8th House (Libra): 505
   Rahu in the 9th House (Scorpio): 506
   Rahu in the 10th House (Sagittarius): 506
   Rahu in the 11th House (Capricorn): 506
   Rahu in the 12th House (Aquarius): 506
9. Ketu 507
   Ketu in the 1st House (Pisces): 507

Ketu in the 2nd House (Aries): 507
Ketu in the 3rd House (Taurus): 507
Ketu in the 4th House (Gemini): 508
Ketu in the 5th House (Cancer): 508
Ketu in the 6th House (Leo): 508
Ketu in the 7th House (Virgo): 508
Ketu in the 8th House (Libra): 509
Ketu in the 9th House (Scorpio): 509
Ketu in the 10th House (Sagittarius): 509
Ketu in the 11th House (Capricorn): 509
Ketu in the 12th House (Aquarius): 510

15. Basics (Terminology) of the 9 Planets 510
Nine planets in astrology and their friendship, neutrality, and enmity: 510
Basics : 512
The main planetary aspects along with brief explanations and examples: 514
The dignities of planets : 516
What is Dasha system? 518
What is Nakshtras? 521
What is Nakshatra-Charan? 525
Nakshatras along with their ruling deity, symbol, and qualities: 528
27 Nakshatras along with the corresponding Rashis and Padas: 533
What is Yogas? 535
   Few combinations of Yogas 536
What is Karan? 539
What is Tithi? 542

What is Mahendra?	544
What is Varna?	546
Determining the Varna	547
What is Vashya?	548
What is Yoni?	552
How to Determine Yoni?	554
What is Gan ?	555
What is Nadi ?	556
What is Dosha?	557
What is Tatva?	559
12 Rashis specific names and corresponding alphabets:	561
What is Paya?	562
What is Navamsha ?	565
How to determine navamsha chart?	567
Analyzing the Navamsha chart for each planet:	568
Transit in astrology:	570
What is Bhav Chalit Chart?	572
Rudraksha beads And Zodiac Signs:	573
List of Nakshatras along with their corresponding Rudraksha beads:	576
Gemstones with specific Rashis (zodiac signs):	580
Gemstones with specific Nakshatras (lunar constellations):	583
Doshas in Astrology:	587
Var (weekday) association for each planet:	589
Numerical associations for the planets:	590
Associations of planets with body parts:	591
Associations of planets with directions:	592

Associations of planets with animals: 593
Associations of planets with flowers: 594
Associations of planets with plants: 596
Associations of planets with colors: 597
Associations of planets with sounds: 599
Mantras associated with each planet:...................600
how to chant mantras effectively: 602
The significance of 108:..604
Associations between planets and food: 605
Association of planets with Vata, Pitta and Kapha:607
Associations between planets and architecture:...608
The associations between planets and chemical elements: 610
Associations between planets and Kundalini chakras: 612
Associations between planets and birds:..............613

16. Conclusion: 615
17. References : 617
   "Please Rate This Book On Amazon To Help Others" 618
   The End 618

Associations Between Planets and Various Factors:

1. Colors: Each planet is associated with specific colors.

2. Gemstones: Certain gemstones are associated with each planet.

3. Metals: Planets are linked to specific metals.

4. Plants and Herbs: Certain plants and herbs are associated with each planet.

5. Animals: Some animals are associated with specific planets.

6. Days of the Week: Each planet is associated with a particular day of the week.

7. Zodiac Signs: Planets rule over certain zodiac signs.

8. Elements: Planets are associated with the classical elements of earth, air, fire, and water.

9. Chakras: Each planet is linked to one or more energy centers in the body.

10. Deities: Certain deities or gods/goddesses are associated with specific planets.

11. Mantras: Each planet has its own mantra for invocation.

12. Yantras: Yantras are geometrical diagrams associated with planets.

13. Numbers: Planets are linked to numerical vibrations.

14. Tastes: Specific tastes are associated with each planet.

15. Body Parts: Planets have associations with different body parts.

In this book, we delve into the fascinating world of astrology, exploring the cosmic symphony and the language of the stars. We unravel the mysteries of the zodiac signs and provide detailed predictions for each ascendant based on the influence of the planets. Additionally, we delve into the fundamentals of the nine planets, discussing their terminology and various associations with colors, gemstones, metals, plants, animals, days of the week, zodiac signs, elements, chakras, deities, mantras, yantras, numbers, tastes, and body parts.

Through this comprehensive exploration, readers will gain profound insights into astrology and its intricate connections with the diverse facets of life. Whether you are a beginner seeking to understand the basics or an experienced astrologer looking to deepen your knowledge, this book offers valuable information and practical guidance to enhance your understanding and application of astrology.

Join us on this enlightening journey as we unlock the secrets of the stars and uncover the profound wisdom embedded within the celestial realm.

Author :

Shivnath

Vedic, Numerology, Palmistry

English, Hindi, Marathi

Exp: 5 Years

★★★★★
2588 orders

[Chat]

Shivnath
Vedic, Numerology, Palmistry, Life Coach, Loshu Grid, Psychologist

English, Hindi, Marathi, German

Exp: 5 Years

About me

Shivnath is a Vedic Astrologer in India. He loves to help his clients when they are in need. His readings are spot on and he works according to Astrology ethics to bring stability to the lives of the people. However, his main motive is to give you clarity and insight regarding your life and also to empower you with the spiritual knowledge of different energies that are revolving around us. Apart from this, you can also contact him regarding Marriage Compatibility, Career and Business, Love and Relationship, Wealth and Prosperity, Career issues and much more. The remedies he provides are very easy and effective and are proven to be accurate most of the time. Moreover, his customers are always satisfied with his solutions and remedies. He helps all his customers on a personal level and tries to build a relationship with them.

Rating & Reviews

4.99
★★★★★
2588 rates

- 5
- 4
- 3
- 2
- 1

About me

Shivnath is a Vedic Astrologer in India. He loves to help his clients when they are in need. His readings are spirit-guided and he works according to Astrology ethics to bring
stability in the lives of the people. However, his main motive is to give you clarity and insight regarding your life and also to empower you with the spiritual knowledge of
different energies that are revolving around us. Apart from this, you can also contact him regarding Marriage Consultation, Career and Business, Love and Relationship,
Wealth and Property, Career issues and much more. The remedies he provides are very easy and effective and are proven to be accurate most of the time. Moreover, his
customers are always satisfied with his solutions and remedies. He treats all his customers on a personal level and tries to build a relationship with them.

Preface:

Astrology, the ancient and profound science of the celestial bodies, has captivated the human imagination for centuries. It is an art that unveils the mysterious dance of the planets and their influence on our lives, offering profound insights into our destiny and the intricate tapestry of the universe.

In my journey as an astrologer, I have delved deep into the realms of astrology, exploring its intricate nuances and unraveling its hidden wisdom. It has been a transformative experience, a path of self-discovery, and a quest for understanding the cosmic forces that shape our existence.

With great pleasure, I present this book, a culmination of my years of study and practice in the realm of astrology. It is a treasure trove of knowledge, comprising a vast array of astrology facts, figures, and insights. Here, I endeavor to offer a comprehensive exploration of this ancient science, inviting readers to embark on a captivating journey of self-discovery and enlightenment.

This book is designed to be a trusted companion, guiding both novice and seasoned astrologers through the intricate web of planetary influences, zodiac signs, houses, and aspects. It provides a solid foundation in the principles and techniques of astrology, while also delving into the fascinating depths of predictive astrology, birth chart analysis, and remedial measures.

Throughout these pages, you will find a harmonious blend of theory and practical wisdom, supported by real-life examples and case studies. It is my earnest desire that this book serves as a guiding light, empowering you to interpret the cosmic symphony and unlock the secrets of the universe within and around you.

Astrology is a timeless science, a language of the heavens that transcends boundaries and connects us with the divine. As you immerse yourself in the pages that follow, may you embark on a transformative journey, embracing the wisdom of the stars and discovering the infinite possibilities that lie within your birth chart.

I extend my heartfelt gratitude to all the masters and teachers who have illuminated my path, and to the cosmic forces that have guided me along this enlightening expedition. May this book be a beacon of light for all those seeking to explore the profound depths of astrology and unravel the mysteries of their own existence.

Shivnath Shinde

Astrologer

Introduction

In a vast universe where planets and stars adorn the cosmic canvas, astrology stands as a timeless and captivating art. It is a language that unveils the intricate interplay between celestial bodies and human destiny, offering profound insights into our lives and the mysterious forces that shape our existence.

Welcome to the world of astrology—a realm where the heavens become our guide and the birth chart unfolds like a sacred map, revealing the blueprint of our souls. It is a captivating journey of self-discovery and a quest for understanding the hidden forces that influence our paths.

This book is an invitation to embark on that journey—an exploration of astrology's profound depths, its rich symbolism, and its transformative power. Whether you are a curious seeker or a seasoned astrologer, this book aims to be your trusted companion, providing a comprehensive understanding of astrology's fundamental principles and practical applications.

Astrology, at its core, is a reflection of the cosmic dance of energy that permeates the universe. It allows us to decipher the unique tapestry of our lives, deciphering the influences of the planets, zodiac signs, and celestial alignments. By studying these celestial patterns, we gain insight into our personalities, relationships, and life events.

Within these pages, you will find a treasure trove of astrological knowledge. We will delve into the intricacies of the zodiac signs, uncovering their characteristics and how they shape our individuality. We will explore the planetary influences, understanding how each planet carries its own unique energy and imparts its wisdom upon us.

Additionally, we will delve into the art of chart interpretation, deciphering the intricacies of the birth chart and revealing its profound insights. We will explore predictive astrology, offering guidance on forecasting future events and understanding the cycles of life.

Throughout this journey, we will also explore the power of astrology as a tool for self-reflection and personal growth. We will delve into the realm of remedial measures, understanding how we can align ourselves with the cosmic energies to create positive shifts in our lives.

As we traverse this intricate web of knowledge, it is essential to approach astrology with an open mind and a spirit of curiosity. It is a field that blends science and intuition, offering both intellectual exploration and a connection to the mysteries of the universe. By embracing this holistic approach, we can unlock the transformative potential that astrology holds.

Astrology is an ever-unfolding tapestry—a constant source of wonder, inspiration, and guidance. As we embark on this journey together, may this book serve as a guiding light, illuminating the path to self-discovery and offering a deeper understanding of the cosmic forces that shape our lives.

So, let us embark on this celestial adventure, diving into the depths of astrology's wisdom, and may it lead us to a profound appreciation of the interconnectedness of all things.

Welcome to the enchanting world of astrology.

1. The Cosmic Symphony: Understanding the Language of the Stars

Unveiling the Hidden Lagna: Correcting Birth Time Mistakes :

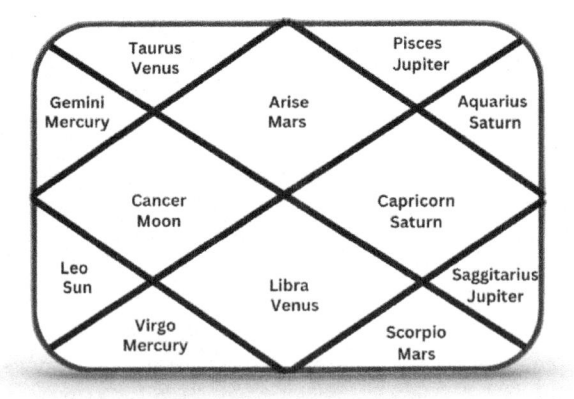

```
           Taurus              Pisces
           Venus               Jupiter
  Gemini           Arise              Aquarius
  Mercury          Mars               Saturn

           Cancer              Capricorn
           Moon                Saturn
  Leo                                 Saggitarius
  Sun              Libra              Jupiter
                   Venus
           Virgo               Scorpio
           Mercury             Mars
```

In the intricate realm of astrology, even a small error in birth time calculation can lead to inaccurate predictions. However, there exists a fascinating method to rectify such mistakes and unveil the true ascendant, despite erroneous watches or careless record-keeping by parents.

What is "lagna"? It refers to the ascendant or the rising sign in astrology. The ascendant is the zodiac sign that was rising on the eastern horizon at the time of an individual's birth. It plays a crucial role in determining the overall personality, traits, and characteristics of a person, as well as influencing various aspects of their life. The discussion in the text revolves around the importance of accurately calculating the lagna and the methodology to rectify any potential errors in determining it.

Let's delve into this intriguing approach. Imagine a scenario where the lagna, or ascendant, is presumed to be Aquarius, but the predicted outcomes fail to align. In such cases, one can explore alternative lagnas, such as Capricorn or Pisces, and study the corresponding results. The lagna that yields accurate predictions shall be deemed correct. By skilfully employing permutations and combinations, the true ascendant can be discovered.

It's essential to consider specific points while undertaking this lagna-casting endeavor:

1. Aries ascendant shall be evaluated in conjunction with Pisces and Taurus.

2. Taurus ascendant shall be assessed in conjunction with Aries and Gemini.

3. Gemini ascendant shall be examined alongside Taurus and Cancer.

4. Cancer ascendant shall be scrutinised in association with Gemini and Leo.

5. Leo ascendant shall be explored with the assistance of Cancer and Virgo.

6. Virgo ascendant shall be appraised in collaboration with Leo and Libra.

7. Libra ascendant shall be examined with the support of Virgo and Scorpio.

8. Scorpio ascendant shall be scrutinised with the aid of Libra and Sagittarius.

9. Sagittarius ascendant shall be studied in conjunction with Scorpio and Capricorn.

10. Capricorn ascendant shall be evaluated alongside Sagittarius and Aquarius.

11. Aquarius ascendant shall be explored with the help of Capricorn and Pisces.

12. Pisces ascendant shall be examined in collaboration with Aquarius and Aries.

This systematic process of considering the neighbouring lagnas empowers astrologers to correct potential errors and unveil the true ascendant with a touch of creative finesse.

By utilising this method, the intricate dance of the zodiac unfolds, and the hidden secrets of one's lagna can be illuminated, transcending the limitations imposed by erroneous birth time recordings.

Distinguishing Factors in Charts: Men and Women

The predictions presented in this book are equally applicable to both men and women, with only a couple of distinctions to bear in mind. Firstly, when interpreting a male horoscope, the predictions concerning the wife should be understood as pertaining to the husband in the case of female horoscopes. Secondly, the predictions concerning the occupations or professions in a female's horoscope will apply to the husband instead.

Predicting Life Events: Vimsottari and Antara Dashas

The timing of significant life events can be accurately predicted using the Vimsottari and Antara dashas. In a male's horoscope, if the Vimsottari Dasha is favorable, it signifies a period of significant progress in one's destiny. In cases where the husband and wife have differing dasha conditions, with one having a good dasha and the other a bad one, it indicates a period of moderate progress. Similarly, when both individuals experience malefic dashas simultaneously, it signifies a harmful period. Conversely, the presence of the Antara (sub-period) of the most auspicious planet within a dasha indicates the most fortunate period.

Addressing Doubts

In instances where a specific matter in a native's horoscope is predicted to bring both benefit and maleficence by different planets, it is important to recognize that both predictions will manifest in some form during their life. The timing and manifestation of these events may vary, but the effects cannot be entirely eliminated. Additionally, it is crucial to understand that the combined influence of all nine planets shapes the life, nature, and inherent characteristics of individuals. Therefore, when contemplating one's destiny, it is advisable to consider the collective impact of all nine planets and their combined effects.

Influence of Planets from the Houses of Occupation:

The aspects of planets from the houses of their occupation provide valuable insights into their influence on various areas of life. Here is a summary of the aspects of each planet from the houses related to their occupation:

Sun: The Sun aspects the 7th house from its house of occupation.

Moon: The Moon aspects the 7th house from its house of occupation.

Mars: Mars has an aspect on the 4th, 7th, and 8th houses from its house of occupation.

Mercury: Mercury aspects the 7th house from its house of occupation.

Jupiter: Jupiter casts its influence on the 5th, 7th, and 9th houses from its house of occupation.

Venus: Venus aspects the 7th house from its house of occupation.

Saturn: Saturn has an aspect on the 3rd, 4th, 7th, and 10th houses from its house of occupation.

Planets as Lords of the Twelve Signs:

Each planet governs specific zodiac signs, and understanding their role as lords of these signs is essential. Here is a summary of the planetary lords for each group of signs:

1st and 8th Signs: Mars
2nd and 7th Signs: Venus
3rd and 6th Signs: Mercury
4th Sign: Moon
5th Sign: Sun
9th and 12th Signs: Jupiter
10th and 11th Signs: Saturn

These associations provide a foundation for analysing the influence of the planets as lords of the different zodiac signs.

Friendship and Enmity among Planets:

Here is a table format summarising the friendship and enmity among planets:

Planets	Deva	Daitya
Sun	Deva	Daitya
Moon	Deva	Daitya
Mars	Deva	Daitya
Jupiter	Deva	Daitya
Venus	Daitya	Deva
Saturn	Daitya	Deva
Dragon's Head	Daitya	Deva
Dragon's Tail	Daitya	Deva
Mercury	Deva	Deva

Note: Mercury is considered a friend of all planets.

In this classification, the Deva planets (Sun, Moon, Mars, and Jupiter) are friends among themselves and are enemies of the Daitya planets (Venus, Saturn, Dragon's Head, and Dragon's Tail). However, Mercury is considered a friend to all planets.

Additionally, the planet that rules a particular zodiac sign is also considered the lord of the house in which that sign is placed.

This table provides a concise overview of the friendship and enmity relationships among the planets based on their classifications as Deva and Daitya, with the exception of Mercury, which is a friend to all.

Exaltation and Debilitation of Planets:

Exaltation and debilitation are significant concepts in astrology that indicate the strengths and weaknesses of planets based on their position in specific zodiac signs. Here are clear sentences to understand the exaltation and debilitation of each planet:

1. Sun:
   - Exaltation: The Sun is exalted in the sign of Aries.
   - Debilitation: The Sun is debilitated in the sign of Libra.

2. Moon:
   - Exaltation: The Moon is exalted in the sign of Taurus.
   - Debilitation: The Moon is debilitated in the sign of Scorpio.

3. Mars:
   - Exaltation: Mars is exalted in the sign of Capricorn.
   - Debilitation: Mars is debilitated in the sign of Cancer.

4. Mercury:

- Exaltation: Mercury is exalted in the sign of Virgo.

- Debilitation: Mercury is debilitated in the sign of Pisces.

5. Jupiter:

- Exaltation: Jupiter is exalted in the sign of Cancer.

- Debilitation: Jupiter is debilitated in the sign of Capricorn.

6. Venus:

- Exaltation: Venus is exalted in the sign of Pisces.

- Debilitation: Venus is debilitated in the sign of Virgo.

7. Saturn:

- Exaltation: Saturn is exalted in the sign of Libra.

- Debilitation: Saturn is debilitated in the sign of Aries.

8. Dragon's Head (Rahu):

- Exaltation: Rahu is exalted in the sign of Gemini.

- Debilitation: Rahu is debilitated in the sign of Sagittarius.

9. Dragon's Tail (Ketu):

- Exaltation: Ketu is exalted in the sign of Sagittarius.

- Debilitation: Ketu is debilitated in the sign of Gemini.

These exaltation and debilitation positions indicate the signs in which the planets are believed to be most potent and weakest, respectively.

The degrees of planets :

The degrees of planets refer to their specific positions within the zodiac at a given time. In astrology, the zodiac is divided into 360 degrees, with each degree representing a unique point in the celestial sphere. The degrees of planets are measured to determine their exact locations within the zodiac.

For example, if a planet is said to be at 15 degrees of Aries, it means that it is positioned 15 degrees away from the beginning of the zodiac sign Aries. Similarly, if a planet is at 25 degrees of Taurus, it signifies its location 25 degrees into the zodiac sign Taurus.

The degrees of planets are crucial for constructing birth charts, analyzing transits, and making astrological predictions. By considering the degrees of planets in relation to other celestial bodies or sensitive points in a chart, astrologers can derive insights into various aspects of an individual's life, including personality traits, relationships, career prospects, and more.

10% Result: Minimal influence or impact from the planet at that degree. It may not significantly contribute to the overall outcome or experience.

25% Result: Mild influence or effect from the planet. It can bring some noticeable but relatively modest changes or manifestations.

50% Result: Moderate influence or effect from the planet. It can have a balanced impact and contribute to significant developments or experiences.

100% Result: Strongest influence or effect from the planet. It can bring powerful transformations, prominent outcomes, or profound experiences.

Planet	0-6 degrees	6-12 degrees	12-18 degrees	18-22 degrees	22-25 degrees	25-30 degrees
Sun	10% Result	25% Result	50% Result	100% Result	50% Result	10% Result
Moon	10% Result	25% Result	50% Result	100% Result	50% Result	10% Result
Mars	10% Result	25% Result	50% Result	100% Result	50% Result	10% Result
Mercury	10% Result	25% Result	50% Result	100% Result	50% Result	10% Result
Jupiter	10% Result	25% Result	50% Result	100% Result	50% Result	10% Result
Venus	10% Result	25% Result	50% Result	100% Result	50% Result	10% Result
Saturn	10% Result	25% Result	50% Result	100% Result	50% Result	10% Result
Uranus	10% Result	25% Result	50% Result	100% Result	50% Result	10% Result
Neptune	10% Result	25% Result	50% Result	100% Result	50% Result	10% Result
Pluto	10% Result	25% Result	50% Result	100% Result	50% Result	10% Result
Rahu	10% Result	25% Result	50% Result	100% Result	50% Result	10% Result
Ketu	10% Result	25% Result	50% Result	100% Result	50% Result	10% Result
Ascendant	10% Result	25% Result	50% Result	100% Result	50% Result	10% Result

2. The Zodiac Tapestry: Exploring the Twelve Signs

The 12 houses in astrology:

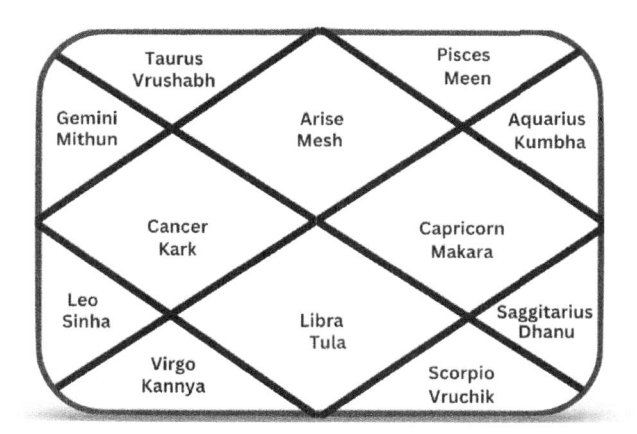

The 12 houses in astrology represent various aspects of life based on their corresponding zodiac signs and ruling planets. Here's a breakdown of each house and its significance:

1. First House (Aries, Ruling Planet: Mars): Represents self-image, personality, and physical appearance.

2. Second House (Taurus, Ruling Planet: Venus): Governs personal finances, possessions, and values.

3. Third House (Gemini, Ruling Planet: Mercury): Relates to communication, siblings, short trips, and learning.

4. Fourth House (Cancer, Ruling Planet: Moon): Signifies home, family, roots, and emotional well-being.

5. Fifth House (Leo, Ruling Planet: Sun): Represents creativity, self-expression, romance, and children.

6. Sixth House (Virgo, Ruling Planet: Mercury): Governs work, health, daily routines, and service to others.

7. Seventh House (Libra, Ruling Planet: Venus): Relates to partnerships, marriage, relationships, and cooperation.

8. Eighth House (Scorpio, Ruling Planets: Mars and Pluto): Signifies transformation, shared resources, sexuality, and the occult.

9. Ninth House (Sagittarius, Ruling Planet: Jupiter): Represents higher education, philosophy, travel, and spiritual pursuits.

10. Tenth House (Capricorn, Ruling Planet: Saturn): Governs career, public image, achievements, and authority.

11. Eleventh House (Aquarius, Ruling Planets: Uranus and Saturn): Relates too friendships, social groups, aspirations, and humanitarian causes.

12. Twelfth House (Pisces, Ruling Planets: Neptune and Jupiter): Signifies spirituality, the subconscious mind, solitude, and hidden matters.

The first house Description :

The first house in a horoscope represents various aspects of an individual's personality, physical appearance, self-expression, and overall approach to life. Here are some possible interpretations and outcomes associated with the first house:

1. Self-Identity: The first house represents the core of your personality and self-image. It reflects how you perceive yourself and how you project that image to the world. It influences your confidence, assertiveness, and overall sense of self.

2. Physical Appearance: The first house is closely associated with your physical body, appearance, and overall vitality. It can provide insights into your natural physical traits, such as facial features, body structure, and overall health.

3. First Impressions: This house is also associated with the first impression you make on others. It reflects how you come across to people when they initially meet you. It may influence how others perceive your personality, energy, and presence.

4. Personal Goals and Ambitions: The first house can reveal your personal aspirations and how you approach achieving your goals. It reflects your motivation, drive, and determination to pursue your desires and make a mark in the world.

5. Self-Expression: This house governs your self-expression, including your communication style, mannerisms, and the way you present yourself to others. It can provide insights into how you express your thoughts, ideas, and emotions.

6. Leadership Abilities: The first house is associated with leadership qualities and the ability to take initiative. It reflects your capacity to assert yourself, take charge, and inspire others. It may indicate your natural inclination towards leadership positions.

7. Independence and Individuality: The first house represents your sense of independence and individuality. It reflects your need for autonomy and freedom to express yourself as a unique individual. It may influence your resistance to conforming to societal norms and your desire to stand out.

8. Approach to Life Challenges: The first house can provide insights into your approach to life's challenges

and how you handle them. It may indicate your resilience, adaptability, and ability to overcome obstacles.

The second house Description :

The second house in astrology represents various aspects related to personal finances, material possessions, values, and self-worth. Here are some potential interpretations and outcomes associated with the second house:

1. Financial Resources: The second house is closely associated with personal finances, including income, earnings, and financial stability. It reflects how you acquire and manage your resources, as well as your overall financial potential.

2. Material Possessions: This house signifies your relationship with material possessions and the importance you place on acquiring and enjoying material comforts. It can provide insights into your attitudes towards money, wealth, and the accumulation of possessions.

3. Personal Values: The second house represents your personal values and what you consider important in life. It influences the principles and beliefs that guide your financial decisions and material pursuits.

4. Self-Worth and Self-Esteem: This house is linked to your sense of self-worth and self-esteem, particularly in

relation to your financial situation and material possessions. It can indicate how your self-worth is influenced by your financial success or the value you place on your possessions.

5. Income and Earnings: The second house reflects your income potential and the ways in which you earn money. It can provide insights into your skills, talents, and resources that contribute to your financial well-being.

6. Spending and Saving Habits: This house also influences you're spending and saving habits. It reflects how you handle money, whether you tend to be a spender or a saver, and your overall financial discipline.

7. Relationship with Material Wealth: The second house can indicate your relationship with material wealth and how you perceive abundance. It may reflect your ability to attract and enjoy material resources and the level of satisfaction you derive from your possessions.

8. Values-Based Decisions: The second house suggests that your financial decisions and material pursuits are influenced by your personal values. It may indicate the importance you place on financial security, stability, or the pursuit of wealth in alignment with your values.

The third house Description :

The third house in astrology represents various aspects related to communication, learning, siblings, short-distance travel, and intellectual pursuits. Here are some potential interpretations and outcomes associated with the third house:

1. Communication and Expression: The third house is closely associated with communication skills, including speaking, writing, and listening. It reflects your ability to articulate your thoughts and ideas effectively and connect with others through communication.

2. Siblings and Close Relatives: This house represents relationships with siblings, cousins, and close relatives. It reflects the dynamics and interactions within these relationships and may provide insights into the nature of your bond with them.

3. Learning and Education: The third house governs learning, education, and intellectual pursuits. It reflects your curiosity, ability to acquire knowledge, and interest in continuous learning. It can indicate your preferred learning styles and areas of interest.

4. Short-Distance Travel: This house is associated with short-distance travel, such as local or regional trips. It reflects your inclination towards exploring nearby places, engaging in short journeys, and the experiences you gain from them.

5. Communication Skills and Professions: The third house influences your communication skills and can indicate potential career paths that involve effective communication, such as writing, journalism, teaching, public speaking, or sales.

6. Sibling Relationships: This house can shed light on the dynamics and relationship with your siblings. It may indicate the level of closeness, communication, and cooperation within these relationships.

7. Mental Abilities and Intellect: The third house represents your mental abilities, including reasoning, logic, and problem-solving skills. It can provide insights into your intellectual potential and how you process information.

8. Curiosity and Adaptability: The third house suggests a natural curiosity and adaptability to new ideas and environments. It reflects your willingness to explore different perspectives, engage in intellectual debates, and embrace changes in your surroundings.

The fourth house Description:

The fourth house in astrology represents various aspects related to home, family, roots, emotions, and the foundation of one's life. Here are some potential interpretations and outcomes associated with the fourth house:

1. Home and Family Life: The fourth house is closely associated with your home environment and family dynamics. It reflects your relationship with your parents, the atmosphere in your childhood home, and the sense of security and comfort you seek in your living space.

2. Roots and Ancestry: This house represents your roots, heritage, and ancestral connections. It reflects your cultural and familial background and the influence it has on your sense of identity and belonging.

3. Emotional Foundation: The fourth house governs your emotional well-being and inner sense of security. It reflects the foundation upon which you build your emotional stability and the need for a nurturing and supportive environment.

4. Private Life and Personal Sanctuary: This house is associated with your private life and personal sanctuary. It reflects the need for a safe and secure space where you can retreat, recharge, and find emotional solace.

5. Real Estate and Property: The fourth house can indicate your inclination towards real estate, property ownership, and matters related to your physical dwelling. It may reflect your desire for stability and investment in properties or your involvement in real estate-related professions.

6. Childhood and Early Memories: This house represents your childhood experiences and early memories. It reflects the influence of your upbringing on

your emotional development and the lasting impact it may have on your present life.

7. Family Traditions and Heritage: The fourth house suggests the importance of family traditions and the preservation of cultural heritage. It may reflect your attachment to family customs, rituals, and the passing down of ancestral wisdom.

8. Sense of Belonging and Security: The fourth house indicates your need for a sense of belonging and emotional security. It reflects your desire for a supportive family or community network that nurtures and protects you.

The fifth house Description :

The fifth house in astrology represents various aspects related to creativity, self-expression, romance, children, and entertainment. Here are some potential interpretations and outcomes associated with the fifth house:

1. Creative Expression: The fifth house is closely associated with creativity and self-expression. It reflects your artistic inclinations, creative talents, and your desire to engage in activities that allow you to express yourself freely.

2. Romance and Love Affairs: This house represents romance, love affairs, and the pursuit of pleasure. It

reflects your approach to romantic relationships, dating, and the enjoyment of life's pleasures and leisure activities.

3. Children and Parenthood: The fifth house governs children, including your relationship with your own children, if applicable, or your role as a parent in the future. It reflects your nurturing qualities, creativity in parenting, and the joy derived from interacting with children.

4. Fun, Entertainment, and Hobbies: This house signifies leisure activities, hobbies, and the pursuit of fun and entertainment. It reflects your need for playfulness, recreation, and activities that bring you joy and a sense of fulfilment.

5. Creative Projects and Pursuits: The fifth house encourages creative projects and endeavours. It may indicate your inclination towards artistic pursuits, such as writing, painting, acting, or any form of self-expression that allows you to showcase your unique creativity.

6. Speculation and Risk-Taking: This house is associated with speculative ventures and risk-taking, such as gambling or investments with an element of chance. It reflects your approach to taking calculated risks and the potential for gains or losses in such endeavours.

7. Confidence and Self-Assurance: The fifth house represents your confidence and self-assurance. It reflects

your ability to express yourself authentically, take pride in your talents and accomplishments, and have the courage to share your creative gifts with others.

8. Playfulness and Inner Child: The fifth house encourages a sense of playfulness and reconnecting with your inner child. It reflects your ability to approach life with a sense of joy, spontaneity, and a willingness to embrace your own unique sense of fun.

The sixth house Description :

The sixth house in astrology represents various aspects related to work, daily routines, health, service, and self-improvement. Here are some potential interpretations and outcomes associated with the sixth house:

1. Work and Employment: The sixth house is closely associated with work, employment, and your approach to daily routines. It reflects your work ethic, job responsibilities, and the satisfaction you derive from your work.

2. Health and Well-being: This house governs health and well-being, both physical and mental. It reflects your

approach to maintaining a healthy lifestyle, self-care practices, and your overall well-being.

3. Service and Helping Others: The sixth house is associated with service to others and the desire to be of assistance. It reflects your inclination towards helping those in need, volunteering, or working in professions that involve serving others.

4. Daily Routines and Habits: This house represents your daily routines, habits, and rituals. It reflects your organisational skills, time management, and the efficiency with which you handle your daily responsibilities.

5. Workplace Relationships: The sixth house may indicate the dynamics and relationships within your workplace. It reflects your ability to collaborate with colleagues, work as a team, and maintain harmonious relationships in your professional environment.

6. Self-Improvement and Personal Development: This house encourages self-improvement and personal development. It reflects your commitment to continuous learning, skill enhancement, and the pursuit of knowledge in order to excel in your work and daily life.

7. Attention to Detail: The sixth house signifies attention to detail and the ability to focus on tasks at hand. It reflects your meticulousness, precision, and the importance you place on thoroughness in your work and daily activities.

8. Work-Life Balance: The sixth house may highlight the importance of achieving a healthy work-life balance. It reflects your ability to manage your time effectively, prioritise self-care, and find harmony between your work responsibilities and personal life.

The seventh house Description :

The seventh house in astrology represents various aspects related to partnerships, relationships, marriage, and collaboration. Here are some potential interpretations and outcomes associated with the seventh house:

1. Marriage and Committed Partnerships: The seventh house is closely associated with marriage and committed partnerships. It reflects your approach to relationships, your desire for a long-term partnership, and the qualities you seek in a partner.

2. Business Partnerships and Contracts: This house represents business partnerships, contracts, and legal agreements. It reflects your ability to collaborate with others in professional settings and establish mutually beneficial relationships.

3. Relationship Dynamics: The seventh house reflects the dynamics within your close relationships. It indicates the balance of power, communication styles, and the ability to form harmonious connections with others.

4. Collaboration and Cooperation: This house is associated with collaboration and cooperation in various

areas of life. It reflects your ability to work well with others, negotiate compromises, and find mutual solutions in partnerships.

5. Relationship Needs and Desires: The seventh house signifies your relationship needs and desires. It reflects the qualities you value in a partner, the level of commitment you seek, and the importance of shared values and goals in a relationship.

6. Diplomacy and Negotiation: The seventh house encourages diplomacy and negotiation skills. It reflects your ability to find common ground, resolve conflicts, and maintain harmony in your relationships.

7. Open Enemies and Opponents: This house may indicate the presence of open enemies or opponents in your life. It reflects challenges or conflicts that arise from opposing viewpoints or conflicting interests.

8. Attraction and Compatibility: The seventh house reflects the level of attraction and compatibility you seek in relationships. It may indicate the qualities, physical or otherwise, that you find appealing in potential partners.

The eighth house Description :

The eighth house in astrology represents various aspects related to transformation, sexuality, shared resources, and the deeper aspects of life. Here are some potential interpretations and outcomes associated with the eighth house:

1. Transformation and Rebirth: The eighth house is closely associated with transformation and rebirth. It reflects your ability to undergo personal growth, embrace change, and experience profound inner transformations.

2. Shared Resources and Finances: This house represents shared resources, such as inheritances, investments, and financial partnerships. It reflects your approach to joint finances, debt, and the management of shared assets.

3. Intimacy and Sexuality: The eighth house governs intimacy, sexuality, and deep emotional connections. It reflects your approach to intimate relationships, the level of trust and vulnerability you are willing to share, and your understanding of the deeper aspects of love.

4. Occult and Mystical Matters: This house is associated with the occult, mysticism, and metaphysical pursuits. It reflects your interest in esoteric knowledge, psychic abilities, and your potential for spiritual growth and transformation.

5. Psychological Depth and Inner Healing: The eighth house represents psychological depth and inner healing. It reflects your ability to confront and transform deep-seated emotional patterns, traumas, and subconscious beliefs.

6. Life and Death: This house signifies the cycle of life and death. It reflects your understanding and acceptance of mortality, your approach to grief and loss,

and your perception of the mysteries of life and the afterlife.

7. Power Dynamics and Control: The eighth house may indicate power dynamics and issues related to control in relationships. It reflects your ability to navigate power struggles, assert your personal boundaries, and establish healthy boundaries in shared spaces.

8. Inheritance and Legacy: This house represents inheritance, both material and spiritual. It reflects the potential for receiving legacies, gifts, or ancestral wisdom that can shape your life and contribute to your personal growth.

The ninth house Description :

The ninth house in astrology represents various aspects related to higher learning, spirituality, philosophy, travel, and expansion of consciousness. Here are some potential interpretations and outcomes associated with the ninth house:

1. Higher Education and Philosophy: The ninth house is closely associated with higher education, academia, and philosophical pursuits. It reflects your desire for knowledge, intellectual curiosity, and the quest for deeper understanding of life's meaning.

2. Spiritual Beliefs and Exploration: This house represents spirituality and religious beliefs. It reflects

your approach to spirituality, your religious or philosophical inclinations, and your exploration of different spiritual practices.

3. Travel and Adventure: The ninth house governs long-distance travel, foreign cultures, and the pursuit of new experiences. It reflects your inclination to explore different countries, cultures, and expand your horizons through travel.

4. Wisdom and Life Philosophy: This house signifies your personal wisdom and life philosophy. It reflects your beliefs, values, and the principles you live by. It may also indicate your ability to impart wisdom and guidance to others.

5. Higher Learning and Teaching: The ninth house encourages higher learning and teaching. It reflects your aptitude for academic pursuits, teaching or mentoring others, and your inclination to share knowledge and wisdom.

6. Law, Ethics, and Justice: This house is associated with law, ethics, and justice. It reflects your sense of fairness, moral compass, and your interest in legal matters or advocacy for social justice causes.

7. Publishing and Media: The ninth house may indicate an affinity for publishing, writing, or engaging with various forms of media. It reflects your ability to disseminate knowledge, share your ideas, and communicate on a broader scale.

8. Spiritual and Philosophical Teachers: This house represents spiritual and philosophical teachers or mentors who have a significant impact on your life. It reflects the guidance and wisdom you receive from these individuals.

The tenth house Description :

The tenth house in astrology represents various aspects related to career, public image, reputation, achievements, and authority. Here are some potential interpretations and outcomes associated with the tenth house:

1. Career and Professional Life: The tenth house is closely associated with career and professional life. It reflects your aspirations, ambitions, and the path you choose to pursue in your professional endeavours.

2. Public Image and Reputation: This house represents your public image and reputation. It reflects how you are perceived by others, your social standing, and the impression you make in the public sphere.

3. Achievements and Recognition: The tenth house governs achievements and recognition. It reflects your potential for success, the recognition you receive for your accomplishments, and the rewards you earn through hard work and dedication.

4. Authority and Leadership: This house is associated with authority and leadership. It reflects your ability to

take on leadership roles, manage responsibilities, and inspire others with your influence and guidance.

5. Professional Goals and Long-Term Plans: The tenth house signifies your professional goals and long-term plans. It reflects your vision for success, your determination to achieve your objectives, and the strategic steps you take to advance in your career.

6. Public Responsibilities and Duties: This house represents public responsibilities and duties. It reflects your involvement in public service, community roles, or positions of responsibility that require you to serve the public interest.

7. Professional Reputation and Success: The tenth house signifies your professional reputation and success. It reflects the impact you have in your chosen field, the level of respect you garner from peers, and your ability to leave a lasting legacy in your career.

8. Career Changes and Advancement: This house may indicate career changes and advancements. It reflects your potential for growth, promotion, or shifts in your professional path that lead to greater success and recognition.

The eleventh house Description :

The eleventh house in astrology represents various aspects related to friendships, social connections, group activities, aspirations, and personal goals. Here are some potential interpretations and outcomes associated with the eleventh house:

1. Friendships and Social Circles: The eleventh house is closely associated with friendships and social connections. It reflects your ability to form meaningful relationships with others, the type of friends you attract, and your involvement in group activities.

2. Networking and Social Influence: This house represents networking and social influence. It reflects your ability to connect with people from various backgrounds, establish beneficial relationships, and leverage your social network for personal and professional opportunities.

3. Community Involvement and Humanitarian Causes: The eleventh house governs community involvement and humanitarian causes. It reflects your inclination to contribute to society, engage in activism, and work towards the betterment of the collective.

4. Group Collaboration and Teamwork: This house encourages group collaboration and teamwork. It reflects your ability to work well within a team, contribute your unique skills and ideas, and achieve common goals through collective efforts.

5. Aspirations and Long-Term Goals: The eleventh house signifies your aspirations and long-term goals. It reflects your vision for the future, the dreams you strive to achieve, and the community support you seek to realise your ambitions.

6. Social Activism and Advocacy: This house is associated with social activism and advocacy. It reflects your passion for social justice, your willingness to speak out against injustice, and your dedication to making a positive impact in the world.

7. Social Events and Gatherings: The eleventh house may indicate involvement in social events and gatherings. It reflects your enjoyment of socialising, attending parties, and being part of social circles where you can connect with like-minded individuals.

8. Group Dynamics and Peer Influence: This house represents group dynamics and peer influence. It reflects the impact of your social environment on your personal growth, decision-making, and the ability to find support and encouragement from your peers.

The twelfth house Description :

The twelfth house in astrology represents various aspects related to introspection, spirituality, subconscious mind, hidden matters, and solitude. Here are some potential interpretations and outcomes associated with the twelfth house:

1. Spirituality and Inner Growth: The twelfth house is closely associated with spirituality and inner growth. It reflects your inclination towards introspection, meditation, and seeking a deeper connection with the divine or higher realms.

2. Subconscious Mind and Dreams: This house represents the subconscious mind and dreams. It reflects your intuition, psychic abilities, and the messages and insights that come through dreams and the hidden realms of the mind.

3. Solitude and Retreat: The twelfth house signifies solitude and retreat. It reflects your need for periods of seclusion, introspection, and self-reflection to recharge and connect with your inner self.

4. Hidden Matters and Secrets: This house is associated with hidden matters and secrets. It reflects the potential for hidden enemies, unresolved issues, or aspects of your life that are kept private or concealed from others.

5. Compassion and Empathy: The twelfth house governs compassion and empathy. It reflects your ability to understand and empathise with the pain and struggles of others, and your inclination towards acts of kindness and service.

6. Karma and Past Lives: This house signifies karma and past lives. It reflects the influence of past experiences on your present life, the lessons you need to learn, and the spiritual growth that comes from resolving karmic patterns.

7. Self-Undoing and Sacrifice: The twelfth house may indicate tendencies towards self-undoing or sacrifice. It reflects the challenges you face in letting go of self-

limiting patterns, addictive behaviours, or the need to rescue others at the expense of your own well-being.

8. Healing and Therapy: This house encourages healing and therapy. It reflects the potential for emotional and psychological healing, the need to address deep-rooted issues, and the benefit of seeking professional help or engaging in therapeutic practices.

3. Predictions of the Planets with Reference to Arise Ascendant

1. Sun in Aries

Sun in the 1st House (Aries):

For individuals with Aries Ascendant, when the Sun is in the 1st house, they tend to be learned and receive a good education. They have a deep understanding of themselves, and their self-knowledge is strong. They are often tall in stature and find happiness in the company of children. Mentally, they are sharp and astute. However, their focus on their spouse may be somewhat lacking, and they might have a diminished interest in sexual matters and occupational pursuits.

Sun in the 2nd House (Taurus):

When the Sun is placed in the 2nd house, individuals may face difficulties in acquiring education, leading to mental worry. Their financial situation might be challenging, and they may find it necessary to work hard for their wealth. Problems with children could also arise during this period.

Sun in the 3rd House (Gemini):

With the Sun in the 3rd house, individuals possess a powerful intellect and excel in their education. They have a commanding influence over others through their speech. Physically, they are strong and hard-working. They maintain harmonious relationships with their siblings and hold strong beliefs in righteousness, faith in God, and adherence to Dharma. They exhibit great courage and communicate bravely.

Sun in the 4th House (Cancer):

In this placement, individuals receive a good education and are blessed with the qualities of a caring mother. They possess a sweet speaking style and are likely to acquire land and property. They may show less interest in matters related to their father. At times, they may become negligent, and they might harbour negative opinions towards the government and society. However, overall, they are wise individuals.

Sun in the 5th House (Leo):

When the Sun is in the 5th house, individuals acquire a good education and become skilled orators. They possess intellect and foresight and have a positive influence on their children. However, there may be a shortage of income, and they may develop a sense of superiority over others.

Sun in the 6th House (Virgo):

Individuals with the Sun in the 6th house may face challenges in education and experience mental worries. They may encounter enemies but will ultimately overcome difficulties and obstacles. They are inclined to guide others in problem-solving. Happiness with children may be limited, and they may receive influence from their maternal grandfather. They tend to spend a lot of money and gain through their intellectual pursuits.

Sun in the 7th House (Libra):

When the Sun is placed in the 7th house, individuals may not find satisfaction in their relationships with their spouse and children. Their educational pursuits may suffer, and they might lack wisdom. Their family life could be troubled, and they may engage in both right and wrong methods to earn more. They may not experience happiness in their sexual life and may be secretive individuals.

Sun in the 8th House (Scorpio):

With the Sun in the 8th house, individuals may face difficulties and misery concerning their children. Their education may suffer, leading to mental worries. They tend to be secretive and follow a routine life. They may acquire wealth through others and display a crooked nature. Their speech can be harsh and impulsive.

Sun in the 9th House (Sagittarius):

Individuals with the Sun in the 9th house receive a good education and improve their destiny through wisdom. They are religiously inclined and experience happiness from their children, siblings, and sisters. They possess energy and may receive unexpected gains. They speak justly, hold influence, and are learned individuals.

Sun in the 10th House (Capricorn):

When the Sun is placed in the 10th house, individuals with Aries Ascendant may exhibit childish behavior and develop conflicts or enmity with their father figure. They may face hindrances in their professional advancement or occupation, encountering opposition from society and the government. Their work might lack decency or ethical conduct. However, they hold a deep respect for their mother and find happiness in matters related to houses and landed property.

Sun in the 11th House (Aquarius):

Individuals with the Sun in the 11th house may feel indifferent towards acquiring education. They might experience dissatisfaction in their relationships with children and prioritize intellectual pursuits over family matters. They may display selfish tendencies, have a tendency towards harsh speech, and possess ambitious aspirations.

Sun in the 12th House (Pisces):

Those with the Sun in the 12th house may have limitations in acquiring a good education and could experience weak eyesight. They may have extravagant spending habits and feel discontented with their children. Their communication style may be roundabout or indirect. They might face mental worries and challenges from enemies. They strive to control their expenses and maintain good contacts.

2. Moon in Aries

Moon in the 1st House (Aries):

When the Moon is in the 1st house, individuals experience happiness and enjoy all kinds of pleasures. They receive affection from their mother and find joy in their land and home. They possess a good-looking appearance and derive happiness from their spouse. Sexual pleasure is fulfilling for them. They achieve success and respect in their chosen occupation or profession. They have contacts with supportive individuals and enjoy a luxurious lifestyle.

Moon in the 2nd House (Taurus):

With the Moon in the 2nd house, individuals acquire wealth, lands, and property. They come from a large family. However, they may find it challenging to fully enjoy their wealth. They experience mental happiness but face disturbances in their daily routine. They receive help from others.

Moon in the 3rd House (Gemini):

When the Moon is placed in the 3rd house, individuals find happiness through their relationships with brothers and sisters. They gain from their mother and enjoy fame. They have a strong faith in God and hold a deep love for righteousness (Dharma). They possess landed property and receive help and support from their siblings.

Moon in the 4th House (Cancer):

Individuals with the Moon in the 4th house receive abundant motherly affection and acquire landed property through her. They are carefree and experience mental happiness. They hold their mother in high regard, considering her superior to their father. They engage in works related to the government and society, enjoying pleasures and luxuries.

Moon in the 5th House (Leo):

When the Moon is in the 5th house, individuals perceive themselves as intelligent. They find happiness through their children and acquire wealth. They possess excellent speaking skills and are considerate of others' feelings. They engage in deep thinking and hold a devoted attitude towards their mother.

Moon in the 6th House (Virgo):

Individuals with the Moon in the 6th house encounter hindrances in their pursuit of happiness. They may lack motherly affection and experience a lack of family happiness. They may not possess substantial landed properties. Mental unhappiness prevails, and they face fears from enemies. They tend to spend a significant amount and receive help from their maternal grandfather.

Moon in the 7th House (Libra):

Those with the Moon in the 7th house enjoy family pleasures and find a good-looking spouse. They experience happiness with their mother and enjoy landed property. They possess physical health and a handsome appearance. They have a fulfilling sexual life and exhibit great skills in maintaining family and worldly affairs.

Moon in the 8th House (Scorpio):

When the Moon is placed in the 8th house, individuals may experience the loss of their mother and unhappiness with maternal relatives. They face disturbances and tend to be narrow-minded. Stomach troubles may be a recurring issue, and they struggle to accumulate wealth. They face financial challenges and difficulties.

Moon in the 9th House (Sagittarius):

Individuals with the Moon in the 9th house are blessed with good luck from their mother's side. They acquire landed property and buildings. They receive divine assistance and feel content and satisfied. They have a strong belief in righteousness (Dharma) and receive support from their siblings. They experience gains in industry.

Moon in the 10th House (Capricorn):

With the Moon in the 10th house, individuals receive affection from their father and acquire landed property. They receive help from the government and society, enjoying their favor. They achieve success in business or their chosen profession. They engage in virtuous deeds, have a good sense of fashion, appreciate beauty and decoration, and hold high aspirations.

Moon in the 11th House (Aquarius):

When the Moon is in the 11th house, individuals experience good income and gain happiness, although they may face some difficulties along the way. They acquire wealth from lands and houses and receive a good education. They possess the ability to speak sweetly and find pleasure in their relationships. They enjoy the comforts and pleasures that life has to offer.

Moon in the 12th House (Pisces):

Individuals with the Moon in the 12th house tend to spend a significant amount on pleasure and indulgence. They may have expenses related to good causes as well. They may experience the loss of their mother and lack substantial landed properties. They have associations with enemies but possess the ability to plan their expenditures with ease. They may experience mental restlessness.

3. Mars in Aries

Mars in the 1st House (Aries):

When Mars is in the 1st house, individuals gain fame and physical greatness. They possess spiritual powers, although their mother may not be supportive. They may lack happiness in their married life and struggle to find pleasure in family relationships. Restlessness is a prominent trait.

Mars in the 2nd House (Taurus):

Individuals with Mars in the 2nd house are always occupied with earning money. However, they may experience financial losses. They may engage in illegal or unethical practices to accumulate wealth. They may face challenges or losses related to their children. Their harsh speech can hinder their progress, and they may have a less religious inclination.

Mars in the 3rd House (Gemini):

When Mars is placed in the 3rd house, individuals are energetic and ambitious. They may not find happiness in their relationships with siblings. However, they gain recognition from the government and society. They achieve success through their own merit and excel in business. They have the ability to overcome obstacles and conquer their enemies.

Mars in the 4th House (Cancer):

Individuals with Mars in the 4th house may have a short stature. They may experience a lack of motherly affection and restlessness. They may face difficulties or losses related to land and property. Happiness in married life may be lacking, and they tend to be hard-working.

Mars in the 5th House (Leo):

With Mars in the 5th house, individuals display wisdom but can also be impulsive. They may not find happiness or satisfaction in their relationships with children. They have a tendency to spend heavily and hold ambitious aspirations.

Mars in the 6th House (Virgo):

Individuals with Mars in the 6th house are influential and gain fame through their industry or work. They may encounter enemies but emerge victorious. They may experience physical ailments or troubles but manage to overcome them. Confidence is not easily shaken. They may have a slightly irreligious inclination and tend to spend a significant amount. They possess bravery, occult powers, and selfish tendencies.

Mars in the 7th House (Libra):

When Mars is placed in the 7th house, individuals face difficulties in fulfilling their duties and encounter constant clashes in their married life. They strive for the betterment of their business or profession. They receive recognition and honour from the government and society. However, they may struggle to improve their financial situation. They may face challenges in enjoying a fulfilling sexual life.

Mars in the 8th House (Scorpio):

Individuals with Mars in the 8th house may have a lean body and a deficiency in physical size. They often feel restless. They can gain wealth through inheritances or by holding power over others' lives, but this may lead to premature ageing. Their relationships with siblings may suffer, but they can become famous.

Mars in the 9th House (Sagittarius):

With Mars in the 9th house, individuals are fortunate but face hindrances in their luck or destiny. They may receive gains from others or distant relatives. They tend to spend a significant amount and may not be happy with their motherly relationships. They may not pay much attention to land, peace, and happiness. Their relationships with siblings may be less harmonious. They have a showy nature.

Mars in the 10th House (Capricorn):

Individuals with Mars in the 10th house possess great physical strength. They attain dignity and supremacy in their daily lives. They have self-respect and pride and gain fame and respect from the government and society. They engage in grand deeds and have a good personality. They are independent and assert themselves, often giving orders. However, they may be careless about seeking pleasure and may not be dutiful towards their parents. They have a mischievous side but excel in education and intellect.

Mars in the 11th House (Aquarius):

Individuals with Mars in the 11th house are hard-working and achieve gains through their efforts. They may adopt aggressive or confrontational approaches in pursuit of their goals. However, they may experience financial losses and face worries and distress within their families. They overcome their enemies but can be somewhat careless. They possess mysterious powers related to knowledge and intelligence.

Mars in the 12th House (Pisces):

Those with Mars in the 12th house often feel restless and unsatisfied in their relationships with siblings. They tend to spend a significant amount of money and may not find happiness in their married life. They experience worries and distress in their daily work or occupation. Overcoming challenges becomes a difficult task for them. They may not find fulfilment in their sexual life and domestic responsibilities. Physically, they may have weaker constitutions.

4. Mercury in Aries

Mercury in the 1st House (Aries):

Individuals with Mercury in the 1st house have friendly relationships with their siblings. They receive support from their maternal grandfather's side and possess the ability to overcome enemies, disputes, and obstacles. They are clever in getting their work done and benefit from the support of their spouse and family. With careful planning and industriousness, they improve their working conditions.

Mercury in the 2nd House (Taurus):

Those with Mercury in the 2nd house earn wealth through their intelligence. They have a mixed relationship with their family and may not receive strong support from their siblings. They are ambitious and strive to earn more.

Mercury in the 3rd House (Gemini):

Individuals with Mercury in the 3rd house are intelligent and strive for perfection. They may not receive significant support from their siblings. However, they improve their wealth through hard work and exert influence. They have the ability to conquer enemies.

Mercury in the 4th House (Cancer):

Energetic and industrious, individuals with Mercury in the 4th house face hindrances from their brothers and sisters. They find happiness through their maternal grandfather but may have problems related to property. They are restless but ultimately overcome their enemies. They experience gains in their occupation and receive honor from the state and society.

Mercury in the 5th House (Leo):

Those with Mercury in the 5th house are careful, judicious, and clever. They find happiness with their children and are successful in conquering their enemies. They earn good wealth. There Lucky Metal is Gold.

Mercury in the 6th House (Virgo):

Individuals with Mercury in the 6th house are influential but may experience conflicts with their brothers. They receive support from their maternal grandfather and are successful in overcoming enemies. They may be careless about their expenditure but are dignified due to their intelligence. They are highly industrious, courageous, and brave.

Mercury in the 7th House (Libra):

Those with Mercury in the 7th house have to work hard and face challenges in their occupation. Despite the difficulties, they make progress. They may not be entirely happy with their spouse but enjoy sexual pleasures. They advance in domestic and worldly affairs and receive help from their maternal grandfather.

Mercury in the 8th House (Scorpio):

Individuals with Mercury in the 8th house may experience weaknesses in their finances. They receive energies from their maternal grandfather but may not have strong affection from their brothers and sisters. They are clever in getting their work done and have faith in occult powers. They work hard to acquire wealth but may suffer from stomach problems and worry in their daily routine.

Mercury in the 9th House (Sagittarius):

Those with Mercury in the 9th house achieve success through industry. They gain fame and power but may not be strong believers in religious principles. They receive help from their brothers and sisters but may struggle to determine the right approach for their betterment.

Mercury in the 10th House (Capricorn):

Individuals with Mercury in the 10th house possess discriminative abilities. They receive help from their brothers, sisters, and father. They gain honour and power in government and society through their hard work. They experience improvement in their industry.

Mercury in the 11th House (Aquarius):

Those with Mercury in the 11th house gain from their relationships with brothers and sisters. They earn wealth and work hard to increase their income. They experience gains in education, possess good speaking skills, and are clever in their endeavours.

Mercury in the 12th House (Pisces):

Individuals with Mercury in the 12th house may lack affection from their siblings. They must keep their expenditures under control. They receive help from unexpected sources, including their enemies. They have occult powers and may be concerned about growing expenses, leading them to be somewhat miserly.

5. Jupiter in Aries

Jupiter in the 1st House (Aries):

These individuals are handsome, fortunate, and respected. They make wise financial decisions, enjoy good health, possess a religious inclination, have children, receive a good education, experience domestic happiness, achieve success in their occupations, demonstrate foresight, and exhibit a kind-hearted nature.

Jupiter in the 2nd House (Taurus):

Individuals are fortunate and accumulate wealth. They receive divine assistance, although there may be slight losses in their accumulated wealth. They are adept at managing their expenses, although there are occasional instances of overspending. They possess a religious outlook, overcome their enemies, and find contentment in their daily routines.

Jupiter in the 3rd House (Gemini):

Fortunate individuals who manage their expenses well. They receive support from their brothers and sisters, work hard, achieve success in their occupations, and enjoy familial happiness.

Jupiter in the 4th House (Cancer):

These individuals experience happiness and gains through their homes. They are fortunate, exhibit a showy nature, and have a religious inclination. They derive pleasure from their mothers but do not find happiness through their fathers.

Jupiter in the 5th House (Leo):

Fortunate individuals who possess intelligence and receive a good education. They have expertise in religious scriptures, are eloquent speakers, find happiness through their children, and receive honors.

Jupiter in the 6th House (Virgo):

Less fortunate individuals who may lack religious inclination. They experience a loss of fame, manage their expenses, face disputes but emerge victorious, may not be dutiful towards their parents, face enmity with the government and society, display cleverness in dealing with enemies, and work with wisdom.

Jupiter in the 7th House (Libra):

These individuals are successful in their daily lives and experience happiness in their domestic life. They find a dignified spouse, live modestly, possess faith in God, achieve success, work energetically, and maintain a righteous outlook.

Jupiter in the 8th House (Scorpio):

Unlucky and irreligious individuals who have a long life but face unpleasantness due to their destiny.

Jupiter in the 9th House (Sagittarius):

Fortunate individuals who achieve success in their endeavors with divine assistance. They possess good intellect and education, find happiness through their children, receive cooperation from their siblings, and have a religious outlook.

Jupiter in the 10th House (Capricorn):

Successful in business but may not hold significant importance in society and government. They spend honorably, find peace and happiness, and receive divine assistance.

Jupiter in the 11th House (Aquarius):

Individuals experience gains with the support of destiny. They receive assistance in their endeavors, cooperation from their siblings, achieve success in their occupations, enjoy sexual pleasures, and excel in education and public speaking.

Jupiter in the 12th House (Pisces):

These individuals possess a religious outlook but are not highly fortunate. They spend generously but also exercise control over their expenses. They may face some losses and direct their expenditures towards religious endeavors. They are dignified and cautious of their enemies.

6. Venus in Aries

Venus in the 1st House (Aries):

Successful profession and wealth accumulation. Beautiful and satisfying marital life.Artistic and clever.Good family and domestic happiness.Skilled, able, and successful in worldly affairs.

Venus in the 2nd House (Taurus):

Accumulates good wealth.Large and loving family.Success in various professions.Enjoyment of sexual pleasures with a satisfying spouse.Honor and respect were received.

Venus in the 3rd House (Gemini):

Clever wealth accumulation and prominent position.Supportive and influential siblings.Attractive and religious spouse.Enjoyment of sexual pleasures and adherence to duty and religion.Esteemed, influential, and pleasing appearance.

Venus in the 4th House (Cancer):

Happiness, wealth, and a good spouse.Respected position and honor from government and society.Affection from mother and worldly pleasures.Clever and refined approach.

Venus in the 5th House (Leo):

Favorable occupation and wealth accumulation.Limited family and marital happiness.Mental worries and exhaustion related to children.Articulate, educated, and preoccupied with sexual thoughts.

Venus in the 6th House (Virgo):

Anxiety regarding wealth and family losses.Dissatisfaction with the spouse and sexual unhappiness.Hard work required.Lack of happiness on the paternal side.Excessive spending, secretive strategies, and health issues.Engages in borrowing and spending practices.

Venus in the 7th House (Libra):

Abundant wealth and a good position.Beautiful spouse and wealthy father-in-law.Strong family ties and enjoyable sexual pleasures. Skilful in earning money and highly respected.Possesses a handsome appearance.

Venus in the 8th House (Scorpio):

Weak health and loss of wealth.Success through foreign collaborations.Dissatisfaction with the spouse and family.Lack of sexual pleasures.Hidden passions.

Venus in the 9th House (Sagittarius):

Great fortune and happiness from the spouse and family.Wealth accumulation and adherence to moral principles.Bravery and courage.

Venus in the 10th House (Capricorn):

Advantages from the father.Happiness in the maternal home and landed property.Tremendous wealth, fame, and wisdom.

Venus in the 11th House (Aquarius):

Significant wealth and professional success.Gains from the spouse and enjoyable sexual experiences.Some dissatisfaction concerning children and education.

Venus in the 12th House (Pisces):

Excessive spending and loss of wealth.Strained family and relative relationships.Dissatisfaction with the spouse.Occupational improvements.Extravagant indulgence in sexual pleasures.Fear from enemies, quarrelsomeness, and unhappiness with the maternal grandfather.

7. Saturn in Aries

Saturn in the 1st House (Aries):

Individuals with Saturn in Aries Ascendant may not be considered attractive in appearance. They may not experience happiness or a close bond with their father. They tend to be dependent on others and often have to work hard to earn money. Despite this, they are very industrious and energetic. They give special importance to their spouse and may display some laziness in their personal life.

Saturn in the 2nd House (Taurus):

People with Saturn in the 2nd House generally earn well and have the potential to gain from government or society. However, they may not receive affection or emotional support from their mother. They may feel restless in their daily life and continuously work hard to increase their wealth.

Saturn in the 3rd House (Gemini):

Individuals with Saturn in the 3rd House are energetic and valorous. They receive education and support from their siblings. They also gain honor and recognition from the government and society. However, they tend to spend a lot and may feel unhappy with their children. They may not show much interest in religion and can be prideful.

Saturn in the 4th House (Cancer):

People with Saturn in the 4th House find happiness and support from their father. They receive help from the government or society. However, they may not experience a strong emotional connection with their mother. They may face challenges from their enemies and need to work hard to overcome them. They can be somewhat careless but still have to put in a lot of effort to achieve their goals.

Saturn in the 5th House (Leo):

Individuals with Saturn in the 5th House may not have a strong bond or receive much happiness from their father. They can gain through education and intellectual pursuits. They work hard to progress in their chosen occupation and derive joy from pursuing sexual pleasures. They give importance to their spouse and dedicate themselves to social activities. However, they may not be entirely satisfied with their children.

Saturn in the 6th House (Virgo):

People with Saturn in the 6th House may not experience happiness with their father. They may worry about their daily routine and face some insecurities in terms of their earnings. They may not have significant problems with enemies but may incur heavy expenses due to circumstances beyond their control. They may receive some help from their siblings.

Saturn in the 7th House (Libra):

Individuals with Saturn in the 7th House tend to do well in business but have to work hard for their earnings. They may feel restless and seek pleasure in sexual activities. They can be proud and have a sense of self-importance.

Saturn in the 8th House (Scorpio):

People with Saturn in the 8th House may experience worries related to their father and often live alone. They work hard to gain from foreign collaborations and exhibit great determination and ability. They may face intellectual challenges and not derive much happiness from children or education. Arrogance can be a prominent trait.

Saturn in the 9th House (Sagittarius):

Individuals with Saturn in the 9th House gain heavily through the house of destiny. They receive a regular fixed income and are fortunate in many aspects of life. They tend to be religious and do not have many enemies. They have the ability to overcome obstacles and challenges.

Saturn in the 10th House (Capricorn):

People with Saturn in the 10th House engage in significant business ventures and enjoy good income. They receive support from the government or society and may spend lavishly. They also find pleasure in sexual activities. They work diligently to progress in their career and have a sense of self-pride.

Saturn in the 11th House (Aquarius):

Individuals with Saturn in the 11th House typically have a stable and firm income. They engage in honorable deeds and receive assistance from the government or society. They are known for their hard work and may prioritize their responsibilities over personal comfort. They may experience intellectual concerns regarding their daily routine.

Saturn in the 12th House (Pisces):

Individuals with Saturn in the 12th House may experience financial losses related to their father. They tend to spend money in various ways and work hard to increase their wealth. They engage in diverse activities to uphold righteousness and maintain influence in challenging situations or with adversaries.

8. Rahu in Aries

Rahu in the 1st House (Aries):

Individuals with Rahu in Aries Ascendant may experience health issues and have a diseased appearance. They exhibit courage and often become popular among others. They tend to make unauthorized efforts and keep their actions secretive. Despite facing calamities, they show bravery and resilience.

Rahu in the 2nd House (Taurus):

People with Rahu in the 2nd House may encounter wealth loss and separation from their family. They possess cleverness in earning money and engage in unauthorized methods discreetly to accumulate wealth. They face domestic problems and conflicts within the family. Courageous and restless, they constantly seek new experiences.

Rahu in the 3rd House (Gemini):

Individuals with Rahu in the 3rd House are courageous and work hard to acquire wealth. They tend to exert control over their siblings. Fearless by nature, they exert influence and pressure on others.

Rahu in the 4th House (Cancer):

People with Rahu in the 4th House may experience the loss of their mother and a lack of peace in their lives. They may also face the loss of property and lands, which leads to mental stress. Their actions may often astonish others.

Rahu in the 5th House (Leo):

Individuals with Rahu in the 5th House may not receive a good education. They feel unhappy with their children and tend to be mentally worried. They may display peevishness and harsh speech, finding it difficult to understand others.

Rahu in the 6th House (Virgo):

People with Rahu in the 6th House overcome challenges and difficulties related to earnings. They have an upper hand in dealing with various obstacles. However, they can be selfish and face hindrances from their maternal grandfather's side.

Rahu in the 7th House (Libra):

Individuals with Rahu in the 7th House may experience problems in their relationships, particularly with their spouse. They find it challenging to manage their household and often achieve success in their occupation only after facing difficulties. They may also experience sexual dissatisfaction and engage in unauthorised gains through worldly affairs.

Rahu in the 8th House (Scorpio):

People with Rahu in the 8th House face worries in their daily life and may suffer a loss of livelihood. They may experience internal diseases in the abdomen and are known for adopting manipulative strategies.

Rahu in the 9th House (Sagittarius):

Individuals with Rahu in the 9th House tend to feel unhappy and face anxieties and nervousness regarding their destiny and progress. They resort to improper and secret schemes to achieve their goals. They may face significant losses in matters related to religion and spirituality, leading to a lack of faith and restlessness.

Rahu in the 10th House (Capricorn):

People with Rahu in the 10th House may not be happy with their father and face hindrances in their career progression and business ventures. However, they possess latent power and determination to overcome obstacles and eventually achieve success through great effort.

Rahu in the 11th House (Aquarius):

Individuals with Rahu in the 11th House have the potential to gain heavily, accumulating income and wealth. They employ secret, and sometimes unauthorized, methods to achieve their desired outcomes.

Rahu in the 12th House (Pisces):

People with Rahu in the 12th House may feel unhappy with their spending habits. They tend to have conflicts with people outside their immediate circle. However, they possess a sense of calmness and are not easily perturbed even when faced with grave difficulties. Ultimately, they succeed in controlling their expenses.

9. Ketu in Aries

Ketu in the 1st House (Aries):

Individuals with Ketu in Aries Ascendant may feel restless and have a weak constitution. They may experience occasional bouts of pain. They possess good patience and are not easily influenced by others. However, they can be rash, obstinate, and lack self-confidence.

Ketu in the 2nd House (Taurus):

People with Ketu in the 2nd House may face losses in their wealth and struggle with financial shortages. They may experience unhappiness within their family.

Ketu in the 3rd House (Gemini):

Individuals with Ketu in the 3rd House may feel unhappy and have conflicts with their siblings. They may resort to improper methods to achieve their goals. However, they do not lose their self-confidence and often act in their own self-interest.

Ketu in the 4th House (Cancer):

People with Ketu in the 4th House may lack a strong bond with their mother and may experience separation from their family. They may face losses in immovable properties such as land and buildings. They feel restless and unhappy but eventually overcome significant challenges and achieve gains and pleasures.

Ketu in the 5th House (Leo):

Individuals with Ketu in the 5th House may feel dissatisfied with their children and may struggle in the realm of education. They find it difficult to communicate their ideas and words effectively and tend to be secretive.

Ketu in the 6th House (Virgo):

People with Ketu in the 6th House conquer their enemies and display bravery. They receive less affection from their maternal grandfather. They face sudden adversaries but ultimately succeed in overcoming them. However, they may also commit sins along the way.

Ketu in the 7th House (Libra):

Individuals with Ketu in the 7th House may experience the loss of a spouse or feel sexually unsatisfied in their relationship. They encounter problems in their occupation but navigate them with care and eventually achieve success.

Ketu in the 8th House (Scorpio):

People with Ketu in the 8th House may experience weakness in their back and lower abdomen. They may be careless in their daily routine and face challenges related to their age. They have a strong sense of pride and contribute to the cooperative aspects of their livelihood. They work hard and eventually gain some fame and influence.

Ketu in the 9th House (Sagittarius):

Individuals with Ketu in the 9th House work diligently towards their destiny's progress. They may explore hidden places and experiment with different approaches.

Although they may not adhere to traditional religious practices, they do not criticise or blame Dharma.

Ketu in the 10th House (Capricorn):

People with Ketu in the 10th House may experience distress, loss, and deficiencies related to paternal sources. They may not find satisfaction in their occupation but achieve success through great effort. They may also face a loss of honor and respect but display bravery in their actions.

Ketu in the 11th House (Aquarius):

Individuals with Ketu in the 11th House gain significantly and continuously strive for further gains. They are always engaged in pursuing financial success. They may sometimes act rashly in their earnings and tend to prioritize their own selfish interests.

Ketu in the 12th House (Pisces):

People with Ketu in the 12th House tend to spend a significant amount and worry about their expenditures. They work with determination to manage their expenses and may face difficulties at times.

4. Predictions of the Planets with Reference to Taurus Ascendant

1. Sun in Taurus

Sun in the 1st House (Taurus):

Individuals with Sun in Taurus Ascendant acquire landed property and experience happiness through their occupation. They find joy in their relationships with their spouse and family, as well as in their sexual pleasures.

Sun in the 2nd House (Gemini):

People with Sun in the 2nd House enjoy wealth, land, and have a strong connection with their mother. They experience happiness within their family and through their ownership of buildings.

Sun in the 3rd House (Cancer):

Individuals with Sun in the 3rd House gain influential happiness from their siblings. They find joy in their properties and buildings and receive assistance from their mother. However, they may have a tendency towards irreligiosity.

Sun in the 4th House (Leo):

People with Sun in the 4th House acquire land and property. They experience happiness through their mother but may not receive much assistance from their father. They establish connections with the government and feel content within their own home.

Sun in the 5th House (Virgo):

Individuals with Sun in the 5th House gain education and wisdom. They find happiness through their children and possess intelligence.

Sun in the 6th House (Libra):

People with Sun in the 6th House face opposition and potential separation from their mother. They may experience loss of land and property and worries caused by enemies. They feel restless and may lose courage.

Sun in the 7th House (Scorpio):

Individuals with Sun in the 7th House experience happiness through their mother, family, and spouse. However, they may encounter some bodily discomfort.

Sun in the 8th House (Sagittarius):

People with Sun in the 8th House feel restless and distressed in relation to their mother. They may leave their country and establish influential friendships and ownership of land in foreign places. They work towards increasing their wealth.

Sun in the 9th House (Capricorn):

Individuals with Sun in the 9th House experience happiness through their mother and acquire lands and buildings. They become more religious and find some joy in their relationships with their siblings. They are also fortunate.

Sun in the 10th House (Aquarius):

People with Sun in the 10th House experience happiness through their mother but may have conflicts with their father. They enjoy the possession of lands and buildings and receive recognition from society and the government. They find satisfaction in their occupation but may experience losses due to occasional laziness.

Sun in the 11th House (Pisces):

Individuals with Sun in the 11th House gain from their mother, acquire lands and buildings, and receive some income. They benefit from education and their children and possess great cleverness and patience.

Sun in the 12th House (Aries):

People with Sun in the 12th House tend to spend a significant amount. They experience happiness through others but may face losses related to buildings and property. They may fear their enemies and feel restless due to heavy expenditures.

2. Moon

Moon in the 1st House (Taurus):

Individuals with Moon in Taurus Ascendant receive support from their brothers and sisters. They possess courage and ambition but may experience some dissatisfaction with their spouse, profession, and sexual pleasures. They feel restless in domestic affairs.

Moon in the 2nd House (Gemini):

People with Moon in the 2nd House accumulate wealth and find happiness in their relationships with their brothers and sisters. They may feel physically weak but gain in their daily life through their career. They put in a lot of effort.

Moon in the 3rd House (Cancer):

Individuals with Moon in the 3rd House engage in industrious work and receive excellent cooperation from their brothers and sisters. They are hardworking and experience mental gains. They have a belief in God and possess patience.

Moon in the 4th House (Leo):

People with Moon in the 4th House find happiness through their brothers and sisters. They acquire lands and buildings and receive help from others. Their relationship with their father may not be very cordial. They are enterprising and experience happiness.

Moon in the 5th House (Virgo):

Individuals with Moon in the 5th House receive a good education and find support from their brothers and sisters and children. They are skilled conversationalists.

Moon in the 6th House (Libra):

People with Moon in the 6th House experience differences with their brothers and sisters. They may feel exhausted and find strength in dealing with enemies.

Moon in the 7th House (Scorpio):

Individuals with Moon in the 7th House are not very happy with their spouse. They may not receive much help from their brothers and sisters and may feel dissatisfied in their occupation and sexual pleasure.

Moon in the 8th House (Sagittarius):

People with Moon in the 8th House may experience separation from their brothers and sisters. They feel strong in their daily routine of life and make efforts to acquire wealth. They have contacts with foreign countries and show interest in occult studies.

Moon in the 9th House (Capricorn):

Individuals with Moon in the 9th House receive favorable outcomes through destiny. They have harmonious relationships with their brothers and sisters, possess a dharmic nature, believe in God, and experience happiness.

Moon in the 10th House (Aquarius):

People with Moon in the 10th House receive help from their brothers and sisters and make progress in their work within the government and society. They find happiness through their mother and cherish pleasing memories.

Moon in the 11th House (Pisces):

Individuals with Moon in the 11th House gain wealth through their hard work and benefit from their relationships with their brothers and sisters. They make progress in education and find happiness through their children. They are clever and intelligent.

Moon in the 12th House (Aries):

People with Moon in the 12th House may experience enmity with their brothers and sisters. They have a significant amount of expenditure but are not harmed by enemies. They may experience mental unrest.

3. Mars

Mars in the 1st House (Taurus):

Individuals with Mars in Taurus Ascendant may experience impurities in their blood and daily life expenditure. They prioritise their wife over their mother, find happiness through lands and buildings, and often wander. They work hard, but may feel somewhat restless within the family.

Mars in the 2nd House (Gemini):

People with Mars in the 2nd House may face difficulties in monetary gains and family matters. They may experience distress in their profession and marital life, as well as troubles in education and with their children.

Mars in the 3rd House (Cancer):

Individuals with Mars in the 3rd House feel distress and deficiencies in their marital life. They may experience separation from their brothers, weakness, and wavering in their occupation. They make efforts to gain influence over their enemies.

Mars in the 4th House (Leo):

People with Mars in the 4th House may experience the loss of their mother and separation from their homeland.

However, they find happiness in their occupation and have strong marital happiness. They work hard to earn more wealth but may experience weakness in sexual pleasures. They gain respect from the government and society.

Mars in the 5th House (Virgo):

Individuals with Mars in the 5th House tend to spend excessively. They may be slightly weak in education and experience loss regarding their children. They make others work hard and feel anxious about worldly affairs and sexual pleasures.

Mars in the 6th House (Libra):

People with Mars in the 6th House face worries in their occupation and have mixed expenditure. They experience concerns about their spouse and are likely to suffer from diabetes. They may have enmity with their maternal grandfather and their household.

Mars in the 7th House (Scorpio):

Individuals with Mars in the 7th House have dignified expenditure and weakness in the dignity of their family. They have mixed relations with their spouse and weakness in sexual pleasures. They may experience loss in wealth but are hardworking.

Mars in the 8th House (Sagittarius):

People with Mars in the 8th House work hard but face many troubles and disputes in their occupation. They may experience loss through their spouse and face many disputes within the family. They may also suffer from financial losses, organic disorders, and have a shorter life expectancy.

Mars in the 9th House (Capricorn):

Individuals with Mars in the 9th House experience huge expenditure due to their profession. They may not be inclined towards religious or moral principles and have disputes with their brothers and sisters. They may experience loss through their mother and feel unhappy regarding their children. They come under the influence of their spouse and feel exhausted.

Mars in the 10th House (Aquarius):

People with Mars in the 10th House excel in their professional work but may experience disorder in their body. They may face loss in their children's side and struggle with education. They may also experience loss through their father and have mixed feelings in sexual pleasures.

Mars in the 11th House (Pisces):

Individuals with Mars in the 11th House earn wealth through their profession but may face some losses concerning their children and education. They are able to control their enemies, but they may feel unhappy with their spouse and experience deficiencies in sexual pleasures. They try to control their expenditure but still tend to spend.

Mars in the 12th House (Aries):

People with Mars in the 12th House may experience loss through their spouse but may indulge in sexual pleasures through extramarital affairs. They may feel weak due to their involvement in excessive sexual connections.

4. Mercury

Mercury in the 1st House (Taurus):

Individuals with Mercury in Taurus Ascendant acquire wisdom and education. They earn wealth through careful considerations, possess a handsome appearance, and command respect within the family and through their spouse. They have desires for sexual pleasure and have the potential to become rich and clever.

Mercury in the 2nd House (Gemini):

People with Mercury in the 2nd House accumulate significant wealth and receive extensive education. They develop strong bonds with their children and excel in planning. They are ambitious and driven in life.

Mercury in the 3rd House (Cancer):

Individuals with Mercury in the 3rd House receive a good education and earnings. They have the power to influence their children and possess good discretion. They gain fame and influence through their siblings. They are skilled conversationalists.

Mercury in the 4th House (Leo):

People with Mercury in the 4th House acquire a good education and experience happiness through their children. They accumulate wealth, including buildings and property. They have decent ideas, enjoy comfort and happiness, engage in positive actions, and possess strong oratorical abilities. They make progress in business.

Mercury in the 5th House (Virgo):

Individuals with Mercury in the 5th House receive a good education and accumulate wealth. They are clever and discriminating in their actions. They find happiness through their children.

Mercury in the 6th House (Libra):

People with Mercury in the 6th House may face deficiencies in education and within the family. However, they are clever in dealing with their enemies. They have concerns about acquiring wealth.

Mercury in the 7th House (Scorpio):

Individuals with Mercury in the 7th House are clever in earning money. They receive support from their children and may experience slight unhappiness with their spouse. They indulge in more sexual pleasures and are interested in accumulating wealth.

Mercury in the 8th House (Sagittarius):

People with Mercury in the 8th House may experience the loss of children and limited education. They face the loss of wealth and mental worries. They may engage in foreign collaborations.

Mercury in the 9th House (Capricorn):

Individuals with Mercury in the 9th House acquire a good education and accumulate wealth. They are fortunate in having children and have strong beliefs in God. They receive help from their siblings.

Mercury in the 10th House (Aquarius):

People with Mercury in the 10th House receive a high level of education. They may secure government jobs and gain from their father and children. They earn substantial wealth and achieve distinction in business. They enjoy gains from the government and society, are respected, and benefit from buildings and lands. They possess cleverness.

Mercury in the 11th House (Pisces):

Individuals with Mercury in the 11th House may face challenges in acquiring wealth and experience some difficulties in education. They feel unhappy with their children and encounter discrimination in their income-related matters. They possess cleverness.

Mercury in the 12th House (Aries):

People with Mercury in the 12th House experience loss through their children and face financial setbacks. They may have limited education and worries. They tend to spend extravagantly and receive help from their paternal grandfather. They face worries from enemies and encounter losses and deficiencies within the family.

5. Jupiter

Jupiter in the 1st House (Taurus):

Individuals with Jupiter in Taurus in the first house are generally clever but may suffer from health problems. Despite this, they usually obtain importance and dignity in their daily lives. These individuals possess a good education but may experience some challenges with their children.

Jupiter in the 2nd House (Gemini):

People with Jupiter in Gemini in the second house typically gain wealth and make progress in the realm of finances. They may experience some unhappiness with their father and have concerns involving the government and society. However, they make attempts to overcome these worries.

Jupiter in the 3rd House (Cancer):

Those with Jupiter in Cancer in the third house are likely to gain substantial wealth and demonstrate courage and influence. They often hold a great deal of dignity in their daily lives and have sway over their siblings. In terms of spirituality, they may not give much importance to faith and divinity.

Jupiter in the 4th House (Leo):

Individuals with Jupiter in Leo in the fourth house are likely to enjoy a long life and achieve fame in their professional and personal lives. They may experience separation from their mother but also benefit from connections with foreign countries. These individuals may have mixed relations with their father, face opposition from the government and society, and possess hidden talents or powers.

Jupiter in the 5th House (Virgo):

People with Jupiter in Virgo in the fifth house may face some challenges in the area of education but work hard to achieve success. They may also possess hidden talents or powers during conversation.

Jupiter in the 6th House (Libra):

Individuals with Jupiter in Libra in the sixth house may struggle to obtain wealth and may experience health issues. They might have conflicts with their father and face disapproval from the government and society. Additionally, they may experience a deficiency in income and may have a tendency to overspend.

Jupiter in the 7th House (Scorpio):

Those with Jupiter in Scorpio in the seventh house take pride in their nobility and may have mixed relations with their spouse. They typically experience success in their daily occupations, receive assistance from foreign countries, perform energetic deeds, and maintain support from their brothers and sisters. They have a knack for utilising effective strategies for achieving worldly gains.

Jupiter in the 8th House (Sagittarius):

Individuals with Jupiter in Sagittarius in the eighth house receive help from foreign countries and tend to spend a lot. They might have mixed relations with their mother, work hard to accumulate wealth, and uphold dignity in their daily routines. Additionally, they may have mixed relations with their family.

Jupiter in the 9th House (Capricorn):

People with Jupiter in Capricorn in the ninth house are likely to experience significant losses concerning their destiny and spirituality, as well as some health problems. They may feel restless in their daily routine and compromise their faith to achieve material gains. These individuals may experience weakness in income and in matters related to divinity, using their cleverness regarding children and attracting some cooperation from their siblings.

Jupiter in the 10th House (Aquarius):

Those with Jupiter in Aquarius in the tenth house often have connections with foreign countries and may experience loss or enmity with their father. They may achieve financial success through hard work, but experience some weakness in their relations with the government and society. These individuals show honorable spending habits and use various methods to improve their wealth and influence. They may face a deficiency in the house of mother but strive to overcome this issue.

Jupiter in the 11th House (Pisces):

Individuals with Jupiter in Pisces in the eleventh house generally enjoy long lives and attain wealth through successful strategies. They may experience some tension with their brothers and sisters and attempt to obtain unauthorised gains in matters of relationships and pleasure. These individuals are also believed to have hidden strength or powers.

Jupiter in the 12th House (Aries):

People with Jupiter in Aries in the twelfth house are prone to spending judiciously while working hard in the pursuit of wealth and success. They may have a good relationship with their mother but face enmity with their maternal grandfather. These individuals might also experience deficiencies in matters related to wealth.

6.Venus

Venus in the 1st House (Taurus):

Individuals with Venus in the first house of their Taurus Ascendant birth chart are known to be proud and possess a strong determination. They have a steady and unwavering approach towards life and are successful in their daily occupation. Their influence is significant in the house of enemies, often allowing them to be victorious against adversaries. Marriage provides financial gains, but they may suffer from occasional health problems. Despite their stubborn nature, they remain resolute in their decisions.

Venus in the 2nd House (Gemini):

When Venus is placed in the second house of a Taurus Ascendant birth chart, the person puts in tremendous effort to accumulate wealth. Although these individuals are determined to increase their financial status, they may face some challenges in the house of wealth and family. There is also a possibility of health issues, but their persistence and dedication help them to overcome difficult situations.

Venus in the 3rd House (Cancer):

The presence of Venus in the third house indicates that a person has to work hard to achieve success. They may face conflicts with siblings, and their fortune is likely to be linked to their maternal grandfather's house. Despite the challenges, their perseverance is the key to their progress.

Venus in the 4th House (Leo):

Individuals with Venus in the fourth house may experience difficulties in their relationship with their mother, leading to a loss in physical happiness. There are potential challenges in the father's house, but they can expect honor and recognition from society and the government. They work diligently to succeed in their business, and issues related to land and buildings may cause some unrest. However, their resilience is their strength in overcoming obstacles.

Venus in the 5th House (Virgo):

With Venus in the fifth house, a person may face trouble when it comes to children and education. They tend to be anxious and find it difficult to communicate their thoughts effectively due to a nervous disposition. Despite their struggles, they refuse to accept defeat, even when dealing with opposition in the house of enemies.

Venus in the 6th House (Libra):

Individuals with Venus in the sixth house exhibit independence and the ability to influence others. Again, health issues could be a concern, but they receive support from their maternal grandfather's side of the family. Their ability to work hard and persevere in the face of adversity enables them to enjoy significant influence over their enemies.

Venus in the 7th House (Scorpio):

A person with Venus in the seventh house tends to have an attractive appearance. They may experience unauthorised gains through their spouse and could be easily tempted by sensual pleasures. While there may be some marital problems, they are diligent in their professional life, navigating through any unrest with patience and determination.

Venus in the 8th House (Sagittarius):

This placement of Venus may bring about physical discomfort and a loss in the side of the maternal grandfather's family. Despite their restlessness, they perform demanding tasks and work diligently to improve their financial situation. Even in the face of adversity, they remain steadfast and resilient.

Venus in the 9th House (Capricorn):

A fortunate disposition characterises individuals with Venus in the ninth house of a Taurus Ascendant birth chart. However, they may struggle to advance in matters related to spirituality or religion. These individuals are intelligent, well-mannered, and receive support from siblings. Their calculated approach helps them succeed in battles against their enemies.

Venus in the 10th House (Aquarius):

When Venus is positioned in the tenth house, a person is likely to progress in the government and society. They may encounter some issues with their father but manage to assert their influence in the house of enemies. Although their relationship with their mother may not be ideal, they receive honour and progress in their career. A tinge of unhappiness may linger, but it does not deter them from their goals.

Venus in the 11th House (Pisces):

With Venus in the eleventh house, an individual may experience substantial financial gains. However, their education may be affected, and they may also face some dissatisfaction regarding their children. Despite these challenges, they remain driven to increase their wealth, relying on their wit and intellect to do so.

Venus in the 12th House (Aries):

Venus positioned in the twelfth house, specifically in Aries, indicates a tendency to spend lavishly, experience concerns, and endure certain ailments. Additionally, individuals with this placement may encounter disrespect in matters of honor and frequently feel a sense of isolation.

7.Saturn

Saturn in the 1st House (Taurus):

When Saturn is positioned in the first house of Taurus Ascendant, it is believed to bring fortune and influence. Individuals with this placement are likely to receive respect from their father, government, and society. They may have a keen interest in politics and work diligently towards progress. However, they may not receive much support from their siblings and may experience conflicts with their spouse. Despite these challenges, they are hardworking and determined individuals.

Saturn in the 2nd House (Gemini):

In the second house, Saturn in Gemini indicates that individuals will accumulate wealth through destiny and receive respect from government and society. They may find some satisfaction through their mother, but may struggle with managing land and property. These individuals are likely to work hard to enjoy their wealth and may be somewhat restless. They may also experience restrictions in their relationships with government, society, and their father.

Saturn in the 3rd House (Cancer):

Saturn in Cancer in the third house suggests that individuals will achieve significant progress and success through hard work. They may become well-known and respected, but may experience dissatisfaction in their relationships with siblings. These individuals are skilled communicators, but may be careless with their spending. They are likely to be religious, influential, and courageous, with support from their father.

Saturn in the 4th House (Leo):

In the fourth house, Saturn in Leo indicates dissatisfaction with one's parents. However, these individuals may gain influence and power in dealing with enemies and receive honour from government and society. They may feel somewhat unhappy and engage in challenging tasks, but they are also religious and committed to their beliefs.

Saturn in the 5th House (Virgo):

With Saturn in Virgo in the fifth house, individuals are likely to gain from their father and achieve success and honour through their intelligence and education. They may acquire knowledge of religious duties and education, and experience some progress in their relationships with their children. However, they may also face dissatisfaction in their marriage and need to work hard to achieve success in their daily occupations.

Saturn in the 6th House (Libra):

In the sixth house, Saturn in Libra suggests that individuals will gain strength from their father and conduct business through influential actions. They are likely to be respected and honored, maintaining influence over their enemies. These individuals are willing to work hard and maintain their progress, but may be careless in their work and spending habits. They may also experience conflicts with their siblings.

Saturn in the 7th House (Scorpio):

Saturn in Scorpio in the seventh house indicates fortune, but also uneasiness within the family. These individuals may not be very religious and may experience unhappiness with their mother. Despite these challenges, they may still gain from the government and society.

Saturn in the 8th House (Sagittarius):

In the eighth house, Saturn in Sagittarius suggests distress in one's relationship with their father and a lack of fame. However, these individuals may achieve progress through diligence and cooperation with foreign countries. They may possess divine power and excel in education.

Saturn in the 9th House (Capricorn):

With Saturn in Capricorn in the ninth house, individuals are likely to experience happiness with their father and gain from government and society. They may achieve dignity in dealing with enemies but may face deceit in their relationships with siblings. These individuals are energetic and committed to their religious duties, earning them honour and respect.

Saturn in the 10th House (Aquarius):

In the tenth house, Saturn in Aquarius indicates great honour in government and society. However, these individuals may be careless and make mistakes in their spending habits. They may experience unhappiness with their mother and conflicts with their spouse. Despite these challenges, they may engage in successful business ventures, albeit with some unhappiness.

Saturn in the 11th House (Pisces):

Saturn in Pisces in the eleventh house suggests significant income and gains for individuals. They are likely to be religious and hardworking, with some success in their relationships with their children.

Saturn in the 12th House (Aries):

In the twelfth house, Saturn in Aries indicates loss in one's relationship with their father and engagement in lowly deeds. These individuals may experience weakness in their spending habits and influence in dealing with enemies. They may also feel unhappy in their interactions with government and society.

8. Rahu

Rahu in the 1st House (Taurus):

When Rahu is in the first house of Taurus, it indicates a weak constitution, leading to worries and anxieties. The individual may be secretive and clever, but also courageous. They may face challenges in maintaining their health and well-being, and may need to work on building their strength and resilience.

Rahu in the 2nd House (Gemini):

In the second house of Gemini, Rahu's presence signifies a strong desire for wealth and material possessions. The individual may work hard and plan meticulously to accumulate wealth, but may sometimes face obstacles in achieving their financial goals. They may need to make significant efforts to secure their financial future and establish a stable foundation for their family.

Rahu in the 3rd House (Cancer):

When Rahu is in the third house of Cancer, it indicates potential loss or separation from siblings. The individual may be secretive and selfish in their dealings with others, which could lead to strained relationships with their brothers and sisters. They may need to work on being more open and honest with their loved ones to maintain harmony in their family life.

Rahu in the 4th House (Leo):

In the fourth house of Leo, Rahu's presence signifies loss in the house of the mother, as well as the loss of land and property. The individual may be unhappy and may leave their birthplace in search of a better life. They may face suffering and challenges in their personal life, but may find happiness through unconventional or secret methods. They may also have deep and hidden plans for their living situation and overall happiness, which could cause them to feel restless and unsettled.

Rahu in the 5th House (Virgo):

When Rahu is in the fifth house of Virgo, it indicates a loss in education and a potential loss of children. The individual may be secretly clever, but may face challenges in their academic pursuits and in starting a family. They may need to work on overcoming these obstacles to achieve their goals and find fulfillment in their personal life.

Rahu in the 6th House (Libra):

In the sixth house of Libra, Rahu's presence signifies a strong influence over enemies and potential loss through the maternal grandfather. The individual may be selfish and cautious in their dealings with others, which could lead to conflicts and challenges in their relationships. They may need to work on being more open and trusting with others to foster stronger connections and alliances.

Rahu in the 7th House (Scorpio):

When Rahu is in the seventh house of Scorpio, it indicates distress in the house of marriage and potential deficiencies in sexual pleasure. The individual may face challenges in their relationship with their spouse and may experience loss in their father-in-law's house. They may also face difficulties in their professional life and daily routine, and may seek unconventional or secretive means to find satisfaction in their personal life. They may be selfish in their pursuits and may need to work on being more considerate and understanding of the needs of others.

Rahu in the 8th House (Sagittarius):

In the eighth house of Sagittarius, Rahu's presence signifies disturbances in the house of longevity and potential abdominal troubles. The individual may feel restless and may sometimes contemplate ending their life due to their suffering. They may need to work on finding inner peace and developing coping mechanisms to deal with their challenges and hardships.

Rahu in the 9th House (Capricorn):

When Rahu is in the ninth house of Capricorn, it indicates a loss in the house of destiny and potential mistakes in matters of religion and spirituality. The individual may not achieve fame and may struggle with their faith in a higher power. They may need to work on developing their spiritual beliefs and finding a sense of purpose in their life.

Rahu in the 10th House (Aquarius):

In the tenth house of Aquarius, Rahu's presence signifies dissatisfaction with one's father and a strong work ethic in pursuit of professional success. The individual may face challenges in their relationship with their father and may work tirelessly to advance their career and social standing. They may also experience anxiety in matters related to government and society, as well as in their business and professional endeavors.

Rahu in the 11th House (Pisces):

When Rahu is in the eleventh house of Pisces, it indicates success in achieving financial gains, but also a tendency to exert more effort than necessary in pursuit of these gains. The individual may be selfish in their financial pursuits and surpassing what is actually necessary. This placement suggests a somewhat self-centered approach to accumulating resources.

Rahu in the 12th House (Aries):

On the other hand, when Rahu is placed in the twelfth house in Aries, individuals may experience losses and significant expenditures. This can lead to worries and difficulties in effectively managing their expenses.

9.Ketu

Ketu in the 1st house (Taurus):

This placement suggests weakness in both the physical body and mental faculties. Individuals may exhibit a backward mindset, restlessness, secrecy, and bravery, but also a tendency towards unfairness.

Ketu in the 2nd house (Gemini):

Expect financial losses and enduring pains, leading to restlessness. There could be a significant decrease in wealth.

Ketu in the 3rd house (Cancer):

Individuals with this placement will engage in energetic actions and work hard for progress. However, they may experience separation from their siblings, restlessness, bravery, worry, and diligence.

Ketu in the 4th house (Leo):

There could be a sense of displacement or separation from one's homeland. Troubles related to property and buildings may arise, leading to various forms of losses and unhappiness. However, happiness may be attained after overcoming significant struggles.

Ketu in the 5th house (Virgo):

Difficulties in education and studies are anticipated, resulting in a deficiency in learning. Communication skills may feel weak, and there may be losses or challenges concerning children. Individuals may exhibit indifference towards obstacles, engage in secretive behavior, and disregard honesty.

Ketu in the 6th house (Libra):

Individuals will confront enemies with courage but may face illnesses and troubles. There may be conflicts with the maternal grandfather, and a somewhat impulsive approach may be observed.

Ketu in the 7th house (Scorpio):

This placement may bring difficulties and losses in marital relationships, as well as challenges related to sexual pleasure. Secret associations or affairs may arise. However, ultimate success in one's occupation can be achieved after overcoming various troubles and obstacles.

Ketu in the 8th house (Sagittarius):

Expect involvement in questionable or shady activities. Hard work may be dedicated to establishing collaborations with foreign entities. Anxieties may arise in life, and there may be a slight reduction in the overall lifespan.

Ketu in the 9th house (Capricorn):

There may be a weakening of religious beliefs and a lack of fame. Individuals may work diligently towards their destiny and its outcomes. However, they may face obstacles and challenges along the way.

Ketu in the 10th house (Aquarius):

Individuals may experience dissatisfaction or unhappiness with their fathers. Challenges may arise in government and societal matters. There may be a strong focus on business and hard work to achieve success.

Ketu in the 11th house (Pisces):

There is potential for earning substantial wealth through dedicated efforts. However, unorthodox or unauthorised methods may be employed, leading to some losses in gains.

Ketu in the 12th house (Aries):

Expect significant expenditures and a disregard for religious principles. Individuals may boldly engage in external relations or affairs.

5. Gemini Ascendant Predictions for Sun in Gemini Ascendant:

1. Sun

Predictions for the Planets with Reference to Gemini Ascendant:

Sun in the 1st House (Gemini):

The individual will engage in influential deeds and have the support of their siblings.

They will exert great strength and influence in their marital house.

There will be an increase in the strength of their sexual pleasures.

Sun in the 2nd House (Cancer):

The individual will work hard to increase their wealth.

There may be some separations or conflicts with their siblings.

They will have influence and success in matters related to wealth.

Their physical strength will primarily contribute to their monetary progress.

Sun in the 3rd House (Leo):

The individual will possess great physical strength.

They will gain dignity and respect through their relationships with their siblings.

They may have less faith in a higher power or a spiritual belief system.

Sun in the 4th House (Virgo):

The individual will experience happiness and harmony with their siblings.

They will benefit from properties and real estate, and their strength will be enhanced through them.

They will make progress and find fulfillment in their work and labor.

They will have influence and respect within their mother's household, as well as with their father.

They may attain honor and influence in connection with the government, society, and business.

Sun in the 5th House (Virgo) for Gemini sign:

The individual finds happiness and creativity through their children, gains strength through their hobbies, and seeks intellectual pursuits for self-expression.

Sun in the 6th House (Scorpio):

The individual will work diligently and use their strength and energy to accomplish tasks.

They will have significant influence and recognition in adversarial situations or with enemies.

There will be a strong connection to their maternal grandfather.

They may experience some uneasiness or challenges in matters related to expenses.

Sun in the 7th House (Sagittarius):

The individual will have a strong influence on their spouse or partner.

Progress and success are likely to be experienced after marriage.

They will have a powerful drive for sexual pleasures.

They can expect support and cooperation from their siblings.

Sun in the 8th House (Capricorn):

There may be a sense of weakness or reduced energy.

Losses or challenges may arise through relationships with siblings.

The individual will make significant efforts, using hidden resources, to improve their financial situation.

They may experience some worries or difficulties in their daily routine.

Sun in the 9th House (Aquarius):

The individual's energy will be directed towards relying on destiny or fate.

They may feel a deficiency in achieving success through their own industry or hard work.

Their siblings will provide support and strength.

They will possess great courage and determination.

Success in their industry or field of work may bring them influence.

They tend to be obstinate or persistent.

Sun in the 10th House (Pisces):

The individual will make substantial progress through their energy and strength.

They will receive the influence and support of their father.

Cooperation from their siblings can be expected.

They will experience progress and influence in matters related to the government, society, and career.

They will achieve success through their hard work and labor.

They have a propensity to do good and display great courage.

Sun in the 11th House (Aries):

The individual will gain significantly from their relationships with siblings.

There may be some weaknesses in the area of education.

They may experience some deficiencies or challenges regarding their children.

They could use improper or harsh language at times.

They tend to be careless and overly joyful.

Sun in the 12th House (Taurus):

The individual may face losses and weakness due to their enemies.

There could be separations or conflicts with their siblings.

They may spend excessively and feel restless in matters related to expenses.

2.Moon

Sure! Here are the predictions for the Moon in Gemini Ascendant without any bullet points:

Moon in the 1st H2use (Gemini):

The individual will acquire wealth, have a pleasing appearance, find beauty in their marriage, succeed in their daily work, and enjoy sexual pleasures. They will also receive respect from their father-in-law and have a stable mind.

Moon in the 2nd House (Cancer):

The individual will accumulate significant wealth, follow righteous principles, and experience progress and prosperity in financial matters.

Moon in the 3rd House (Leo):

The individual will engage in valuable work, earn wealth through their efforts, face obstacles in relationships with siblings, and gain fame and courage.

Moon in the 4th House (Virgo):

The individual will accumulate wealth, properties, and assets, have a strong bond with their mother and home, find success in business and wealth, and receive honor in governmental and societal spheres.

Moon in the 5th House (Libra):

The individual will attain education, make progress in matters related to children, and make clever efforts to acquire wealth.

Moon in the 6th House (Scorpio):

The individual may feel restless, experience family losses (often related to the mother), face worries from enemies, encounter financial losses, have conflicts, experience health issues, spend excessively, and gain through secret strategies.

Moon in the 7th House (Sagittarius):

The individual will earn wealth through their work, have a prosperous mindset, gain honor and dignity, experience harmony in their marriage, have a strong sexual drive, and generally be content.

Moon in the 8th House (Capricorn):

The individual may face loss of wealth, weakness in the body, family losses, gain through hidden endeavors, and experience progress in matters related to age.

Moon in the 9th House (Aquarius):

The individual will acquire wealth through destiny, uphold righteous principles, respect siblings, be fortunate, believe in a higher power, receive honor within the family, and society.

Moon in the 10th House (Pisces):

The individual will inherit wealth through their father, achieve significant wealth through business, gain respect in government and society, have a desire for progress, and experience limitations in wealth matters.

Moon in the 11th House (Aries):

The individual will earn significant wealth, make progress in education, experience gains from their family, and find happiness through their children.

Moon in the 12th House (Taurus):

The individual will acquire wealth through connections and collaborations, face significant family losses, but benefit from secret endeavors. They may experience challenges in their family life and may not pay much attention to their health.

3.Mars

Predictions for Mars in Gemini Ascendant:

Mars in the 1st House (Gemini):

- Gains through physical labor and achieves significant gains.
- May experience some health issues and weakness in the body.
- Restlessness and disturbances in the relationship with the mother.
- Some obstacles in finding peace and happiness.
- Influential in dealing with enemies.
- Some anxiety in the relationship with the spouse and can be somewhat impulsive.

Mars in the 2nd House (Cancer):

- Heavy losses in wealth and family matters.
- Weakness in the maternal and paternal side.
- Works hard to acquire wealth.
- May gain through secretive and intricate strategies.

- Some distress in matters related to children.
- Obstacles in adhering to righteous principles (Dharma).

Mars in the 3rd House (Leo):

- Great influence over enemies.
- Significant gains through hard work and labor.
- Tendency towards pride and enmity with siblings.
- Gains influence and recognition in government and society.
- Potential enmity with the father.
- Brave and courageous, but may struggle with adhering to righteous principles (Dharma).

Mars in the 4th House (Virgo):

- Mixed gains and losses in the relationship with the mother.
- Support from the maternal grandfather's side.
- Gains from land and property.
- Mixed emotions regarding happiness.
- Indifference towards enemies, but still benefits from them.
- Mixed relations in the marital sphere.
- Involvement in industry, government, and societal matters.

Mars in the 5th House (Libra):

- Gains through intellectual labor and education.
- Overcomes enemies and obstacles.
- Challenges from children.
- Some anxieties present.

Mars in the 6th House (Scorpio):

- Strength from the mother's side and maternal grandfather's house.
- Obstacles in adhering to righteous principles (Dharma).
- Prone to diseases.
- Strong gains in the house of income.
- Unhappiness with expenses and insufficient income.
- Very courageous.

Mars in the 7th House (Sagittarius):
- Gains wealth through hard work in the daily occupation.
- Some gains from government and society.
- Possible enmity present.
- Gains influence from the father.
- Some deficiencies within the family.
- May experience health issues related to sexual pleasures.

Mars in the 8th House (Capricorn):

- Progress in longevity.

- Permanent gains through hard work in foreign countries.
- Deficiency in matters of wealth.
- Maintains income but has mixed relations with siblings.

Mars in the 9th House (Aquarius):

- Gains through destiny.
- Tends to spend more and may experience worries in expenditure.
- Careless approach.
- Deficiency in matters related to spirituality and faith.

Mars in the 10th House (Pisces):

- Influential and laborious actions.
- Gains from government and society.
- Victory and gains from enemies.
- Difficulties in the relationship with the father.
- Success through hard work in education.
- Some gains with difficulty in matters related to children.
- Deficiency in maternal happiness.

Mars in the 11th House (Aries):

- Significant gains and income.
- Gains from the maternal grandfather's side.
- Heavy gains and influential strength from enemies.

- Gains through industry.
- Weakness in accumulated wealth.
- Gains with authority and influence.
- Some worries related to children.

Mars in the 12th House (Taurus):

- Worries and weakness in matters of income.
- Achieves work through enemies.
- Perplexity in relationships with siblings.
- Restlessness in the marital sphere.
- Excessive spending.
- May experience some sexual disorders.

4. Mercury

Mercury in the 1st House (Gemini):

Individual with Mercury in the 1st House is handsome and possesses a good physique. They have a strong connection to land and buildings, as well as support from others. They find happiness in their occupation, gain self-knowledge, and experience joy from their spouse. This placement brings honor and a sense of fulfillment.

Mercury in the 2nd House (Cancer):

With Mercury in the 2nd House, there is a tendency to accumulate significant wealth. The individual gains properties and lands, experiences maternal happiness, and sees an increase in family and material possessions.

They find contentment in their daily routines and activities.

Mercury in the 3rd House (Leo):

People with Mercury in the 3rd House enjoy harmonious relationships with their siblings. They acquire land and have a positive relationship with their mother. This placement brings honor and respect, and the individual is known for their fair and thoughtful nature. They possess courage, enthusiasm, and fame.

Mercury in the 4th House (Virgo):

Individuals with Mercury in the 4th House lead a happy life and have a good physique. However, there may be a deficiency in the relationship with their father. They are not particularly concerned about government and societal matters but acquire buildings and property. They find happiness through spiritual practices but can be somewhat careless.

Mercury in the 5th House (Libra):

People with Mercury in the 5th House possess deep intellectual capabilities. They derive happiness from their children and receive support from their mother. They value peace but may experience occasional mental worries. However, there is a tendency to overlook the needs of their children.

Mercury in the 6th House (Scorpio):

Those with Mercury in the 6th House may experience unhappiness, worries, and dependence on others. There could be losses in terms of properties, lands, and residential affairs. They tend to spend generously and bring happiness to others. However, they possess wisdom and discernment.

Mercury in the 7th House (Sagittarius):

Individuals with Mercury in the 7th House find happiness in their occupation and enjoy a harmonious relationship with their spouse. They have strong desires for spiritual progress and derive great pleasure from sexual life and indulgences. They may have a sense of self-pride.

Mercury in the 8th House (Capricorn):

People with Mercury in the 8th House may experience a deficiency in physical strength. They may make some progress in their spouse's domain and find happiness in their daily routine. There may be progress and success in accumulating wealth, but there could also be a lack of properties and lands. They may find happiness in foreign countries but may face an unsettled environment. This placement brings a sense of forcefulness.

Mercury in the 9th House (Aquarius):

Individuals with Mercury in the 9th House are considered fortunate. They possess a good physique and acquire buildings and property. They uphold righteousness, have faith in God, and strive for greatness and contentment. They experience happiness through their relationships with siblings and possess foresight.

Mercury in the 10th House (Pisces):

Those with Mercury in the 10th House may experience weakness in their relationship with their father. However, they gain honor and recognition in society. There may be physical weaknesses, and they may face obstacles in social and governmental spheres. They may be perceived as lazy and encounter hindrances in their progress.

Mercury in the 11th House (Aries):

People with Mercury in the 11th House achieve significant gains through their physical efforts. They experience great happiness and acquire buildings and property. They find joy through their children and education. They are highly intelligent and clever

Mercury in the 12th House (Taurus):

Individuals with Mercury in the 12th House may experience a deficiency in physical pleasures and a weakness in their body. They may have a tendency to wander and travel to different places. There may be a sense of unhappiness or discontent with their mother and homeland. They tend to spend money freely but have the ability to get things done efficiently. They possess a wandering nature.

5.Jupiter

Jupiter in the 1st House (Gemini):

Jupiter gains prominence in the realm of the spouse, holds an occupation that carries special significance, receives support from the father, benefits from the government and society, enjoys the strength and well-being of children, attains a good education, possesses a healthy body, and demonstrates diligence and hard work.

Jupiter in the 2nd House (Cancer):

Jupiter experiences an increase in wealth through personal efforts, receives assistance from the father, encounters some bonds and support from the spouse's family, faces worries in daily routines, wields considerable influence in adversarial situations, acquires wealth through involvement in governmental and societal affairs, and comes from a financially well-off family background.

Jupiter in the 3rd House (Leo):

Jupiter attains a special position, strength, and attractiveness through the spouse, establishes connections with the government and society, derives substantial pleasure from sexual experiences, receives support from siblings, experiences a deficiency in adhering to righteous conduct (Dharma), and exhibits high levels of energy and courage.

Jupiter in the 4th House (Virgo):

Jupiter finds happiness in business and occupation, receives honor from the mother's side of the family, as well as joy from the father's side, performs daily tasks with dignity and nobility, derives happiness from involvement in governmental and societal matters, gains strength from lands and properties, and is known for being industrious and honorable.

Jupiter in the 5th House (Libra):

Jupiter acquires extensive education, possesses great skills and cleverness, experiences the joy of having children, gains knowledge of business and occupation through the spouse, enjoys the respect and sexual pleasures associated with a dignified marital life, receives honor from the government and society, and is blessed with good fortune.

Jupiter in the 6th House (Scorpio):

Jupiter engages in dependent occupations, achieves significant influence and honor in adversarial situations, encounters challenges in the context of the spouse, experiences progress in matters related to wealth, and may face limitations in terms of sexual pleasures.

Jupiter in the 7th House (Sagittarius):

Jupiter's daily endeavors involve public service, earns substantial respect and progress in business-related occupations, benefits from the government and society, receives support from the father, spouse, and siblings, exhibits passion, enthusiasm, and great fortune.

Jupiter in the 8th House (Capricorn):

Jupiter may experience losses in relation to the spouse and father, encounters difficulties in business occupations, faces challenges from foreign countries, witnesses weakness in matters concerning the government and society, feels restless, and finds some maternal happiness.

Jupiter in the 9th House (Aquarius):

Jupiter may experience some dissatisfaction in relation to the father and spouse, feels a sense of discontentment, gains power in matters related to destiny, receives support from children, and attains education.

Jupiter in the 10th House (Pisces):

Jupiter enjoys great respect and dignity in business endeavors, makes progress in the chosen occupation, receives support from the father, gains honor in governmental and societal spheres, benefits from the spouse, and exhibits great authority in worldly matters.

Jupiter in the 11th House (Aries):

Jupiter brings significant gains, dignity, and a healthy father, but may experience a loss in relation to the spouse, gains respect in daily occupations, benefits from the father and gains recognition in governmental and societal arenas, receives support from siblings, enjoys ample sexual pleasures, possesses ambition, attains happiness through wealth, children, and education, and demonstrates cleverness.

Jupiter in the 12th House (Taurus):

Jupiter may face some weakness in relation to the father, significant loss in the context of the spouse, challenges in obtaining honor from the government and society, as well as in the chosen occupation. However, there may be some strength associated with land and property matters. There might be a sense of restlessness in daily routines, and a decrease in the enjoyment of sexual pleasures.

6. Venus

Predictions for Venus in Gemini Ascendant are as follows:

Venus in the 1st House (Gemini):

Individuals with Venus in the 1st house of Gemini are likely to have a healthy body and possess mental strength. They are clever and articulate. However, there may be a tendency towards experiencing difficulties or losses related to children. They may frequently talk about their spouse and sexual pleasures.

Venus in the 2nd House (Cancer):

When Venus is placed in the 2nd house of Cancer, there may be some financial losses, but these individuals can earn wealth through careful planning. They are likely to prioritize education and may face occasional mental worries. They are hardworking when it comes to accumulating wealth.

Venus in the 3rd House (Leo):

Individuals with Venus in the 3rd house of Leo may experience challenges in their relationships with siblings. They may also face difficulties in education and may not be satisfied with their children. However, they are very clever and courageous.

Venus in the 4th House (Virgo):

Those with Venus in the 4th house of Virgo may experience losses or separations related to their mother or their birthplace. However, they may progress well in government or society. They may feel mentally worried due to domestic unhappiness and may not be satisfied with their children's situation. They may also face some challenges in education.

Venus in the 5th House (Libra):

Individuals with Venus in the 5th house of Libra are likely to receive a good education. However, they may not be entirely happy with their children. They may gain through expenditures, possibly indicating a tendency to spend on pleasurable activities.

Venus in the 6th House (Scorpio):

In the case of Venus in the 6th house of Scorpio, there may be weaknesses in education. These individuals may face difficulties or sufferings related to their children and may incur significant expenditures. They may also encounter challenges from enemies or face some suffering. They tend to be secretive.

Venus in the 7th House (Sagittarius):

Individuals with Venus in the 7th house of Sagittarius gain strength in their daily occupation or work.

However, they may face some weaknesses or challenges regarding their children. They may also experience worries or conflicts related to their spouse. They tend to derive sexual pleasures and may spend heavily on their family and spouse.

Venus in the 8th House (Capricorn):

When Venus is placed in the 8th house of Capricorn, individuals may experience weaknesses in education. They may also face losses concerning their children. They strive to increase their wealth but may face some financial deficiencies.

Venus in the 9th House (Aquarius):

Those with Venus in the 9th house of Aquarius may experience deficiencies in education. However, they possess the strength and ability to overcome these challenges. They may exhibit decent cleverness in acquiring knowledge and progress in their destiny. They may gain through their children but may not derive much happiness from their relationships with siblings.

Venus in the 10th House (Pisces):

Individuals with Venus in the 10th house of Pisces are likely to attain education and have strong and successful children. They may find satisfaction and strength in their profession or business. However, they may experience weaknesses in various aspects of their lives, including finances, relationships with their mother, and the pursuit of pleasure. They are highly clever and influential.

Venus in the 11th House (Aries):

When Venus is placed in the 11th house of Aries, individuals are predicted to gain a significant amount of education. However, there may be some deficiencies in their relationship with their children. They have a clever

Venus in the 12th House (Taurus):

Individuals with Venus in the 12th house of Taurus may experience considerable weaknesses in their educational pursuits. They may face losses related to their children and tend to spend a significant amount of money. However, they possess cleverness in getting tasks accomplished, particularly in challenging situations or with adversaries. They may have a somewhat suspicious intellect.

7. Saturn

Predictions for Saturn in Gemini Ascendant are as follows:

Saturn in the 1st House (Gemini):

Individuals with Saturn in the 1st house of Gemini are fortunate in many aspects of life. However, they may have concerns regarding their progress and may experience worries. They tend to have good longevity but may also face challenges in their relationships with siblings.

Saturn in the 2nd House (Cancer):

When Saturn is placed in the 2nd house of Cancer, individuals may experience losses in accumulated wealth. They may exhibit a tendency to be lazy in their daily routine and face weaknesses or hindrances within their family. Financial matters may pose challenges.

Saturn in the 3rd House (Leo):

Those with Saturn in the 3rd house of Leo are hardworking individuals. However, they may feel unhappy or unsatisfied with their relationships with siblings. They tend to follow a Tammasic Dharma (lower virtue) and may toil extensively while also spending a significant amount of money.

Saturn in the 4th House (Virgo):

Individuals with Saturn in the 4th house of Virgo may experience some loss or lack of maternal affection. They spend their daily routine with influence and may encounter both worries and fortune. They may be engaged in acquiring buildings or real estate.

Saturn in the 5th House (Libra):

When Saturn is placed in the 5th house of Libra, individuals possess great wisdom. They gain strength through their children and acquire education. However, there may be a deficiency in their income. They may feel restless in their marital life.

Saturn in the 6th House (Scorpio):

Those with Saturn in the 6th house of Scorpio accomplish tasks through grand and laborious means. They may have religious practices or devices to improve their lives but may not prioritize religion itself. They may experience enmity with siblings and have influence in the house of enemies. They tend to spend a significant amount of money and may lack faith in God. They may also have some level of fame.

Saturn in the 7th House (Sagittarius):

Individuals with Saturn in the 7th house of Sagittarius make progress in their daily occupation or work. They may gain fame in their chosen field. They experience more happiness and sexual pleasures and enjoy good longevity. They are considered fortunate overall.

Saturn in the 8th House (Capricorn):

When Saturn is placed in the 8th house of Capricorn, individuals have good longevity. However, they may face hindrances or challenges in their progress and destiny, particularly through foreign countries. They gain fame in their occupation and experience progress in marriage. They exhibit a special force in matters related to intellect and education. There may be a deficiency in the house of children but progress in government and society.

Saturn in the 9th House (Aquarius):

Those with Saturn in the 9th house of Aquarius have a long life and are considered fortunate. They may face weaknesses in matters of Dharma (righteousness) and may experience deficiencies in income. They have significant influence in the house of enemies and may feel unhappy or unsatisfied with their relationships with siblings. They may have contacts with foreign countries.

Saturn in the 10th House (Pisces):

Individuals with Saturn in the 10th house of Pisces may experience losses in matters related to their father. However, they rise in their line of progress and strive to earn respect in government and society through their grand achievements. They may face worries and spend a significant amount of money. Progress in their daily occupation is indicated, but there may be some enmity within their family. They possess influence and are considered influential overall.

Saturn in the 11th House (Aries):

When Saturn is placed in the 11th house of Aries, individuals may experience some weakness in matters of income. They may also face worries or concerns. However, they possess special strength in the house of education and intellect. They receive support from their children and tend to be ambitious in their pursuits.

Saturn in the 12th House (Taurus):

Those with Saturn in the 12th house of Taurus may lead restless lives. They may experience weaknesses in matters of Dharma (righteousness) and incur higher levels of expenditure. They strive to increase their wealth and possess significant influence in dealing with enemies. There may be some loss of wealth and deficiencies in fame. They tend to have a somewhat impersonal approach to life.

8. Rahu

Rahu in the 1st House (Gemini):

Indicates a tall stature, harbors deep and bitter thoughts, possesses self-pride, achieves fame, tends to excessively pursue his ideas, and possesses spiritual knowledge.

Rahu in the 2nd House (Cancer):

Brings losses in wealth, experiences great worries and distress related to financial matters, faces significant challenges within the family, engages in secretive schemes for acquiring wealth, and may have a tendency to exploit others.

Rahu in the 3rd House (Leo):

Signifies loss and distress concerning siblings, but maintains courage and perseverance, works hard despite fatigue, displays timidity and selfishness, yet possesses significant courage.

Rahu in the 4th House (Virgo):

Indicates unhappiness in the realm of the mother, experiences losses related to property and real estate matters, and faces domestic dissatisfaction. This placement also suggests a serious nature.

Rahu in the 5th House (Libra):

Brings deficiencies in wisdom and education, as well as some losses and worries concerning children.

Rahu in the 6th House (Scorpio):

Exerts a strong influence in adversarial situations, experiences loss in the maternal grandfather's house, shows indifference towards physical ailments and moral principles (Dharma), tends to engage in sinful and criminal activities, and displays both selfishness and bravery.

Rahu in the 7th House (Sagittarius):

Signifies loss and difficulties in the realm of the spouse, deep worries in daily occupations, and deficiencies and sorrows in matters of sexual pleasures, albeit in a secretive and improper manner. This placement may also indicate laziness.

Rahu in the 8th House (Capricorn):

Brings excessive worries, occasional encounters with severe and nerve-wracking troubles, indulges in secretive thinking, experiences deficiencies in daily routines, and may suffer from stomach-related troubles.

Rahu in the 9th House (Aquarius):

Indicates weakness in relation to the father, deficiency in upholding moral principles (Dharma), and a lack of faith in God. However, there may be some eventual stability in matters related to destiny.

Rahu in the 10th House (Pisces):

Causes worries in the realm of the father, employs troublesome methods for personal progress, experiences weakness and challenges in matters concerning the government and society, but manages to navigate the situation carefully and eventually achieves progress.

Rahu in the 11th House (Aries):

Brings significant income and gains, but also signifies selfishness in the realm of friendships and associations.

Rahu in the 12th House (Taurus):

May occasionally face troubles due to excessive expenditure, exhibits carelessness in other places, operates with secretive tactics and remote thinking.

9.Ketu

Ketu in the 1st House (Gemini):

Signifies significant weakness and anxiety in the body, a lack of beauty, potential for sudden danger or accidents, experiences weakness in the heart, possesses patience, and displays secretive and obstinate tendencies.

Ketu in the 2nd House (Cancer):

Brings great losses and frustrations in matters of wealth, experiences distress within the family, works hard to acquire wealth, and eventually achieves some success.

Ketu in the 3rd House (Leo):

Brings great worries and difficulties related to siblings, diminishes the bond with brothers and sisters, requires serious labor and perseverance.

Ketu in the 4th House (Virgo):

Indicates losses and deficiencies in the realm of the mother, encounters obstacles concerning land and property matters, but eventually achieves stability and happiness after overcoming various disturbances and challenges.

Ketu in the 5th House (Libra):

Creates difficulties in acquiring education, leads to mental worries, brings losses concerning children, struggles to communicate ideas effectively, tends to speak in a somewhat bitter manner, possesses a selfish intellect, and lacks gentleness.

Ketu in the 6th House (Scorpio):

Exerts significant influence in adversarial situations, brings losses in the maternal grandfather's domain, utilizes inner strength and boldness to overcome difficulties and worries, displays selfishness and fearlessness.

Ketu in the 7th House (Sagittarius):

Indicates a strong connection with a spouse possessing special strength, provides excessive sexual pleasures, accomplishes great deeds in daily occupations, but faces some deficiencies in managing domestic affairs peacefully.

Ketu in the 8th House (Capricorn):

Causes restlessness and worries in daily routines, involves hard work and encounters difficulties in professional life, and may experience some stomach-related complaints.

Ketu in the 9th House (Aquarius):

Brings worries in matters of destiny, requires intense labor for progress, faces some losses in matters of moral principles (Dharma), encounters challenges in attaining fame, and tends to be unsuccessful and selfish.

Ketu in the 10th House (Pisces):

Signifies some losses and worries regarding social status, engages in hard work to achieve honor in governmental and societal affairs, and ultimately gains some inner strength and power.

Ketu in the 11th House (Aries):

Provides strength in matters of income, indicates progress in the realm of gains, may acquire some unauthorized gains, and achieves success through hidden strengths.

Ketu in the 12th House (Taurus):

Tends to spend excessively, engages in hard work to manage expenses.

In the house of Taurus, Ketu brings a focus on material possessions, financial matters, and stability. However, with Ketu's presence, there can be a sense of detachment or dissatisfaction with material wealth and a tendency to detach from material pursuits.

6.Cancer Ascendant Predictions for Sun in Cancer Ascendant:

1.Sun

Sun in Cancer Ascendant:

Sun in the 1st House (Cancer)

This placement indicates dignity, wealth, and glory. However, there may be some dullness in gains related to the wife, occupation, and hindrances to overcome. You possess a strong sense of family.

Sun in the 2nd House (Leo):

With Sun in the 2nd House, you are likely to be very wealthy and have a large family. There may be anxieties in your daily routine, but you have a positive influence on your wealth and enjoy respect in society.

Sun in the 3rd House (Virgo):

This placement brings wealth, fame, and religious progress. You are considered lucky and have supportive brothers and sisters. You work diligently and are highly respected, with the ability to influence others.

Sun in the 4th House (Libra):

With Sun in the 4th House, you may experience troubles related to wealth. There is restlessness in your house of happiness, and deficiencies in both the father and mother's houses. Despite this, you gain respect in business, though cash possessions may be lacking. There may also be challenges concerning land and property. Overall, there is restlessness in your family and wealth.

Sun in the 5th House (Scorpio):

This placement indicates wisdom, wealth, and tremendous gains. You have a large family and possess great foresight. However, there may be some bondage concerning children, and your influence is strong in the field of education. You are ambitious and have a fiery temper.

Sun in the 6th House (Sagittarius):

With Sun in the 6th House, you are influential and earn wealth through diligence. You are not bothered by enemies and difficulties, and in fact, you gain from them. However, you may experience deficiencies in wealth and some influence from the maternal grandfather's side. There may be health issues and deficiencies in family pleasures, but you are respected.

Sun in the 7th House (Capricorn):

In this placement, you pursue your daily occupation despite difficulties with wealth. Gaining wealth may be challenging, and you may face hardships in your relationship with your spouse. However, you are considered rich and secure a respectable job. There is some dullness and bondage regarding sexual pleasures.

Sun in the 8th House (Aquarius):

With Sun in the 8th House, you earn wealth through painful means and may feel a deficiency in wealth. You may acquire ancestral wealth or wealth from a deceased person. There can be sudden loss of wealth as well.

Sun in the 9th House (Pisces):

This placement indicates great luck, religiousness, and wealth. You are energetic, have brothers, and enjoy various advantages in life.

Sun in the 10th House (Aries):

In this placement, you possess powerful influence but may be somewhat careless about land and property. You earn wealth and gain respect from your father. You accumulate wealth through trade or a respectable job, though there may be hindrances related to the mother. You face obstacles to peace but gain respect from the government and society. You have a high-status family and are dignified and influential.

Sun in the 11th House (Taurus):

With Sun in the 11th House, you have the power to accumulate wealth and gains. You make money through financial endeavors, acquire jewels and ornaments, and possess great brilliance. You enjoy advantages in education, with children, and are an influential orator.

Sun in the 12th House (Gemini):

In this placement, you may spend excessive amounts of wealth and struggle to accumulate it. Wealth may come from external sources, and you exert influence over your enemies through spending.

2.Moon

Predictions for Moon in Cancer Ascendant are as follows:

Moon in the 1st House (Cancer):

Individuals with Moon in the 1st house of Cancer have a fair complexion and a symmetrical body. They have strong control over their desires and possess stability. They prioritize their family circumstances, day-to-day affairs, and occupation. They seek and attain pleasures, earn respect, act independently, and have a stable mind. However, there may be some issues in their married life. They tend to be famous and respected.

Moon in the 2nd House (Leo):

Those with Moon in the 2nd house of Leo earn significant wealth and maintain an aristocratic lifestyle. They uphold their dignity in their daily routines and engage themselves in worldly affairs. They receive respect but may exhibit a selfish nature.

Moon in the 3rd House (Virgo):

Individuals with Moon in the 3rd house of Virgo are energetic and work whole-heartedly for their development. They are consistently happy and have faith in Dharma (righteousness). They are fortunate, have a strong bond with their siblings, possess a handsome physique, gain fame, and peacefully accomplish their tasks. They exhibit strong willpower.

Moon in the 4th House (Libra):

When the Moon is placed in the 4th house of Libra, individuals live happily in their birthplace. They have a pleasant physical appearance and experience happiness related to land and property. They engage in significant endeavors, bring joy to others, respect their parents, feel reluctant to travel abroad, receive recognition and appreciation from government and society, live in peace, and achieve success.

Moon in the 5th House (Scorpio):

Those with Moon in the 5th house of Scorpio may have weaknesses in education and intellect. They encounter some difficulties in matters related to children and tend to feel restless. They may have a narrow perspective, struggle to express themselves clearly, and may resort to lying. They may also have a shorter stature.

Moon in the 6th House (Sagittarius):

Individuals with Moon in the 6th house of Sagittarius may experience weakness and ailments in their bodies. They often depend on others, feel restless, prefer to live with their grandparents, spend a significant amount of money, fear enemies, and possess a calm and courageous nature.

Moon in the 7th House (Capricorn):

When the Moon is placed in the 7th house of Capricorn, individuals receive admiration. They handle their daily affairs with keen interest, have passionate desires, seek and enjoy sexual pleasures, have a beautiful spouse, prioritize their partner, work under pressure, find pleasure in their occupation due to strong willpower, face significant troubles, travel to foreign countries, experience health issues, and remain cautious about acquiring wealth.

Moon in the 8th House (Aquarius):

Those with Moon in the 8th house of Aquarius may have deficiencies in beauty. They encounter obstacles in their occupation and achieve progress through physical labor.

Moon in the 9th House (Pisces):

Individuals with Moon in the 9th house of Pisces are considered lucky and religious. They have a handsome physique, are always happy and energetic, have siblings, and gain fame and virtue.

Moon in the 10th House (Aries):

When the Moon is placed in the 10th house of Aries, individuals are majestic. They benefit from their parents, engage in significant occupations, live a lavish lifestyle, experience happiness, desire land and property, perform good deeds, and receive respect from government and society.

Moon in the 11th House (Taurus):

Those with Moon in the 11th house of Taurus may have a bulky physique and possess influence. They earn significant wealth and experience substantial gains. They have sharp intelligence and live a luxurious life, displaying their influence. They have children but may face deficiencies in the area of education.

Moon in the 12th House (Gemini):

Individuals with Moon in the 12th house of Gemini may experience weaknesses and physical ailments. They may reside in foreign places and receive honor there. They may encounter physical and mental distress, incur significant expenses, strive to exert influence in the realm of enemies, and have a suspicious nature.

3.Mars

Mars in the 1st House (Cancer)

When Mars is in the first house of Cancer, it is not very influential. Individuals with this placement may not receive much respect from their parents, but they pay great attention to their occupation. They may receive some respect in their spouse's house but may be unhappy with their children. These individuals may lack education and experience dullness in life, but they may desire some sexual pleasures.

Mars in the 2nd House (Leo)

Mars in the second house of Leo signifies that the individual will perform great and valuable deeds in their life through wisdom. They will earn a significant amount of wealth and experience happiness with their children. These individuals will receive education and respect in the government, society, and family. They will enjoy gains due to their cleverness and may experience some restlessness in their daily life. They are also very witty.

Mars in the 3rd House (Virgo)

Individuals with Mars in the third house of Virgo are very dignified and receive much respect in government and society. They also receive respect in their father's house and maintain influence in the house of their enemies. These individuals never feel nervous or lose courage and do not care for their brothers, children, father, or Dharma. They are successful, brave, and very skillful.

Mars in the 4th House (Libra)

Mars in the fourth house of Libra indicates that the individual will gain much intelligence and have a vast business and significant undertakings. They are experts in conducting domestic and worldly affairs and gain profit in their daily routine of life. These individuals receive much honor and influence in their own house and their spouse's side. They experience happiness from their father, son, and mother and acquire land and property. They desire more sexual pleasures and gain fame in government and society, as well as enjoy special sexual pleasures.

Mars in the 5th House (Scorpio)

Individuals with Mars in the fifth house of Scorpio possess special knowledge of political science. They are mentally overjoyed due to their children and spend more than they gain. These individuals speak importantly and are respectable businesspeople.

Mars in the 6th House (Sagittarius)

Mars in the sixth house of Sagittarius signifies that the individual is brave and influential. They maintain their dignity and glory and achieve victory over their enemies and diseases. However, they may experience some trouble in their body and spend a lot. There may be some deficiency in their education and children.

Mars in the 7th House (Capricorn)

Individuals with Mars in the seventh house of Capricorn have splendid occupations and receive a raise through their wisdom. They have good luck with their spouse and have influential and majestic partners. These individuals receive respect from the government and society, but they may have some weakness in their body. They enjoy sexual pleasures and receive help from their father and son. They are respected and influential.

Mars in the 8th House (Aquarius)

Mars in the eighth house of Aquarius indicates that the individual will bear the losses of their son and father. They will perform big and difficult tasks and receive little education. These individuals may tell lies and speak bitterly, following unrighteous methods to gain wealth and rise in society. They may feel dissatisfied with the government and society and may be somewhat lazy.

Mars in the 9th House (Pisces)

Individuals with Mars in the ninth house of Pisces are very fortunate and enjoy the pleasures of their son and father. They have a good knowledge of mathematics and accountancy and receive fame and respect from the government and society. They receive a good education and are famous and farsighted.

Mars in the 10th House (Aries)

Mars in the tenth house of Aries signifies that the individual has great managerial ability and works for the government and society. They are very wise and speak intellectually, receiving honor and respect. These individuals are very beautiful but may have weakness in their body. They are very dignified and influential.

Mars in the 11th House (Taurus)

Individuals with Mars in the eleventh house of Taurus receive huge gains due to their wisdom and occupation. They benefit from their son and father and make great efforts to gain wealth through business. They have a good education and good children, and they are very influential and selfish.

Mars in the 12th House (Gemini)

Mars in the twelfth house of Gemini indicates that the individual will receive some respect but may experience troubles from their son. They may have weakness in their education and intelligence and spend a lot. These individuals enjoy sexual pleasures but may experience losses in significant occupations. They are very courageous and energetic.

4.Mercury

Predictions of Mercury in Cancer Ascendant: An In-Depth Analysis

Mercury, the planet of communication, intelligence, and analytical abilities, plays a significant role in shaping an individual's life when placed in different houses of the birth chart. In this essay, we will explore the various predictions of Mercury in Cancer Ascendant, focusing on its placement in each of the twelve houses and the subsequent effects on an individual's life.

Mercury in the 1st House (Cancer)

When Mercury is placed in the first house of Cancer Ascendant, the individual is likely to have a good physique and a majestic demeanour. They may be involved in business and exhibit courage in their professional and personal life. Their strength lies in their occupation and domestic affairs, but they may experience some deficiency in their relationships with siblings. These individuals are often respected and may travel to foreign countries.

Mercury in the 2nd House (Leo)

In the second house, Mercury bestows the individual with the ability to earn money and gain respect. However, they may experience some incomplete happiness in their relationships with siblings. They are likely to be conscious of their expenditure and try to control it.

Mercury in the 3rd House (Virgo)

Individuals with Mercury in the third house are highly energetic and enjoy the support of their siblings. They may not be very religious but possess a good height and the power to manage their expenses. They exhibit great courage, ambition, and modesty in their endeavors.

Mercury in the 4th House (Libra)

With Mercury in the fourth house, individuals can efficiently manage their work and expenditure, leading to happiness. However, they may face some deficiencies in their relationships with parents and siblings, as well as experience losses in land and property. Their success and failures in dealing with the government and society may vary.

Mercury in the 5th House (Scorpio)

The fifth house placement of Mercury empowers individuals in the realms of education and intelligence. They are likely to spend on education and be very clever and wise. However, they may face some deficiencies in their relationships with children and siblings. They are skilled in winning people over to their side.

Mercury in the 6th House (Sagittarius)

Individuals with Mercury in the sixth house may face hindrances in their expenditure and may be involved in dependent work. They tend to spend a lot and face various troubles in life. They may be somewhat restless and try to curtail their expenditure.

Mercury in the 7th House (Capricorn)

In the seventh house, Mercury enables individuals to manage their expenditure through hard work. They may experience more happiness from their sister than their brother and have power and courage in their marital life. Their professional life may be a mix of strengths and weaknesses, but they are likely to succeed in worldly affairs.

Mercury in the 8th House (Aquarius)

With Mercury in the eighth house, individuals may experience weakness in their energy and strength. However, they are likely to be devoid of enemies and possess hidden power. They can manage their expenditure and may resort to difficult means to acquire money. They may experience separation from their siblings and exhibit both carelessness and gentleness.

Mercury in the 9th House (Pisces)

Individuals with Mercury in the ninth house may have some devotion to God but experience incomplete happiness from their siblings. They may have some weakness in their religious beliefs and face deficiencies in their expenditure. They may also suffer from a loss of fame and fortune and possess narrow discernment.

Mercury in the 10th House (Aries)

In the tenth house, Mercury enables individuals to work on a large scale using their power of discrimination. They may experience both greatness and weakness in their relationships with their siblings and father. They are likely to spend a lot on happiness and face some weakness in their relationship with their mother. They may also experience some deficiency in success related to the government and society.

Mercury in the 11th House (Taurus)

Individuals with Mercury in the eleventh house gain much due to their physical strength and enjoy some advantages from their power of expenditure. They may feel some weakness in their house of gains and experience both losses and gains in their relationships with their children. They possess strong, discriminating arguments and speak majestically.

Mercury in the 12th House (Gemini)

In the twelfth house, Mercury bestows individuals with the power to spend a lot. They may maintain distant relationships with their siblings and experience deficiencies in their strength. They may have some influence in their house of enemies and spend on diseases and hardships. They are unlikely to put any obstacles in their house of expenditure.

5.Jupiter

Predictions of Jupiter in Cancer Ascendant

Jupiter in the 1st House (Cancer)

Individuals with Jupiter in the first house of Cancer are self-conscious, dignified, and fortunate. They possess a strong sense of virtue and bravery, appreciating justice and truth. These individuals have a deep understanding of right and wrong and are highly respected by others. They have a golden complexion and are considered handsome, with high intelligence and a broad forehead. They are tall in stature and blessed with children, but may experience some deficiency in sexual pleasures. They may be somewhat careless regarding family matters but possess the power of influence. They are learned, loving, and clever, with the ability to defeat their enemies.

Jupiter in the 2nd House (Leo)

In the second house of Leo, Jupiter brings great wealth and the ability to perform influential deeds. These individuals work hard and receive much honor and respect, although they may face some difficulties with the government, society, and their father.

Jupiter in the 3rd House (Virgo)

Those with Jupiter in the third house of Virgo experience success due to their physical strength and vigor. They place great importance on their spouse and enjoy merriment, but may have a small family. They possess the power of brotherly support and achieve great success against their enemies. They are always busy and may experience some deficiency in sexual pleasures and anxiety within their family.

Jupiter in the 4th House (Libra)

Individuals with Jupiter in the fourth house of Libra are considered lucky, but may spend excessively and face mixed troubles related to their mother.

Jupiter in the 5th House (Scorpio)

In the fifth house of Scorpio, Jupiter bestows wisdom and virtue. These individuals are highly religious and possess extensive knowledge of astrology. They experience good fortune and triumph over their enemies, prioritizing truth above all else. However, they may face some animosity from their children and have a tendency towards political involvement.

Jupiter in the 6th House (Sagittarius)

Those with Jupiter in the sixth house of Sagittarius struggle to uphold their Dharma properly. They defeat their enemies and gain influence in government and society, but may spend excessively. They are highly influential and work diligently to achieve progress.

Jupiter in the 7th House (Capricorn)

In the seventh house of Capricorn, Jupiter brings confusion and hardship related to destiny and marriage. These individuals are careful in their daily occupations and have siblings, but may make mistakes in upholding their Dharma. They may experience restlessness and deficiency in their relationships with their spouse and in sexual pleasures.

Jupiter in the 8th House (Aquarius)

Individuals with Jupiter in the eighth house of Aquarius struggle to uphold their Dharma and tend to spend excessively. They maintain civility with their enemies but may experience a lack of fame and follow obscure religious practices.

Jupiter in the 9th House (Pisces)

In the ninth house of Pisces, Jupiter bestows great fortune and intelligence. These individuals possess the power of children and education, successfully upholding their Dharma and achieving victory over their enemies.

Jupiter in the 10th House (Aries)

Those with Jupiter in the tenth house of Aries are highly influential and fortunate, with exceptional managerial abilities. They can solve complex business problems and gain influence in government, society, and with their father. They work hard to rise in position and become leaders in their circles, demonstrating great cleverness.

Jupiter in the 11th House (Taurus)

In the eleventh house of Taurus, Jupiter brings energy and some carelessness. These individuals may experience deficiency in their relationships with their spouse and in sexual pleasures. They are blessed with education and children, as well as support from their siblings. However, they may face humiliation and obstacles in their daily occupations, despite their intelligence and cleverness.

Jupiter in the 12th House (Gemini)

Individuals with Jupiter in the twelfth house of Gemini tend to spend excessively and may experience some weakness in their destiny. They rely on their labor and destiny to manage their expenditures but may struggle to achieve fame. They may also face obstacles in their happiness and daily routines.

6.Venus

Predictions of Venus in Cancer Ascendant: An In-Depth Analysis

Venus, the planet of love, beauty, and wealth, plays a significant role in shaping our lives. When Venus is in

Cancer Ascendant, it influences various aspects of our lives, such as relationships, career, and finances. In this essay, we will explore the impact of Venus in each house of the Cancer Ascendant and how it affects our lives.

Venus in the 1st House (Cancer)

When Venus is in the first house of Cancer Ascendant, it bestows the individual with a charming and attractive appearance. The person enjoys a comfortable life, with access to properties and buildings. They experience happiness in their marital life and gain success in their family and worldly affairs. Their calm and composed nature helps them maintain harmony in their relationships.

Venus in the 2nd House (Leo)

In the second house, Venus struggles to accumulate wealth, leading to some losses in the native's homeland and mother's happiness. However, the individual enjoys a respectable position in society and maintains an aristocratic lifestyle.

Venus in the 3rd House (Virgo)

With Venus in the third house, the native may face financial challenges and have a strained relationship with their siblings. They may also experience some difficulties in their mother's house and property matters.

Despite these challenges, the individual finds happiness in their spiritual pursuits and may be somewhat lazy.

Venus in the 4th House (Libra)

When Venus is in the fourth house, the native enjoys significant benefits from land and property. They have a comfortable income and access to luxurious items. However, they may have a strained relationship with their father and may be restless at times. The individual is respected and humble, enjoying happiness from the government and society. They engage in noble deeds and contribute positively to their community.

Venus in the 5th House (Scorpio)

In the fifth house, Venus blesses the native with exceptional intelligence and wisdom. They enjoy the happiness of having children and owning property. The individual is respected and honorable, with a strong educational background. They are also very clever and maintain a peaceful demeanor.

Venus in the 6th House (Sagittarius)

With Venus in the sixth house, the native tends to spend excessively, leading to financial challenges. They may face obstacles in their mother's house and experience a lack of peace and happiness in their property matters. The individual may also suffer from health issues and struggle with enemies. Despite these challenges, they are secretly very clever and resourceful.

Venus in the 7th House (Capricorn)

In the seventh house, Venus enables the native to enjoy a happy and fulfilling married life. They experience great pleasure in their relationships and achieve success in their endeavors. The individual is very clever and tactful in their approach to life.

Venus in the 8th House (Aquarius)

When Venus is in the eighth house, the native gains advantages through strategic planning and tactics. They may experience dissatisfaction in their mother's house but enjoy good longevity. The individual is highly intelligent and resourceful.

Venus in the 9th House (Pisces)

In the ninth house, Venus bestows great fortune upon the native. They experience progress in their financial gains and acquire land and property. The individual may have a strained relationship with their siblings but places great faith in divine intervention. They are highly spiritual and rely on their connection with the divine for guidance and support.

Venus in the 10th House (Aries)

With Venus in the tenth house, the native gains support from their parents and enjoys power and recognition from the government and society. They engage in noble deeds and acquire land and property. The individual also owns vehicles and is skillful and clever in their pursuits.

Venus in the 11th House (Taurus)

In the eleventh house, Venus allows the native to enjoy a steady income without any worries. They acquire land and property, receive a good education, and experience the joy of having children. The individual places great importance on financial stability and security.

Venus in the 12th House (Gemini)

When Venus is in the twelfth house, the native may experience some losses in their mother's house and tend to spend excessively. They derive pleasure from spending their income and may be careless in dealing with their enemies. The individual may also be somewhat restless and anxious.

8.Saturn

Predictions of Saturn in Cancer Ascendant: An In-Depth Analysis

Saturn, the slow-moving planet, is known for its significant impact on an individual's life. In Vedic astrology, Saturn is considered the planet of karma, discipline, and justice. When Saturn is placed in different houses of the Cancer Ascendant, it brings various effects on the native's life. This essay will explore the predictions of Saturn in Cancer Ascendant in each house and its implications on the individual's life.

Saturn in the 1st House (Cancer)

When Saturn is placed in the first house of Cancer Ascendant, the native is diligent in their daily occupation and enjoys good longevity. However, they may not be satisfied with their spouse and may indulge in high and obscure tactics for sexual pleasures. They may face hardships in their occupation and show carelessness in government and father's house. Such individuals are often avaricious and careless.

Saturn in the 2nd House (Leo)

With Saturn in the second house, the native enjoys good longevity and may experience restlessness concerning their spouse and family. They may exhibit aristocratic behavior in their daily life and inherit accumulated wealth, making them delightful.

Saturn in the 3rd House (Virgo)

In the third house, Saturn makes the native energetic and dedicated to their daily occupation. They may face some challenges concerning their children but enjoy power and pleasure with their spouse. They may experience confusion in their relationships with siblings and tend to be selfish and bitter in their speech, causing harm to their Dharma.

Saturn in the 4th House (Libra)

When Saturn is in the fourth house, the native experiences great happiness and joy, along with good longevity. However, they may face deficiencies in their social and government-related matters. They may find happiness in their daily occupation through solemn delusion and experience growth in their enemies' house. They enjoy a happy married life and family pleasures.

Saturn in the 5th House (Scorpio)

With Saturn in the fifth house, the native may experience mental confusion regarding their occupation, children, and spouse. However, they find happiness in their married life and sexual pleasures. They are always careful, speak somewhat bitterly, and are very industrious.

Saturn in the 6th House (Sagittarius)

In the sixth house, Saturn blesses the native with good longevity and diligence in their daily occupation. They may experience distress in their married life and face deficiencies in their sexual pleasures. Such individuals are often very wrathful.

Saturn in the 7th House (Capricorn)

When Saturn is in the seventh house, the native follows a laborious daily occupation and gains influence in their married life and work. They enjoy good longevity and may experience changes in their sexual pleasures. They may face physical troubles and tend to be selfish, passionate, and harmful to their Dharma. However, they may also experience an increase in land, property, and happiness.

Saturn in the 8th House (Aquarius)

In the eighth house, Saturn causes anxiety in the native's life concerning their spouse, father, and children. They may face deficiencies in honor and experience weakness and confusion in their business and daily occupation. They may receive help from foreign countries, speak somewhat bitterly, and be secretly very industrious.

Saturn in the 9th House (Pisces)

With Saturn in the ninth house, the native spends their daily routine in a fortunate way and enjoys a long life. However, they may experience dissatisfaction in their fate and tend to be careless.

Saturn in the 10th House (Aries)

In the tenth house, Saturn brings great trouble to the native's father's house and makes them undertake laborious and intricate deeds in their daily occupation. They may face strange struggles concerning their spouse and family but enjoy happiness, property, and buildings. They may experience artificial happiness in their mother's house, spend a lot, and enjoy gains through secret devices in government and society. They may face deficiencies in their sexual desires and tend to be somewhat lazy.

Saturn in the 11th House (Taurus)

When Saturn is in the eleventh house, the native experiences a significant rise in longevity and gains in their daily occupation. They may earn a lot of wealth, face deficiencies in some parts of their body, and enjoy sexual pleasures. They may take undue profits, speak bitterly, and face challenges with their children. They may also gain from foreign countries.

Saturn in the 12th House (Gemini)

In the twelfth house, Saturn makes the native spend a lot and progress in their destiny through troublesome devices and secret tactics. They may experience weakness in their happiness with their spouse and family, face loss of wealth, and deficiencies in their family life.

8. Rahu

(Rahu) in Cancer Ascendant

Rahu, also known as the Dragon's Head, is a shadow planet in Vedic astrology that represents the north node of the Moon. Its placement in the birth chart can have significant effects on an individual's life, depending on the house it occupies. In this essay, we will explore the predictions of Rahu in each house for those with a Cancer Ascendant.

Rahu in the 1st House (Cancer)

When Rahu is in the 1st house, it can cause some deficiencies and calamities in the body. The individual may experience mental distress and anxiety in their thoughts, leading to struggles in finding happiness. Despite these challenges, the person may still strive for personal growth and self-improvement.

Rahu in the 2nd House (Leo)

In the 2nd house, Rahu can lead to a loss of wealth and financial worries. The individual may find themselves taking loans and feeling anxious about their financial situation. This placement may also cause the person to be more focused on material possessions and financial security.

Rahu in the 3rd House (Virgo)

With Rahu in the 3rd house, the individual may experience unhappiness in their relationships with siblings. They may not follow the path of justice and instead engage in unjust actions. Despite this, the person can be very clever, careful, patient, and courageous in their endeavors.

Rahu in the 4th House (Libra)

When Rahu occupies the 4th house, it can create obstacles to peace and happiness. The individual may have strained relationships with their mother and may experience losses in land, buildings, and property. They may also feel unhappy in their residence but may find some happiness towards the end. This placement also indicates a very clever and resourceful nature.

Rahu in the 5th House (Scorpio)

In the 5th house, Rahu can cause significant hardships and losses related to children. However, the individual may find success in the realm of education and display bravery in the face of adversity. This placement may also indicate a strong desire for knowledge and intellectual pursuits.

Rahu in the 6th House (Sagittarius)

With Rahu in the 6th house, the individual may use secretive methods to achieve their goals and may not care about justice or injustice in the pursuit of their selfish desires. They may also have a secret policy with enemies and experience losses in their maternal grandfather's house. This placement indicates a selfish and cautious nature.

Rahu in the 7th House (Capricorn)

In the 7th house, Rahu can cause some trouble in the individual's marital life, leading to nervousness and anxiety. They may also face significant losses in their career but can achieve success through hard work and determination. This placement may also indicate deficiencies in sexual pleasures and daily affairs, as well as a selfish nature.

Rahu in the 8th House (Aquarius)

When Rahu is in the 8th house, the individual may gain power in their daily routine and work promptly. However, they may also experience some stomach-related issues and anxiety in their daily life. This placement may indicate a strong ability to adapt and overcome challenges.

Rahu in the 9th House (Pisces)

In the 9th house, Rahu can cause significant losses in the individual's destiny. Despite this, they may be able to put on a good outward appearance and achieve success after experiencing great nervousness. This placement also indicates a tactful and strategic nature.

Rahu in the 10th House (Aries)

With Rahu in the 10th house, the individual may face troubles in their relationship with their father and may have to endure significant hardships in their career. However, they may eventually gain respect from the government and society after overcoming these challenges. This placement also indicates a creative and industrious nature.

Rahu in the 11th House (Taurus)

In the 11th house, Rahu can bring substantial financial gains in the individual's career. They may be intelligent and cautious in their approach, taking more profits than they are entitled to. This placement also indicates a dignified and ambitious nature.

Rahu in the 12th House (Gemini)

When Rahu occupies the 12th house, the individual may spend their money lavishly and have high-class schemes in their expenditures. They may be able to manage their expenses easily and possess great power. This placement indicates a strong ability to adapt and overcome challenges in the realm of finances and material possessions.

9.Ketu

Predictions of Dragon's Tail (Ketu) in Cancer Ascendant

Ketu, also known as the Dragon's Tail, is a shadow planet in Vedic astrology that represents the south node of the Moon. It is believed to have a significant impact on an individual's life, depending on its placement in the birth chart. In this essay, we will explore the predictions of Ketu in Cancer Ascendant, as it moves through the twelve houses.

Ketu in the 1st House (Cancer)

When Ketu is in the first house of Cancer Ascendant, it may cause weakness in the body and a lean physique.

The individual may face some fatal troubles but will exhibit courage and obstinacy in overcoming them.

Ketu in the 2nd House (Leo)

In the second house, Ketu bestows the individual with immense physical and energetic strength. Through patience and perseverance, the person achieves success and gains courage due to their hard work.

Ketu in the 3rd House (Virgo)

The presence of Ketu in the third house may lead to significant losses in wealth. The individual will have to work hard to increase their earnings and may face difficulties in accumulating wealth.

Ketu in the 4th House (Libra)

In the fourth house, Ketu causes loss and deficiency in the areas of motherly love and happiness. The person may experience hardships related to their residence and face obstacles in attaining happiness. However, they will eventually find contentment.

Ketu in the 5th House (Scorpio)

When Ketu is in the fifth house, the individual may face problems and losses related to their children. They may also experience great difficulties in the realm of education and have a tendency to use harsh speech and words, leading to mental anxiety.

Ketu in the 6th House (Sagittarius)

In the sixth house, Ketu makes the person very brave and grants them a powerful influence over their enemies. The individual may use secret tactics for personal advancement, disregarding virtues and sins in the pursuit of their goals. They may be dangerous, fearless, dissatisfied, and ultimately victorious.

Ketu in the 7th House (Capricorn)

The presence of Ketu in the seventh house may cause distress in the individual's marital life and create obstacles in their professional progress. Despite facing setbacks, the person remains unshaken and eventually achieves stability in their occupation. They may possess secret powers in the realm of sexual pleasures and may not be satisfied with a single partner.

Ketu in the 8th House (Aquarius)

In the eighth house, Ketu may cause the individual to suffer from chronic stomach issues. However, they will lead a life without anxiety and will be willing to work hard.

Ketu in the 9th House (Pisces)

Ketu's presence in the ninth house may bring great distress to the individual's destiny. They may experience a loss of Dharma (righteousness) in their pursuit of success. The person may resort to secret consultations and display superficial religiosity.

Ketu in the 10th House (Aries)

In the tenth house, Ketu may cause losses related to the individual's father and create hardships in their professional life. The person will work hard to improve their trade and may face difficulties in dealing with government and society. However, their industrious nature will help them overcome these challenges.

Ketu in the 11th House (Taurus)

When Ketu is in the eleventh house, the individual will enjoy substantial income and profits. They may be selfish, but their enterprising and energetic nature will help them succeed.

Ketu in the 12th House (Gemini)

In the twelfth house, Ketu may cause great restlessness and difficulties in managing expenses. The individual may face calamities related to their expenditures and may struggle with impatience.

7. Leo Ascendant Planetary Predictions with Reference to Leo Ascendant

1. Sun

Predictions of Sun in Leo Ascendant

Sun in the 1st House (Leo):

The individual with Sun in the first house of Leo is likely to possess great dignity and achieve fame. They are often majestic and tall in stature, with a strong sense of self-worth and pride. However, they may not show much interest in their occupation or domestic affairs and may face opposition in their pursuit of sexual pleasures. Despite these challenges, they are brave and courageous.

Sun in the 2nd House (Virgo):

With the Sun in the second house of Virgo, the individual is likely to accumulate wealth and be considered very rich. They maintain an aristocratic lifestyle and are likely to have a long life. Their influence extends to their family, and they are often seen as a pillar of strength and support.

Sun in the 3rd House (Libra):

The person with Sun in the third house of Libra is considered to be very lucky and has a strong faith in God. They give importance to Dharma and uphold their religious beliefs. However, they may experience dissatisfaction in their relationships with their siblings and may feel a lack of vigor and enthusiasm in their life. Despite these challenges, they remain courageous and hopeful.

Sun in the 4th House (Scorpio):

The individual with Sun in the fourth house of Scorpio has a strong connection with their mother and derives happiness from land and property. They are content living in their own place, but may face some issues in their relationship with their father and in their business endeavors. Foreign travel may not bring them happiness, but they remain fearless, seeking peace and maintaining their pride.

Sun in the 5th House (Sagittarius):

With the Sun in the fifth house of Sagittarius, the person possesses exceptional abilities in the realm of education. They are highly respected, learned, and influential. Their dignity extends to their children, and they are likely to have a strong bond with them.

Sun in the 6th House (Capricorn):

The individual with Sun in the sixth house of Capricorn is likely to achieve victory over their enemies and is not deterred by obstacles or challenges. They may be extravagant in their spending habits, but their determination and resilience remain strong.

Sun in the 7th House (Aquarius):

The person with Sun in the seventh house of Aquarius may experience some unhappiness in their marriage, but they are likely to be successful in their business endeavors. They may feel dissatisfied in their pursuit of sexual pleasures and may be restless in their search for fulfillment.

Sun in the 8th House (Pisces):

With the Sun in the eighth house of Pisces, the individual may find themselves living in a different location than their birthplace. They are cautious in their approach to accumulating wealth and may experience some physical fatigue. They may also feel a sense of isolation and seclusion in their life.

Sun in the 9th House (Aries):

The person with Sun in the ninth house of Aries is likely to be very attractive, with a prominent forehead. They may not be particularly close to their siblings but possess a unique sense of Dharma and spirituality. They are highly respected and may hold a high position in religious institutions, earning fame and recognition.

Sun in the 11th House (Gemini):

With the Sun in the eleventh house of Gemini, the individual is likely to experience significant gains and financial success. They have a strong physique and are able to maximize their profits in various endeavors. They are blessed with children and power, are well-educated, and possess a high level of satisfaction and foresight in their life.

Sun in the 12th House (Cancer):

The person with Sun in the twelfth house of Cancer may have a lean body and may reside in a foreign country. They may experience weakness in their heart and may be prone to excessive spending. Despite these challenges, they have a keen ability to observe their enemies and may feel a sense of loneliness. They possess the power of travel and may feel physically weak at times.

2. Moon

Predictions of Moon in Leo Ascendant

Moon in the 1st House (Leo)

Individuals with the Moon in the first house of Leo are likely to have a strong desire to travel and explore various places. They may experience some physical weakness and tend to spend their money in a majestic and influential manner. These individuals may also face some challenges in their daily occupation and marital life, as they possess a weak heart and a suspicious mind.

Moon in the 2nd House (Virgo)

People with the Moon in the second house of Virgo may experience some loss and weakness in their financial situation and family life. Despite these challenges, they are fully engaged mentally in accumulating wealth and maintaining an aristocratic lifestyle.

Moon in the 3rd House (Libra)

Those with the Moon in the third house of Libra may face losses and weaknesses in their relationships with their siblings. They tend to spend on their brothers and sisters, which may lead to a decrease in their vigor due to heavy expenditure. However, they remain calm and energetic in their approach to life.

Moon in the 4th House (Scorpio)

Individuals with the Moon in the fourth house of Scorpio may experience weakness and deficiency in their relationship with their mother. They may face many obstacles in achieving peace and happiness and may suffer losses in their property and possessions. These individuals are likely to bear mental worries and stress.

Moon in the 5th House (Sagittarius)

People with the Moon in the fifth house of Sagittarius are likely to gain knowledge and wisdom. They are skilled at managing their expenses, but may face loss and weakness in their relationships with their children and in their educational pursuits.

Moon in the 6th House (Capricorn)

Those with the Moon in the sixth house of Capricorn may experience some dependence in their financial situation and may feel mentally fatigued. They tend to get their work done politely but may be careless in dealing with their enemies. These individuals are likely to spend on healthcare and medical expenses.

Moon in the 7th House (Aquarius)

Individuals with the Moon in the seventh house of Aquarius may face loss and weakness in their marital life and family relationships. They may experience challenges in their local occupation and may feel weak in their pursuit of sexual and other pleasures. These individuals may be somewhat anxious and may commit sins, leading to weakness in their everyday tasks.

Moon in the 8th House (Pisces)

People with the Moon in the eighth house of Pisces are likely to manage their expenses well but may feel some deficiency in their daily routine. They may experience weakness in their financial savings and may feel some anxiety about their age and longevity.

Moon in the 9th House (Aries)

Those with the Moon in the ninth house of Aries are likely to manage their expenses well but may experience some weakness in their spiritual and religious pursuits. They may have a restless mind and may face some deficiency in their relationships with their siblings. These individuals may also experience some weakness in their strength and energy levels.

Moon in the 10th House (Taurus)

Individuals with the Moon in the tenth house of Taurus may face losses in their local business and may experience some weakness in their relationship with their father or local position. They may also face challenges in their property and possessions and may experience weakness in their pursuit of happiness. These individuals tend to spend excessively in a royal manner and may have the power to influence the government and society through their expenditure.

Moon in the 11th House (Gemini)

People with the Moon in the eleventh house of Gemini are likely to gain success through the concentration of their mind and may earn money through their power of expenditure. They may have the strength to spend heavily but may experience some weakness in their relationships with their children and in their educational pursuits.

Moon in the 12th House (Cancer)

Those with the Moon in the twelfth house of Cancer are likely to spend excessively and may struggle to control their expenditure. They may be somewhat restless and possess a scrupulous mind, which may lead to challenges in their personal and professional lives.

3.Mars

Predictions of Mars in Leo Ascendant: An In-Depth Analysis

Mars in the 1st House (Leo):

Land and Property, Ideal Mother, and Happiness

Individuals with Mars in the 1st house of their Leo ascendant are likely to acquire land and property, enjoy the presence of an ideal mother, and have high means and influence to achieve happiness. They possess a good physique but may experience dullness in their spouse's, family's, and daily occupation's house.

Mars in the 2nd House (Virgo):

Fortune, Wealth, and Domestic Happiness

Those with Mars in the 2nd house of their Virgo ascendant are very fortunate, experiencing an increase in natural wealth, land, and property. However, they may create some disturbances in their domestic happiness and mother's side. They enjoy the pleasures of having children and exhibit gentleness in their educational pursuits.

Mars in the 3rd House (Libra):

Success, Courage, and Sibling Power

Individuals with Mars in the 3rd house of their Libra ascendant are very fortunate, achieving great success through their physical strength and vigor. They have significant influence in their enemy's house and show little concern for diseases and difficulties. These individuals are very courageous, possess the power of their siblings, and are highly influential.

Mars in the 4th House (Scorpio):

Land, Property, and Motherly Power

Those with Mars in the 4th house of their Scorpio ascendant gain power through land, property, and their mother. They enjoy good luck, peace, and happiness but may experience insipidness in their business and occupation. They may also feel some dissatisfaction in their government and society dealings, promotion of honor, and their spouse and father's house. However, they remain happy and joyous.

Mars in the 5th House (Sagittarius):

Education, Children, and Secret Knowledge

Individuals with Mars in the 5th house of their Sagittarius ascendant happily acquire education and enjoy the happiness of having children. They may experience some deficiency in their expenditure but possess knowledge of secret service and science.

Mars in the 6th House (Capricorn):

Defeating Enemies and Building Power

Those with Mars in the 6th house of their Capricorn ascendant can defend against their enemies but may experience some weakness in their mother's house. They may face hindrances in peace and happiness but possess the power of buildings. They may also experience deficiency in their expenditure.

Mars in the 7th House (Aquarius):

Dullness in Relationships and Domestic Success

Individuals with Mars in the 7th house of their Aquarius ascendant may experience dullness in their relationships with their mother and spouse. They may also feel some dissatisfaction in their domestic happiness but achieve success in their daily occupation.

Mars in the 8th House (Pisces):

Hindrances, Troubles, and Secret Knowledge

Those with Mars in the 8th house of their Pisces ascendant may face many hindrances in happiness and peace, troubles in their mother's house, and weakness in their residential building. They may experience deficiency in acquiring fame but possess knowledge of secret methods.

Mars in the 9th House (Aries):

Fortune, Land, Property, and Faith

Individuals with Mars in the 9th house of their Aries ascendant are very fortunate, acquiring lands and property, and experiencing great happiness. They may face deficiency in their expenditure but have strong faith in God and receive great respect.

Mars in the 10th House (Taurus):

Business Success, Property, and Influence

Those with Mars in the 10th house of their Taurus ascendant achieve progress and happiness through business, possess good property and land, and observe religious formalities. They receive great respect in government and society, succeed in education, and enjoy peace, happiness, and good health from their children. They are very influential.

Mars in the 11th House (Gemini):

Wealth Accumulation, Motherly Advantage, and Intelligence

Individuals with Mars in the 11th house of their Gemini ascendant accumulate wealth, enjoy the advantage of their mother, and gain from buildings and land. They have great influence in their enemy's house, can see the happiness of their family, and work intelligently in their educational pursuits. They may experience some adventures with their children and exhibit both piety and selfishness.

Mars in the 12th House (Cancer):

Weakness, Loss, and Restlessness

Those with Mars in the 12th house of their Cancer ascendant may experience great weakness in their destiny, loss in their mother's house, and loss of lands, buildings, and residential places. They may feel restless in their expenditure and have influence in their enemy's house.

4.Mercury

Here are the predictions for Mercury in Leo ascendant:

Mercury in the 1st House (Leo):

This placement indicates heavy gains and much wealth, great success in daily occupation, and advantage in the house of the wife. The native is likely to have success in worldly affairs and sexual pleasures, and is respectable and clever.

Mercury in the 2nd House (Virgo):

With Mercury in the 2nd house, the native accumulates much wealth and has a big family. However, there may be carelessness in daily routines, and income opportunities may be limited. The native is likely to earn respect.

Mercury in the 3rd House (Libra):

This placement indicates wealth accumulation and many ways of gaining, as well as advantage from siblings. The native may have a lot of confidence in God and is very clever.

Mercury in the 4th House (Scorpio):

The native with Mercury in the 4th house may accumulate wealth and have the power of building and property. They may have their every want satisfied while sitting at home, and get good garments and ornaments. Business success may come through the power of wealth, and respect may be earned in government and society. The native is likely to be a clever worker.

Mercury in the 5th House (Sagittarius):

Those with this placement are likely to acquire education and possess great art in their intellect. They may earn much money and get great advantage from their children. Drawing valuable plans, gaining respect and honor, serving their purpose with politeness, and being very clever are also predicted.

Mercury in the 6th House (Capricorn):

This placement may indicate weakness in accumulating wealth and limited advantage due to wealth in connection with enemies and diseases. The native may spend much but is very clever.

Mercury in the 7th House (Aquarius):

Those with Mercury in the 7th house may experience great success and rise in daily occupation, earn much wealth and gains from the father-in-law's family, and get great pleasure in the house of the wife and family. Pursuing decent occupation with grace and being very clever are also predicted.

Mercury in the 8th House (Pisces):

This placement indicates great loss in the house of wealth and accumulation of wealth through very difficult deeds. The native may experience restlessness in the house of longevity and daily routine of life, and anxiety in life.

Mercury in the 9th House (Aries):

Those with this placement are likely to gain wealth due to the power of destiny, have great reliance in God, and get advantage from siblings. The native may be very respectable.

Mercury in the 10th House (Taurus):

This placement indicates progress in trade and business, gaining power of wealth, and getting great respect in government and society. The native may see an increase in wealth and in the profession of the father's house, and acquire gains from the side of the mother. Strength of lands and buildings may also be gained.

Mercury in the 11th House (Gemini):

The native with Mercury in the 11th house is likely to get huge gains and earn much money. There may be confined dignity in the house of income and advantage from the side of children. Art and earning wealth in the house of education, as well as getting the opportunity and appreciation of their cleverness, are also predicted.

Mercury in the 12th House (Cancer):

Those with this placement may spend a lot of money and not give importance to accumulating wealth. They may take the help of money to drive away enemies, diseases, and difficulties and experience some distress in the store of wealth.

5. Jupiter

Predictions of Jupiter in Leo Ascendant: An In-Depth Analysis

Jupiter, the largest planet in our solar system, is known for its expansive and benevolent nature. In astrology, it is considered the planet of wisdom, knowledge, and spirituality. When Jupiter is placed in the Leo ascendant, it can have a significant impact on various aspects of an individual's life, such as education, relationships, and overall well-being. In this essay, we will explore the predictions of Jupiter in Leo ascendant when it is placed in different houses.

Jupiter in the 1st House (Leo):

When Jupiter is placed in the first house of Leo, the individual is likely to have a long life and acquire a vast amount of education. They will have strong connections with their children and lead a life of prominence. However, there may be some lack of physical attractiveness, and the family environment may be somewhat dull. Despite these minor setbacks, the individual will exhibit great scholarship and knowledge.

Jupiter in the 2nd House (Virgo):

With Jupiter in the second house, the individual will lead an aristocratic lifestyle, but there may be some weaknesses and challenges related to their children. They may also experience confusion and uncertainty in certain aspects of their life.

Jupiter in the 3rd House (Libra):

In this position, Jupiter bestows good longevity upon the individual, but there may be some difficulties in their relationships with siblings. Nevertheless, the individual will still be able to acquire education and knowledge.

Jupiter in the 4th House (Scorpio):

When Jupiter is placed in the fourth house, the individual will experience great happiness in their daily life. However, there may be some deficiencies in their relationship with their mother and their ability to have children. Additionally, they may face some challenges in finding local pleasures and enjoyment.

Jupiter in the 5th House (Sagittarius):

In this position, Jupiter blesses the individual with the happiness of having children and acquiring education. They are considered somewhat fortunate and receive honor and respect for their physical appearance. They lead a joyful life and engage in traditional and intricate conversations.

Jupiter in the 6th House (Capricorn):

With Jupiter in the sixth house, the individual may experience restlessness in their daily life and spend a significant amount of money. They will use diplomacy when dealing with enemies and work hard to increase their wealth.

Jupiter in the 7th House (Aquarius):

In this position, Jupiter may cause confusion and challenges in the individual's marital life. They may face difficulties in managing their business and acquiring the power to do so. There may also be some issues related to education, children, siblings, and a lack of respect.

Jupiter in the 8th House (Pisces):

When Jupiter is placed in the eighth house, the individual will have an increased lifespan but may face troubles with their children. There may be some deficiencies in their education and losses related to their mother and overall happiness.

Jupiter in the 9th House (Aries):

In this position, Jupiter enables the individual to acquire a vast amount of education and have strong connections with their children. They will be respected and promote religious ideas in a complex manner. However, there may be some deficiencies in achieving fame, but they will lead a fortunate and intelligent life.

Jupiter in the 10th House (Taurus):

With Jupiter in the tenth house, the individual may face challenges in their relationship with their father but will have strong connections with their children. They may use secretive tactics when dealing with enemies and work hard to gain honor in government and society. They are likely to be self-confident and skillful in their endeavors.

Jupiter in the 11th House (Gemini):

In this position, Jupiter bestows good longevity, education, and strong connections with children upon the individual. They will lead a cheerful life but may face significant inconveniences in their daily life, relationships with their spouse and family, and their relationships with siblings.

Jupiter in the 12th House (Cancer):

When Jupiter is placed in the twelfth house, the individual may spend a significant amount of money and acquire limited education and few children. However, they will still have a good lifespan and may experience some losses in their overall happiness.

6.Venus

Here are the predictions for Venus in Leo ascendant:

Venus in the 1st House (Leo):

With Venus in the 1st house, the native works with strength and energy, achieving honor and progress in trade and occupation. There is honor and strength in the house of the spouse, as well as special powers and sexual pleasures. The native exerts effort to secure honor in government and society, tactfully getting their work done. They are industrious.

Venus in the 2nd House (Virgo):

This placement may indicate some weakness in the house of wealth and family.

Venus in the 3rd House (Libra):

The native with Venus in the 3rd house gains power from siblings and father. They experience honor in connection with government and society, fame, and engage in religious deeds. Business progress is predicted, and the native is industrious, courageous, and skillful.

Venus in the 4th House (Scorpio):

Having Venus in the 4th House in Scorpio suggests a deep emotional connection to one's home and family. There is a desire for intensity and passion in domestic affairs, leading to a transformative and sometimes tumultuous environment. Family relationships may be complex, yet profoundly intimate and transformative. The home is likely to be decorated with sensual and mysterious elements, reflecting the owner's taste for the enigmatic. This placement also indicates a need for privacy and secrecy within the home, as well as a potential for intense emotional healing and transformation through the family dynamics.

Venus in the 5th House (Sagittarius):

Those with Venus in the 5th house embark on a great business and experience happiness from siblings and father. They gain power from government and society and have great strength in buildings and property. Happiness and skilled work are predicted.

Venus in the 6th House (Capricorn):

This placement indicates some enmity in the house of the father and hindrances in the house of honor. There is ordinary strength in government and society, and the native may spend much and face difficulties in conducting their occupation. Influence in the house of enemies is present, and acquiring progress feels challenging.

Venus in the 7th House (Aquarius):

Those with Venus in the 7th house gain great power in daily and permanent trade and occupation. They have power from siblings and in the house of the father, as well as great respect and influence in connection with government and society. There is a great power and grandeur in the house of the spouse and family, as well as a strong power of sexual pleasure. The native is skilled, courageous, clever, and possesses vigor.

Venus in the 8th House (Pisces):

This placement indicates conducting business in far-off foreign countries and a curious sort of happiness in connection with siblings and father. There may be a deficiency in the house of wealth.

Venus in the 9th House (Aries):

Those with this placement experience grand success and progress through the progress of destiny. They enjoy the company of siblings and father and perform religious functions. There is honor and success in government and society.

Venus in the 10th House (Taurus):

This placement indicates advantage from siblings and father, fame, appreciation for success, honor and success in government and society, and great success in business. There is a rise in prestige, power in buildings and property, and success in business. The native is ambitious, majestic, industrious, and self-conceited.

Venus in the 11th House (Gemini):

The native with Venus in the 11th house earns much wealth, enjoys advantages from government and society, achieves success in the house of education, and gains power from the father and in the house of children. They are zealous workers.

Venus in the 12th House (Cancer):

Those with this placement may spend much and experience loss in the house of father and siblings. There may be loss in business and weakness in the house of government and society.

7. Saturn

Predictions of Saturn in Leo Ascendant: An In-Depth Analysis

Saturn, the sixth planet from the Sun, is known for its slow movement and its influence on an individual's life. In astrology, Saturn is considered a malefic planet, often associated with discipline, hard work, and challenges. When Saturn is placed in the Leo Ascendant, it can have various effects on different aspects of an individual's life, depending on its position in the twelve houses. This essay will explore the predictions of Saturn in Leo Ascendant in each house and its impact on an individual's life.

Saturn in the 1st House (Leo)

When Saturn is in the first house of Leo Ascendant, it indicates that the individual may be involved in a laborious daily occupation that requires physical effort. The person may find happiness in their family and married life, but they may also experience some health issues. The individual may have strong sexual desires and show great determination and hard work in their endeavors.

Saturn in the 2nd House (Virgo)

In the second house, Saturn may bring mixed results in terms of wealth, with both gains and losses. The individual may face obstacles in their relationship with their mother and in finding happiness in their home. There may be some restlessness in their living environment and in their married life, as well as challenges in their daily occupation.

Saturn in the 3rd House (Libra)

When Saturn is in the third house, the individual may experience victory over their enemies and show great strength in their daily work. They may be courageous and determined, but they may also face some restlessness in their relationships with their children and in their financial expenditures.

Saturn in the 4th House (Scorpio)

In the fourth house, Saturn may cause a loss of affection from the individual's mother and create some discord in their married life. The person may be hardworking, persistent, and determined to overcome life's challenges and health issues.

Saturn in the 5th House (Sagittarius)

With Saturn in the fifth house, the individual may be diligent and intelligent in their daily work. They may have strong sexual desires and fantasies, but they may also experience dullness in their relationships with their children. The person may have hidden strategies in their pursuit of knowledge and wisdom, and they may be mentally troubled, skillful, and influential over their enemies.

Saturn in the 6th House (Capricorn)

In the sixth house, Saturn may cause confusion and dissatisfaction in the individual's married life and may lead to a decrease in sexual pleasure. However, the person may gain influence over their enemies and achieve success in their daily work after overcoming significant challenges.

Saturn in the 7th House (Aquarius)

When Saturn is in the seventh house, the individual may achieve stability and success in their daily work through hard work and strategic planning. They may have intense sexual desires, but they may also face some hostility in their married life. The person may neglect their religious duties and suffer from health issues, and they may also encounter obstacles in their relationships with their mother and in finding happiness.

Saturn in the 8th House (Pisces)

In the eighth house, Saturn may cause the individual to experience difficulties in their married life and daily work. They may collaborate with foreign countries and face distress in their relationships with their children.

The person may also suffer losses in their career and feel hopeless about their longevity. However, they may put in significant effort to contribute to government and society.

Saturn in the 9th House (Aries)

With Saturn in the ninth house, the individual may experience weakness in their destiny and a lack of faith in God. However, they may still acquire sufficient wealth.

Saturn in the 10th House (Taurus)

In the tenth house, Saturn may grant the individual success and respect in their daily work, as well as progress and recognition in government and society. The person may enjoy a happy married life and sexual pleasure, but they may also face obstacles in achieving peace and happiness. The individual may be skillful and hardworking.

Saturn in the 11th House (Gemini)

When Saturn is in the eleventh house, the individual may earn significant wealth in their daily affairs and career. They may suffer from health issues but enjoy the benefits of hard work. The person may have a happy married life and strong sexual desires, as well as considerable influence over their enemies.

Saturn in the 12th House (Cancer)

In the twelfth house, Saturn may cause the individual to spend excessively and suffer losses in their married life. They may remain under the influence of their enemies and have little faith in God and destiny. The person may also spend money on treating their health issues.

8. Rahu

Here are the predictions for Rahu (Dragon's Head) in Leo ascendant:

Rahu in the 1st House (Leo):

The native may experience weakness in the body, anxiety, stress in the brain, inner fear, and selfishness. They have a tendency to exert influence.

Rahu in the 2nd House (Virgo):

This placement may indicate some loss in the house of wealth and weakness in the family. The native may resort to secretive means to acquire wealth and feel somewhat restless.

Rahu in the 3rd House (Libra):

Those with Rahu in the 3rd house gain power and influence. There may be some separations and restlessness. However, they possess great patience and diplomatic skills, allowing them to accomplish difficult tasks. They are clever and eventually see an increase in wealth.

Rahu in the 5th House (Scorpio):

This placement may lead to loss or separation related to the mother or in the house of mother. The native may experience difficulties in acquiring happiness and resort to secretive actions to find happiness. There may be distress in the domestic environment, and happiness is achieved after a long time and many challenges.

Rahu in the 6th House (Capricorn):

The native possesses great influence in the house of enemies and may disregard politeness, gentility, and contentment. They are influential and brave.

Rahu in the 7th House (Aquarius):

Restlessness is experienced in the house of the mother, and there is great perplexity in daily occupation. There may be some defects related to sexual organs, and a desire to satisfy unsatisfied passions. Secret schemes are used for sexual pleasure and occupational pursuits. Some strength is gained in the end.

Rahu in the 8th House (Pisces):

There are many perplexities in the daily routine of life and inner troubles in the stomach. Fatal losses may occur in the house of longevity after bearing many hardships.

Rahu in the 9th House (Aries):

Losses are predicted in the house of fortune, and there may be a deficiency in faith and reliance on God. The native employs intricate and secretive methods for success and faces great obstacles. Fame may be lacking.

Rahu in the 10th House (Taurus):

This placement indicates great difficulties in the house of the father and troubles related to government and society. The native works through secret means to achieve progress but faces hindrances in reputation and fortune. They find a way to progress through diplomatic tactics after enduring many hardships.

Rahu in the 11th House (Gemini):

Those with Rahu in the 11th house acquire a large income, great courage, and find ways to maximize profits. They have a tendency towards greed and are never satisfied in acquiring wealth.

Rahu in the 12th House (Cancer):

The native with this placement may spend much and manage their expenditure with great hardships and anxieties. Sometimes they encounter hostile calculations in the house of expenditure.

9. Ketu

Predictions of Dragon's Tail (Ketu) in Leo Ascendant

Ketu in the 1st House (Leo)

When Ketu is placed in the first house of a Leo Ascendant, it can cause some weakness in the body and may even pose life-threatening dangers. Despite these challenges, individuals with this placement are known to be courageous, proud, and possess great sexual prowess. They are also hardworking and often engage in physically demanding labor.

Ketu in the 2nd House (Virgo)

In the second house, Ketu can cause some deficiency in wealth and may create weaknesses in the family structure. However, individuals with this placement are known to be patient and diligent in their pursuit of worldly wisdom.

Ketu in the 3rd House (Libra)

When Ketu is in the third house, it can cause restlessness and tension among siblings. Despite this, individuals with this placement can experience a significant rise in influence and power. They may not be overly concerned with politeness or gentility and are often driven by their selfish desires.

Ketu in the 4th House (Scorpio)

In the fourth house, Ketu can create a sense of deficiency in the relationship with one's mother and may lead to separation from one's homeland or birthplace. Individuals with this placement may face significant obstacles in finding happiness and may experience difficulties related to their residence or property.

Ketu in the 5th House (Sagittarius)

When Ketu is in the fifth house, individuals may need to put in considerable intellectual effort to acquire education. They may also experience distress related to their children and may struggle to express their true opinions or views effectively.

Ketu in the 6th House (Capricorn)

In the sixth house, Ketu can grant individuals great influence over their enemies and help them overcome diseases and difficulties. These individuals may not be overly concerned with modesty and are often driven by their selfish desires. They are also known to be brave and courageous.

Ketu in the 7th House (Aquarius)

When Ketu is in the seventh house, it can cause loss in the area of marriage and relationships. However, individuals with this placement may possess special powers and enjoy sexual pleasures. They may also work hard in their daily occupations.

Ketu in the 8th House (Pisces)

In the eighth house, Ketu can create confusion and complexity in one's daily life. Individuals with this placement may experience internal stomach issues and may face a significant loss in terms of their lifespan.

Ketu in the 9th House (Aries)

When Ketu is in the ninth house, it can cause significant challenges in one's destiny and may hinder progress. There may be deficiencies in one's spiritual and religious life, but after overcoming these obstacles, individuals may eventually find stability and firmness in their destiny.

Ketu in the 10th House (Taurus)

In the tenth house, Ketu can cause some loss in the relationship with one's father. Individuals with this placement may need to work hard and endure hardships in their careers and occupations. They may face significant challenges in rising through the ranks of government and society but are known to be industrious and possess a hidden source of energy.

Ketu in the 11th House (Gemini)

When Ketu is in the eleventh house, individuals may experience an increase in income with relatively less effort. They may also enjoy some definite gains but may not be overly concerned with the profits or losses of others. These individuals are known to be secretly patient.

Ketu in the 12th House (Cancer)

In the twelfth house, Ketu can cause restlessness in terms of expenditure and may create challenges related to work in foreign lands. However, individuals with this placement are known to be internally patient and can overcome these obstacles, eventually finding stability in their financial situation

8. Virgo Ascendant Predictions for Sun in Virgo Ascendant:

1. Sun

Here are the predictions for Sun in Virgo ascendant:

Sun in the 1st House (Virgo):

The native may spend a lot, have a weak and emaciated body, manage their expenditure through physical labor, and conduct daily occupation with a focus on expenses. There may be weakness in the house of the spouse, losses and weakness in the occupation, and a haughty nature.

Sun in the 2nd House (Libra):

This placement suggests great loss of wealth, unnecessary spending, and potential loss within the family. The native may have some influence in their daily routine and achieve their goals through deep and intricate strategies.

Sun in the 3rd House (Scorpio):

The native manages their expenditure independently and may cause harm to their brothers. They may experience anxieties and have a weak destiny. However, they are industrious in their pursuits.

Sun in the 4th House (Sagittarius):

There may be management of expenditure with a deficiency in the means of happiness. Separation in the house of the mother and weakness in the house of the father and in significant business ventures are indicated. The native may also experience a lack of honor and difficulties in government and societal affairs.

Sun in the 5th House (Capricorn):

There is a deficiency in the house of education, troubles related to children, mental worries, weakness in profits, haughtiness, difficulty in expressing ideas clearly, and cleverness.

Sun in the 6th House (Aquarius):

The native manages their expenditure properly through dependent actions but struggles to control expenses even when they desire to do so. They may have to spend on matters of illness.

Sun in the 7th House (Pisces):

Expenditure is managed through the daily occupation, but there may be weakness in the house of occupation. Delay and restlessness in the family are experienced, along with happiness and restlessness due to expenses. The native may have an emaciated figure.

Sun in the 8th House (Aries):

There is significant spending, weakness in the pursuit of accumulated wealth, weakness in the house of family, and association with foreign countries, among other factors.

Sun in the 9th House (Taurus):

The native experiences weakness in destiny and anxiety about fate. There may be a deficiency in devotion to God and some loss in the house of brothers.

Sun in the 10th House (Gemini):

Losses are predicted in the house of the father. The native spends magnificently from their income and business, faces some loss in the house of the mother, and experiences some deficiency in the rise of respect. Honor is gained through business activities.

Sun in the 11th House (Cancer):

Expenditure is based on income, and gains are derived from other houses. There may be losses in relation to children and deficiencies in education. The native may exhibit bitterness and roughness in speech.

Sun in the 12th House (Leo):

There is significant spending, influence over enemies, expenditure on disputes and illness, and a great power of influence in the house of expenditure.

2.Moon

The Moon in Virgo Ascendant: An Exploration of its Influence on Various Aspects of Life

Moon in the 1st House (Virgo)

When the Moon is in the first house of Virgo Ascendant, it bestows physical and mental happiness, making the individual attractive and calm by nature. Such a person is likely to have a beautiful spouse and enjoy a prosperous career. They experience various pleasures and enjoyments in life and are highly respected by others. Their delightful nature makes them interested in their spouse's family, and they may gain from their father-in-law's house. They are very cautious about their income and daily occupation and may have a strong desire for unique sexual experiences.

Moon in the 2nd House (Libra)

A person with the Moon in the second house of Libra is likely to accumulate vast wealth and have a large family. They experience immense happiness from their gains throughout their life and enjoy a long life. They are deeply involved in politics and hold a respectable position in society.

Moon in the 3rd House (Scorpio)

The Moon in the third house of Scorpio signifies that the individual will achieve moderate gains through hard mental labor. They are considered fortunate due to their diligent work ethic and have a strong faith in God and Dharma. However, they may experience distress in their relationships with their siblings.

Moon in the 4th House (Sagittarius)

When the Moon is in the fourth house of Sagittarius, the individual enjoys a comfortable income and gains from land and property. They experience the pleasure of having supportive parents and succeed in their business or occupation. They also receive gains from the government and society, feel mentally content, and enjoy beautiful possessions, clothing, and jewelry. They derive happiness from their mother's house.

Moon in the 5th House (Capricorn)

A person with the Moon in the fifth house of Capricorn benefits from their wisdom, has children, and receives a good education. They possess a strong intellect and gain from their intellectual prowess and wisdom. They are also very sensible individuals.

Moon in the 6th House (Aquarius)

The Moon in the sixth house of Aquarius indicates some weakness in connection with gains, leading to mental anxieties and increased spending. The individual may experience some dependence on others for income or gains and receive little from their maternal grandfather. They may find their mind somewhat preoccupied and have an amiable disposition.

Moon in the 7th House (Pisces)

When the Moon is in the seventh house of Pisces, the individual enjoys significant gains in their daily occupation and has a beautiful spouse. They indulge in splendid sexual pleasures and engage in family-related activities. They are attractive, gain from their father-in-law's house, succeed in worldly affairs, and are intelligent.

Moon in the 8th House (Aries)

A person with the Moon in the eighth house of Aries may experience worries about gains due to associations with challenging situations. They put in considerable effort to accumulate wealth and may endure mental distress. However, they always desire an increase in wealth, family, and destiny.

Moon in the 9th House (Taurus)

The Moon in the ninth house of Taurus signifies a very fortunate individual who gains significantly due to the power of destiny. They have a strong faith in God and Dharma, achieve fame, and may experience some deficiency in their relationships with their siblings. They are farsighted, accept truths, are influential, and secure substantial increments in gains after the age of twenty-four.

Moon in the 10th House (Gemini)

When the Moon is in the tenth house of Gemini, the individual gains majestically from their business and receives significant gains from their father, government, and society. They live a luxurious life, possess expensive items, and enjoy various pleasures. They also gain from their mother's house, land, and property, and experience family enjoyment.

Moon in the 11th House (Cancer)

A person with the Moon in the eleventh house of Cancer enjoys decent gains spontaneously and without much effort. They experience some happiness regarding their children and possess the power of education and wisdom.

Moon in the 12th House (Leo)

The Moon in the twelfth house of Leo indicates an individual who spends a lot and has a fickle and restless mind. They may think about distant matters and spend their entire income on securing gains or dealing with issues related to illness or disputes. They approach their enemies with a cool mind to get their work done, experience some weakness in gaining

3.Mars

Here are the predictions for Mars in Virgo ascendant:

Mars in the 1st House (Virgo):

The native gets a long life, may experience some distress in the body, possesses great power, faces some loss in the house of the mother, feels some distress in the spouse's side, and receives efficiency and cooperation from siblings.

Mars in the 2nd House (Libra):

The native leads a life surrounded by wealth, enjoys a long life, experiences some deficiency in relation to siblings, faces some loss in accumulating wealth, and may have talkative tendencies.

Mars in the 3rd House (Scorpio):

The native works hard, may cause harm to the father, experiences weakness in maintaining influence over enemies.

Mars in the 4th House (Sagittarius):

The native has a long life and enjoys the entire period of life. There may be some loss in the house of the mother, gains wealth, causes some injury to the spouse's side, experiences some deficiency in income, and faces deficiency in relation to the father.

Mars in the 5th House (Capricorn):

The native lives a grand life, gains fame, possesses honor and influence, uses diplomacy wisely, spends a lot, has skill in speech, experiences a mix of strong happiness and unhappiness regarding children, and may exhibit haughty behavior.

Mars in the 6th House (Aquarius):

There may be losses on the maternal grandfather's side, enmity or separation with siblings, causes uneasiness to enemies and opponents, and lives in a sort of bondage.

Mars in the 7th House (Pisces):

The native bears distress in the spouse's house, achieves success in their industry, faces worries related to occupation, plans secret policies for occupational gains, experiences some trouble and distress in the father's house, and encounters deficiency in relation to siblings.

Mars in the 8th House (Aries):

The native enjoys a long life, experiences some deficiency in gains, faces some loss on the sibling's side, and encounters deficiency in handling wealth and hard work.

Mars in the 9th House (Taurus):

The native enjoys a long life, spends a lot, faces some loss in the house of the mother, experiences deficiency in happiness and weakness in matters of righteousness and destiny, and has less faith in God.

Mars in the 10th House (Gemini):

There may be troubles in the father's house, pleasures and sufferings in social and professional progress, special power related to children, rough speech, some deficiency in the mother's house and happiness.

Mars in the 11th House (Cancer):

There may be deficiency in the house of income and gains, deficiency in relation to siblings, progress in education, intelligence, and children, and some loss in the accumulation of wealth.

Mars in the 12th House (Leo):

The native faces some loss on the enemy and maternal grandfather's side, experiences loss of brother and spouse, and encounters loss in daily occupation.

4. Mercury

Predictions of Mercury in Virgo Ascendant: An In-Depth Analysis

Mercury in the 1st House (Virgo)

Individuals with Mercury in the 1st House are tall and symmetrical in appearance, enjoying a sense of royal grandeur. They are highly influential and often experience progress in their father's house. These individuals are skilled in conducting business and may face some deficiencies in their marital life and sexual pleasures. They are clever, wise, and skillful, often excelling in politics. Diligent and well-mannered, they are respected by others.

Mercury in the 2nd House (Libra)

With Mercury in the 2nd House, individuals are likely to amass significant wealth and prosper in their business endeavors. They are instrumental in linking the progress of their family and wealth, leading to a rich and long life.

Mercury in the 3rd House (Scorpio)

Individuals with Mercury in the 3rd House are handsome and energetic, enjoying the support of their siblings. Their success is often attributed to their efficiency and determination. They live with decency, possess self-pride, and have a strong belief in God.

Mercury in the 4th House (Sagittarius)

Those with Mercury in the 4th House live happily and own beautiful, well-decorated homes. They enjoy the happiness of their parents and conduct business peacefully and successfully. They are respected and honored by both the government and society, known for their cleverness and jovial nature.

Mercury in the 5th House (Capricorn)

Individuals with Mercury in the 5th House are highly intelligent and well-educated, enjoying the power and happiness of their children. They are proud and dutiful, living in beautifully decorated homes. They are self-conscious and well-versed in the laws of government and society.

Mercury in the 6th House (Aquarius)

With Mercury in the 6th House, individuals may experience dependency and face enmity in their father's house, leading to hindrances in their progress. They may suffer from illnesses and discomfort caused by their enemies. Despite their gentle nature, they may have to endure the consequences of their sins and spend excessively.

Mercury in the 7th House (Pisces)

Individuals with Mercury in the 7th House may face worries in their family life and experience deficiencies in their relationships with their father and spouse. They may also suffer from physical weakness but are capable of safeguarding their honor. Their influence in matters related to sexual pleasures may be limited, but they are highly industrious in their occupations, often engulfed in worries.

Mercury in the 8th House (Aries)

With Mercury in the 8th House, individuals may experience loss or distress in their physical and emotional well-being, as well as in their relationships with their father. They may feel unhappy and weak-hearted in matters of progress and may reside in foreign countries. Despite facing challenges in their business, they remain engaged in schemes to increase their wealth.

Mercury in the 9th House (Taurus)

Individuals with Mercury in the 9th House are fortunate, receiving help and honor from their father's house. They are respected by the government and society and possess a handsome, attractive appearance. They enjoy the company of their siblings and achieve success in their business endeavors, maintaining a strong faith in God and receiving divine assistance.

Mercury in the 10th House (Gemini)

With Mercury in the 10th House, individuals have a handsome appearance and excel in their business pursuits. They enjoy pleasure and progress from the government and their father's house, as well as the happiness of their mother, properties, and buildings. They are skilled managers.

Mercury in the 11th House (Cancer)

Individuals with Mercury in the 11th House earn substantial wealth and enjoy significant gains from their father's house. They prosper in their business and experience gains connected to the government. They wear beautiful clothes and ornaments, skillfully executing their tasks. They are well-educated and enjoy the pleasures of having children.

Mercury in the 12th House (Leo)

With Mercury in the 12th House, individuals tend to spend excessively and may reside in foreign countries. They may experience some weakness in their father's house and display courage when dealing with their enemies. They exercise discretion in their expenditures.

5. Jupiter

Here are the predictions for Jupiter in Virgo ascendant:

Jupiter in the 1st House (Virgo):

The native experiences domestic happiness, gets a clever wife, enjoys pleasant occupation, is considered fortunate, is diligent in matters of righteousness and family affairs, may face some deficiency in relation to children, experiences some weakness in wisdom and education, has intellectual concerns related to the wife and family, has a well-built body, owns property, and is clever and happy.

Jupiter in the 2nd House (Libra):

The native gains honor and power through wealth, finds pleasure in property, experiences some attachment to pleasures related to the mother and wife, gains wealth from daily occupation, receives assistance from the father's house, finds honor and happiness in government and society, enjoys a long life, has influence over enemies, and experiences happiness in the maternal grandfather's family.

Jupiter in the 3rd House (Scorpio):

The native gains heavily through various pleasant occupations, gets a beautiful and influential wife, possesses a good stature, enjoys sufficient sexual pleasures, takes care of the family well, has faith in righteousness, has siblings, receives support from the mother's house, works hard, gains power from the father-in-law's house, experiences growth after marriage, and is fortunate.

Jupiter in the 4th House (Sagittarius):

The native finds happiness through the mother and wife, acquires property, enjoys occupational happiness, spends generously, performs occupation with joy, experiences happiness through the father's house, and enjoys family pleasures.

Jupiter in the 5th House (Capricorn):

The native may feel unhappy in relation to family pleasures, experiences weakness and deficiency in various aspects (mother, wife, children), faces worries in daily occupation, encounters weaknesses in education and wisdom, hesitates while speaking, faces hindrances in happiness and peace, has improper ideas about sexual pleasures, and feels distressed.

Jupiter in the 6th House (Aquarius):

The native faces hindrances in family pleasure, bears some distress related to the mother and wife, experiences deficiencies in peace and happiness, encounters obstacles in daily occupation, has a family, spends generously, handles enemies with politeness, faces hindrances in sexual affairs, experiences deficiencies in residential places, and receives some assistance from large business concerns.

Jupiter in the 7th House (Pisces):

The native enjoys great pleasures, engages in dignified occupation, finds honor and happiness through daily occupational activities, experiences an increase in pleasure after marriage, enjoys peace in married life, has siblings, and achieves success through good strength.

Jupiter in the 8th House (Aries):

The native faces significant suffering in family life, encounters some deficiency in the mother's house, experiences distress and separation on the wife's side, achieves success in daily occupation despite great obstacles, spends generously, and strives to accumulate wealth.

Jupiter in the 9th House (Taurus):

The native is fortunate, pays attention to God, experiences family pleasures due to the power of destiny, acquires buildings and property, has siblings, faces some distress regarding children, encounters weakness in education and intellect, utters faulty and weak words, and possesses peace and foresight.

Jupiter in the 10th House (Gemini):

The native is dignified, industrious, and enjoys luxurious sexual pleasures, engages in significant business ventures, accumulates substantial wealth, owns landed property, finds pleasure in parents, receives respect in government and society, experiences happiness through the spouse, and gains respect through occupation.

Jupiter in the 11th House (Cancer):

The native gains heavily through daily occupation, has the pleasure of an extraordinarily beautiful wife, experiences decent sexual pleasure, gains heavily in terms of mother, land, and buildings, enjoys happiness with siblings

Jupiter in the 12th House (Leo):

Spiritual Growth and Inner Expansion: Jupiter in the 12th House suggests a strong potential for spiritual growth and inner expansion. You may have a deep interest in exploring the realms of spirituality, mysticism, and metaphysics. This placement can bring a sense of wisdom and insight gained through introspection and inner exploration.Compassion and Service: Jupiter in the 12th House in Leo often signifies a compassionate and humanitarian nature. You may feel a strong urge to serve others, particularly those who are less fortunate or in need. Your generosity and empathy may shine through in your interactions with others.

6.Venus

Predictions of Venus in Virgo Ascendant: An In-Depth Analysis

Venus in the 1st House (Virgo)

When Venus is positioned in the first house of a Virgo Ascendant, the native may experience some physical weakness or health issues. Despite this, they are likely to have a fortunate spouse who supports them in their endeavors. The individual may be involved in a significant daily occupation and may indulge in sensual pleasures. Their career is likely to progress after marriage, indicating a strong connection between their personal and professional lives.

Venus in the 2nd House (Libra)

A person with Venus in the second house of their Virgo Ascendant birth chart is likely to be very wealthy, fortunate, and well-respected. They may come from a prominent family and enjoy a luxurious lifestyle. This placement of Venus indicates a strong affinity for material possessions and a desire to maintain a high social status.

Venus in the 3rd House (Scorpio)

The presence of Venus in the third house of a Virgo Ascendant birth chart suggests that the native will experience an increase in wealth due to their destiny. They are likely to be well-known, religious, and have strong relationships with their siblings. This placement also indicates that the individual will be influential and highly regarded in their community.

Venus in the 4th House (Sagittarius)

Individuals with Venus in the fourth house of their Virgo Ascendant birth chart are likely to accumulate wealth and be very fortunate. They may be hardworking and industrious, with a strong focus on acquiring land and property. This placement also suggests that the native will benefit from their parents' support and guidance.

Venus in the 5th House (Capricorn)

When Venus is positioned in the fifth house of a Virgo Ascendant birth chart, the native is likely to be highly intelligent, fortunate, and skilled in various fields. They may be particularly adept at religious discourse, astrology, and politics. This placement also indicates a strong connection to their children and a deep enjoyment of family life. The individual is likely to be well-respected and admired for their talents and accomplishments.

Venus in the 6th House (Aquarius)

A person with Venus in the sixth house of their Virgo Ascendant birth chart may be a successful politician and accumulate wealth throughout their life. However, they may struggle with their moral compass and face challenges related to their destiny. This placement suggests that the native will be able to overcome their enemies through their adherence to their principles and beliefs.

Venus in the 7th House (Pisces)

Individuals with Venus in the seventh house of their Virgo Ascendant birth chart are likely to be very fortunate and enjoy a high standard of sensual pleasure. They may accumulate significant wealth and be involved in a substantial daily occupation. This placement also indicates a beautiful spouse and a wealthy father-in-law, further contributing to the native's overall prosperity.

Venus in the 8th House (Aries)

When Venus is positioned in the eighth house of a Virgo Ascendant birth chart, the native may experience some challenges related to their family and destiny. They may also struggle with their religious beliefs and find success in foreign countries. This placement suggests a need for resilience and adaptability in the face of adversity.

Venus in the 9th House (Taurus)

Individuals with Venus in the ninth house of their Virgo Ascendant birth chart are likely to be very fortunate, religious, and wealthy. They may enjoy strong family bonds and close relationships with their siblings. This placement also indicates a deep belief in a higher power and a strong connection to their spiritual beliefs.

Venus in the 10th House (Gemini)

A person with Venus in the tenth house of their Virgo Ascendant birth chart is likely to be highly respected and considered very fortunate. They may experience success in their career due to their father's support and their own cleverness in business. This placement suggests a strong drive for achievement and recognition in their professional life.

Venus in the 11th House (Cancer)

When Venus is positioned in the eleventh house of a Virgo Ascendant birth chart, the native is likely to accumulate significant wealth and be highly intelligent. They may be deeply committed to their moral principles and enjoy strong connections with their children. This placement also indicates that the individual will benefit from their family's support and enjoy a life filled with beautiful possessions and experiences

Venus in the 12th House (Leo)

Romantic Imagination: Venus in the 12th House suggests a romantic and imaginative nature. You may have an idealistic view of love and may seek a soulful, deep connection in your relationships. You might daydream about romance and have a tendency to idealize your partners.

ntense Emotional Connections: This placement can bring about intense emotional experiences in relationships. You may be drawn to passionate and dramatic connections. However, there is also a possibility of emotional complexities or hidden dynamics in your relationships that may require careful navigation.

7.Saturn

Here are the predictions for Saturn in Virgo ascendant:

Saturn in the 1st House (Virgo):

The native is victorious, serious, and engages in deep intricate planning. They have capable children and receive education. They make progress in their daily occupation but may experience enmity and separation from their children. Some health issues may also arise.

Saturn in the 2nd House (Libra):

The native earns significant wealth and accomplishes grand deeds. There may be some harm to the mother's house and a sense of carelessness with age. Progress is achieved with some difficulties in relation to children, leading to restlessness.

Saturn in the 3rd House (Scorpio):

The native engages in energetic deeds guided by wisdom. There may be bitterness in plans for special expenses. They are victorious over enemies and maintain influence over siblings. They possess a quarrelsome nature but are courageous and influential.

Saturn in the 4th House (Sagittarius):

The native wields immense influence through their properties. They receive honor but may experience deficiency and distress regarding parental happiness. Another lady may provide assistance in the mother's house. There is a lack of peace and happiness.

Saturn in the 5th House (Capricorn):

The native possesses sharp intelligence and faces some hindrances in the progress of their children. They employ various strategies in matters of wealth and occupation. They overcome enemies but may not be satisfied with one spouse. There is distress and toil related to daily occupation and the spouse.

Saturn in the 6th House (Aquarius):

The native defeats enemies and does not engage in quarrels and diseases. There is constant opposition with siblings, restlessness, distress in expenditure, significant troubles related to children, deficiency in education, and a tendency to speak in a crooked manner.

Saturn in the 7th House (Pisces):

The native enjoys sexual pleasures in various ways but experiences distress regarding the spouse and children. They receive support similar to a mother from another lady in matters of happiness and occupation. They gather significant education and engage in criticism of righteousness.

Saturn in the 8th House (Aries):

There is great distress on the side of children, limited education, skillfulness in business occupation, talkativeness, and health issues related to the stomach and anus.

Saturn in the 9th House (Taurus):

The native is highly intelligent and clever, appears influential and industrious, achieves substantial gains, excels in quarrelsome matters and diseases, defeats enemies through intellectual power, shows deep interest in matters of righteousness, has enmity with siblings, and possesses courage and arrogance.

Saturn in the 10th House (Gemini):

The native increases their influence through their abilities, receives honor through intellectual power, gains respect from children but faces some difficulties, possesses great skill in political affairs, achieves progress from the father's house with some challenges, succeeds in business, experiences bitterness in expenditure, and is highly skilled.

Saturn in the 11th House (Cancer):

The native gains significantly through intellectual tactics, constantly feels restless, is intellectual and clever, possesses the art of earning wealth, and maintains influence over enemies.

Saturn in the 12th House (Leo):

The native worries due to tasteless expenditure, experiences loss and distress on the side of children, faces deficiencies in intellect and education, formulates grand schemes for wealth increase, constantly worries, and speaks less.

8. Rahu

Rahu in the 1st House (Virgo):

When Rahu is placed in the first house of a Virgo Ascendant, the individual is likely to be cunning and clever in their speech, using their intelligence to maintain influence over others. They may achieve significant success through the use of occult powers, but may also experience physical ailments as a result. Such individuals are likely to be highly attentive to their spouse and matters related to the occult, and they are often willing to work hard to achieve their goals.

Rahu in the 2nd House (Libra):

With Rahu in the second house, a person may experience financial instability and family troubles. They may manage their affairs temporarily by taking loans, but are at risk of sudden losses in wealth.

Rahu in the 3rd House (Scorpio):

When Rahu is placed in the third house, the individual is likely to be hardworking and courageous. However, they may face difficulties in their relationships with siblings and may exhibit selfish tendencies.

Rahu in the 4th House (Sagittarius):

Rahu's placement in the fourth house can lead to restlessness in one's personal life and losses related to their mother. They may also experience difficulties related to land, buildings, and their place of residence. Despite these challenges, they may possess and enjoy occult powers.

Rahu in the 5th House (Capricorn):

Individuals with Rahu in the fifth house may struggle with education and may be prone to dishonesty. They may indulge in substances such as hemp, tobacco, and other stimulants. They may also be quick to anger and rely on their intuition to accomplish tasks. Additionally, they may face challenges related to their children.

Rahu in the 6th House (Aquarius):

With Rahu in the sixth house, a person is likely to be successful in defeating their enemies and overcoming diseases. They may gain wealth through unethical means and may experience internal weaknesses. Such individuals are often selfish and cunning.

Rahu in the 7th House (Pisces):

When Rahu is placed in the seventh house, the individual may face difficulties in their marriage and family life. They may experience significant challenges and worries in their career, resorting to complex tactics to manage their occupation. They may also use hidden powers to succeed in their work.

Rahu in the 8th House (Aries):

Rahu's placement in the eighth house can lead to a life filled with challenges and unhappiness. The individual may experience health issues related to their stomach and anus, as well as difficulties in matters related to their lifespan.

Rahu in the 9th House (Taurus):

With Rahu in the ninth house, a person may experience weaknesses in their destiny and may initially struggle in matters related to their Dharma. However, they may eventually find stability and develop the ability to discern truth from falsehood.

Rahu in the 10th House (Gemini):

When Rahu is placed in the tenth house, the individual is likely to achieve success and recognition in their career. They may experience worries but can gain influence in government and societal matters through strategic planning and tactics.

Rahu in the 11th House (Cancer):

Rahu's placement in the eleventh house can lead to gains, albeit accompanied by some worries. The individual may experience a lack of material possessions, such as clothing and jewelry, and may feel a sense of deficiency in their physical body.

Rahu in the 12th House (Leo):

With Rahu in the twelfth house, a person is likely to face significant challenges related to their expenditures. They may experience worries and difficulties in managing their finances, but may ultimately achieve stability in this area.

9.Ketu

Here are the predictions for Dragon's Tail (Ketu) in Virgo ascendant:

Ketu in the 1st House (Virgo):

The native is self-conceited and experiences weakness in the body. There is a peculiar kind of weakness in their physique, but they maintain a firm outward appearance. They are clever, respectable, and tend to act rashly.

Ketu in the 2nd House (Libra):

The native is unable to accumulate wealth and faces family distress. There is an internal weakness despite appearing financially stable. They manage to increase their wealth through great efforts.

Ketu in the 3rd House (Scorpio):

The native works hard, experiences losses and separation in relation to siblings, and displays great courage. They are fearless and determined.

Ketu in the 5th House (Sagittarius):

The native possesses buildings and property, experiences some pleasures, but lacks true inner peace. They have a patient disposition.

Ketu in the 6th House (Capricorn):

The native faces many troubles during their educational life. They have harshness in their mind, experience distress in matters related to children, display some pride, and have intellectual worries. They sometimes disregard modesty and exhibit a political nature.

Ketu in the 6th House (Aquarius):

The native possesses great power and energy. They consider themselves fearless and defeat their enemies. They work with pride, overcome diseases, and do not pay much attention to justice or injustice. They are selfish and influential.

Ketu in the 7th House (Pisces):

The native experiences distress in their married life, faces difficulties in managing the family, engages in hard labor for their occupation, exhibits keenness in sexual pleasures but finds them incomplete.

Ketu in the 8th House (Aries):

The native leads a highly restless life, faces significant difficulties, experiences diseases in the lower parts of the stomach or anus, encounters major accidents frequently, and lives with anxiety. They engage in hard labor.

Ketu in the 9th House (Taurus):

The native experiences weakness in matters of destiny. They follow their own path of righteousness (Dharma) and actively work towards the rise of their fortune.

Ketu in the 10th House (Gemini):

The native faces loss and distress in the father's house, encounters worries in government-related matters, and experiences hindrances in the progress of their business.

Ketu in the 11th House (Cancer):

The native achieves significant gains but also endures worries related to income. They establish firmness in matters of gains.

Ketu in the 12th House (Leo):

The native faces great difficulty in matters of expenditure but eventually overcomes it.

9.Libra Ascendant: Planetary Predictions with Reference to Libra Ascendant

The Libra Ascendant, or rising sign, is an important aspect of an individual's astrological chart. It represents the sign that was rising on the eastern horizon at the time of their birth. This essay will explore the predictions of the planets with reference to the Libra Ascendant, focusing on the placement of the Sun in various houses.

1.Sun

Sun in the 1st House (Libra)

When the Sun is in the first house of a Libra Ascendant, the individual is likely to derive their income through physical labor. However, this may also result in some weakness in their income and physical health. They are likely to be steadfast in their daily occupation and enjoy special gains in the areas of their spouse and family life. Additionally, they may experience heightened sexual pleasure and possess a lean and thin body.

Sun in the 2nd House (Scorpio)

With the Sun in the second house, a Libra Ascendant individual is likely to accumulate significant wealth and enjoy a substantial income. They may benefit from their family's wealth and appear to be affluent, earning them respect and admiration from others.

Sun in the 3rd House (Sagittarius)

In this position, the Sun bestows great power, influence, and courage upon the Libra Ascendant individual. They are likely to benefit from their siblings and gain wealth and success from their adherence to their principles and values. They are also likely to be highly energetic.

Sun in the 4th House (Capricorn)

When the Sun is in the fourth house, the Libra Ascendant individual may experience some deficiencies and uneasiness in their plans for financial gain. However, they are likely to benefit from both their father and mother, albeit with some shortcomings. They may also enjoy happiness related to their mother and their home.

Sun in the 5th House (Aquarius)

In this position, the Sun grants the Libra Ascendant individual gains from education and benefits from their children. However, they may also experience some mental fatigue and selfishness due to their pursuit of wealth. They are likely to be intelligent and possess a quick wit.

Sun in the 6th House (Pisces)

With the Sun in the sixth house, the Libra Ascendant individual is likely to achieve victory over their enemies and spend generously. They are likely to be well-mannered, brilliant, and fearless.

Sun in the 7th House (Aries)

In this position, the Sun enables the Libra Ascendant individual to pursue influential occupations and gain from their spouse. They are likely to have a beautiful spouse and enjoy special sexual pleasures. They may also experience significant influence in their spouse's life. However, they may feel physically fatigued due to excessive work or peculiar income sources and may experience some weakness due to excessive sexual indulgence. They are likely to be hardworking.

Sun in the 8th House (Taurus)

When the Sun is in the eighth house, the Libra Ascendant individual may experience worries about their income and gain in foreign countries. They are likely to be cautious about accumulating wealth and may receive hereditary gains. They may lead a laborious life and contribute to the growth of their family.

Sun in the 9th House (Gemini)

In this position, the Sun bestows great fortune upon the Libra Ascendant individual, resulting in substantial gains due to the power of destiny. They are likely to be brilliant, influential, and carefree.

Sun in the 10th House (Cancer)

With the Sun in the tenth house, the Libra Ascendant individual is likely to earn income with respect and engage in large-scale business ventures. They may enjoy significant gains in their father's house and benefit from government-related matters. They may be less enthusiastic about gains related to land and buildings and employ foresight in their business and occupational pursuits.

Sun in the 11th House (Leo)

In this position, the Sun grants the Libra Ascendant individual substantial gains and a consistent income. However, they may experience some deficiencies in their children's lives. They are likely to be well-educated, acquire enmity, and use harshness and irritation in their conversations.

Sun in the 12th House (Virgo)

When the Sun is in the twelfth house, the Libra Ascendant individual is likely to spend excessively, often depleting their entire profit. They may entertain thoughts of renunciation and gain from their enemies.

2.Moon

Here are the predictions for Moon in Libra ascendant:

Moon in the 1st House (Libra):

The native is dignified, majestic, and respected. They make progress in the father's house, enjoy high-class sexual pleasures, experience the happiness of a spouse, work in a majestic manner in their occupation, and receive honor from the government and society.

Moon in the 2nd House (Scorpio):

There is weakness in matters of wealth, potential loss of fortune through business, an increase in longevity, and a tendency to work secretly to acquire wealth.

Moon in the 3rd House (Sagittarius):

The native has a close bond with their brothers and sisters, is fortunate and successful, upholds righteousness (Dharma), possesses strong faith in God, and is clever and industrious.

Moon in the 5th House (Capricorn):

The native owns their own property, receives honor and respect, experiences happiness from parents, enjoys the pleasure of a successful business, possesses noble and intellectual ideas, and is esteemed by the government and society.

Moon in the 6th House (Aquarius):

The native is educated, thinks of ambitious plans for progress, has children who become a source of progress for them, and holds managerial responsibilities.

Moon in the 6th House (Pisces):

There may be some deficiencies in the father's house, but the native excels in business. They have more expenditures than income, but they maintain dignity in the face of worries and enemies. They have connections with foreign places.

Moon in the 7th House (Aries):

The native has a beautiful spouse and enjoys sexual pleasures. They experience progress and honor after marriage. They are clever, skilled workers who find success in their occupation. They may have preoccupations with sexual matters but engage in good business.

Moon in the 8th House (Taurus):

There is weakness in the father's house and in matters of wealth. The native receives honor from foreign countries but may experience a painful death. They are praised after their demise.

Moon in the 9th House (Gemini):

The native is very fortunate, upholds religious and moral values, experiences progress in matters related to government and society, has supportive siblings, gains fame, and holds strong beliefs in God.

Moon in the 10th House (Cancer):

The native is respected in the government, receives support from their father, engages in significant business ventures, derives pleasure from their respect and honor, has a strong sense of self-pride, finds happiness in the mother's house, owns property, and is highly industrious.

Moon in the 11th House (Leo):

The native acquires decent and influential gains, benefits from their father, possesses wisdom and education, finds pleasure in their children, excels in their work, gains respect from the government, conducts significant business ventures, and receives benefits from society.

Moon in the 12th House (Virgo):

There are losses in business occupations, setbacks in matters related to the government, weakness in matters of honor and respect, creates an impact in dealings with enemies, and may experience mental deficiencies.

3.Mars

Predictions of Mars in Libra Ascendant: An Exploration of the Effects of Mars in Different Houses

Mars in the 1st House (Libra)

When Mars is in the first house of Libra, the individual is likely to be very wealthy and respected in society. They may have a lean physique but will be engaged in valuable occupations. They are likely to have a beautiful and capable spouse, enjoying ideal pleasures and great happiness in their life. They will also benefit from household profits, buildings, and other properties.

Mars in the 2nd House (Scorpio)

In the second house, Mars brings an increase in wealth through business and occupation. The individual will possess great power, but there may be a deficiency in happiness from their spouse. They will experience an excess of sexual pleasures and some happiness from their children.

Mars in the 3rd House (Sagittarius)

Mars in the third house indicates influential labor, progress, and influence in connection with one's occupation. The individual will have an influential and beautiful spouse, but there may be some restrictions in their relationship with their spouse and siblings. There may be some dissatisfaction in their relationship with their father, and they may experience some weakness in terms of sexual pleasures, occupation, wealth, and power. They may also face some challenges in dealing with the government and society and may have some difficulties with their enemies.

Mars in the 4th House (Capricorn)

When Mars is in the fourth house, the individual will experience happiness and significant wealth due to their daily occupation. They will acquire land and property and enjoy the happiness of their spouse. Their wealth will increase after marriage, and their spouse may have a dominant role in their household. They will also experience happiness from their mother, but there may be some weakness in their relationship with the government. Their rise in position may be somewhat weak, but they will enjoy sexual pleasures and happiness in their family.

Mars in the 5th House (Aquarius)

In the fifth house, Mars brings wealth, education, and intelligence. However, there may be some opposition from their children. The individual will have an intelligent spouse but may be somewhat selfish.

Mars in the 6th House (Pisces)

Mars in the sixth house indicates weakness in wealth and occupation, and the individual may experience some distress from their spouse and family. They may spend a lot, but they will have influence over their enemies. There may be a deficiency in their sexual pleasures.

Mars in the 7th House (Aries)

In the seventh house, Mars brings significant wealth and respect. The individual will have a strong-willed spouse, but there may be some deficiency in their relationship with their father and the government. They may also experience weakness in their occupation.

Mars in the 8th House (Taurus)

Mars in the eighth house may cause the loss of current wealth and confusion in occupation. The individual may experience distress in their relationship with their spouse and family and may face some restrictions in their relationship with their siblings.

Mars in the 9th House (Gemini)

In the ninth house, Mars brings wealth due to the individual's and their spouse's luck. They will progress through their daily occupation, spend a lot, and enjoy great happiness from land and property. They will be fortunate and respected in society.

Mars in the 10th House (Cancer)

Mars in the tenth house indicates weakness in wealth and occupation, and the individual may face challenges in dealing with the government and society. They may experience insults in their relationship with their spouse and father due to a lack of wealth. They may also face difficulties and troubles in their relationship with their father and spouse, who may have a low standard of occupation. There may be a deficiency in their sexual pleasures, but they will be respected in the government and receive help from their father. They will be involved in significant business ventures, enjoy great pleasure due to their respect and honor, and be filled with self-pride. They will also experience happiness in their relationship with their mother and be very hardworking.

Mars in the 11th House (Leo)

In the eleventh house, Mars brings significant influential gains, gains from their father, wisdom, and education. The individual will enjoy the pleasure of having children, be a good worker, and be respected in the government. They will be involved in significant business ventures, gain from society, and acquire substantial income due to their occupation. They will also enjoy the happiness of their spouse.

Mars in the 12th House (Leo)

Mars in the 12th house indicates a complex and dynamic energy that manifests in the realm of spirituality, subconsciousness, and hidden aspects of life. People with Mars in the 12th house of Virgo are likely to have a strong drive to explore the depths of their psyche and seek spiritual enlightenment.

4.Mercury

Here are the predictions for Mercury in Libra ascendant:

Mercury in the 1st House (Libra):

The native is fortunate and enjoys physical well-being. They have a slim and lean body, experience domestic happiness through their spouse, achieve success in their occupation, possess cleverness and wisdom, uphold justice, have influence, and display a gentle nature.

Mercury in the 2nd House (Scorpio):

The native is wealthy and respectable, finds pleasure in life through their financial power and destiny, and makes progress with some weakness in the family domain.

Mercury in the 3rd House (Sagittarius):

Considered very fortunate, the native is courageous, possesses a gentle physique, renews contact with siblings after a period of weakness, and is respected and reserved.

Mercury in the 4th House (Capricorn):

The native enjoys pleasures, spends comfortably, experiences some deficiencies in the mother's house, finds pleasure in their mother and homeland, and practically upholds righteousness (Dharma).

Mercury in the 5th House (Aquarius):

The native possesses deep and extensive knowledge of Dharma, attains progress through intellect and speech, experiences happiness with some deficiencies in matters related to children, manages their expenditures wisely, and excels in political matters.

Mercury in the 6th House (Pisces):

There is significant weakness and dishonor in their destiny, as well as losses in their fortune. The native experiences restlessness in dealings with enemies and worries related to expenditure. They may employ secret tactics.

Mercury in the 7th House (Aries):

The native is very fortunate and enjoys family pleasures. They experience progress in their occupation after marriage, gain control over their expenditures, derive good and decent pleasures with some deficiencies in matters related to their spouse, and possess favorable means of sexual pleasures. They achieve decent progress in their occupation with some success.

Mercury in the 8th House (Taurus):

The native experiences distress in their destiny, weakness, and restlessness in matters of expenditure. They display some firmness in their older age and have a peaceful death.

Mercury in the 9th House (Gemini):

The native is highly fortunate, gains fame, progresses according to their destiny, possesses financial power, displays courage, and has supportive siblings.

Mercury in the 10th House (Cancer):

The native exudes valor and grandeur, conducts splendid business ventures, receives honor through their good deeds, spends majestically, and is respected and prestigious.

Mercury in the 11th House (Leo):

The native achieves significant success through the power of their destiny, increases their income through wisdom, acquires education and knowledge, possesses great wisdom and foresight, achieves success with some weaknesses in matters related to children, and is fortunate and clever.

Mercury in the 12th House (Virgo):

There is high expenditure, losses in matters related to destiny, significant spending on pilgrimages due to religious inclinations, and the use of wise tactics in dealing with enemies.

5. Jupiter

Predictions of Jupiter in Libra Ascendant: An In-Depth Analysis

Jupiter in the 1st House (Libra)

When Jupiter is positioned in the first house of Libra, it indicates that the individual will be involved in influential deeds and will possess great courage. They are likely to engage in hard physical labor and exhibit wisdom in their actions. These individuals are known to follow shrewd policies and tactfully handle their occupations. They are also careful about their religious behavior, which may lead to some enmity in the house of children. However, they can expect dignity and support from their spouse.

Jupiter in the 2nd House (Scorpio)

Individuals with Jupiter in the second house of Scorpio are likely to amass significant wealth and earn respect from others. They will have a strong influence in the house of enemies and may experience progress in their relationship with their father. These individuals are also known for their wisdom and intelligence.

Jupiter in the 3rd House (Sagittarius)

When Jupiter is positioned in the third house of Sagittarius, it indicates that the individual will engage in influential and energetic deeds. They are likely to experience gains in their occupation and be considered fortunate by others. These individuals will also have power and authority in the house of siblings, which can lead to strong bonds and support from their brothers and sisters.

Jupiter in the 4th House (Capricorn)

Individuals with Jupiter in the fourth house of Capricorn may experience loss in the house of their mother and may not find peace even in their own home. They may also experience restlessness in their relationship with their siblings and may have a tendency to overspend. However, they are capable of defeating their opposition and overcoming challenges.

Jupiter in the 5th House (Aquarius)

When Jupiter is positioned in the fifth house of Aquarius, it indicates that the individual will derive strength from their intellect and children. However, they may face some difficulties in attaining happiness from their children and may struggle with acquiring education. These individuals are courageous, have brave children, and are known for their cleverness, wisdom, and skill.

Jupiter in the 6th House (Pisces)

Individuals with Jupiter in the sixth house of Pisces are known for their bravery and hard work. They can achieve success and defeat their opponents through their determination and efforts. However, they may also be prone to overspending and may feel restricted in their work, leading to carelessness.

Jupiter in the 7th House (Aries)

When Jupiter is positioned in the seventh house of Aries, it indicates that the individual will be successful in their daily occupation and may excel in the industrial sector. They will enjoy great power through their spouse and receive the best cooperation from their siblings.

These individuals can defeat their enemies and achieve victory through their strong willpower.

Jupiter in the 8th House (Taurus)

Individuals with Jupiter in the eighth house of Taurus may experience weakness and may work with secret policies. They may also overspend and feel a sense of weakness in the house of their mother, land, and happiness.

Jupiter in the 9th House (Gemini)

When Jupiter is positioned in the ninth house of Gemini, it indicates that the individual will derive power from the house of destiny and receive cooperation from their siblings, albeit with some obstacles. They will not be bothered by quarrels and enemies and will acknowledge the power of justice. These individuals will also have children and enjoy the support of their family.

Jupiter in the 10th House (Cancer)

Individuals with Jupiter in the tenth house of Cancer are likely to be influential and may experience separation in the house of their mother while progressing in the house of their father. They may not engage in much business but will be brave, powerful, and have siblings. These individuals are also experts in intricate policies and strategies.

Jupiter in the 11th House (Leo)

When Jupiter is positioned in the eleventh house of Leo, it indicates that the individual will be energetic and amass significant wealth. They will achieve success in their occupation and be considered a successful and industrious worker. These individuals will be influential, enjoy the support of their siblings, and have a strong bond with their spouse. However, they may experience some deficiencies in the area of children.

Jupiter in the 12th House (Virgo)

Individuals with Jupiter in the twelfth house of Virgo may experience weakness in their strength and energy. They may have enmity with their siblings

6.Venus

Here are the predictions for Venus in Libra ascendant:

Venus in the 1st House (Libra):

The native faces some non-cooperation in their progress but enjoys a long life. They are highly respectable, gain fame, experience some weakness in the body, possess good self-awareness, have foresight, display diplomatic skills, and hold influence.

Venus in the 2nd House (Scorpio):

The native benefits from wealth and enjoys a long life. They use their strength to increase their wealth but may also experience occasional losses in matters of wealth. They experience a mix of pleasures and struggles in their family life and may be dependent on others.

Venus in the 3rd House (Sagittarius):

The native is very energetic, works hard, experiences some deficiencies in the relationship with siblings, and is highly clever.

Venus in the 4th House (Capricorn):

The native lives comfortably and happily in their own place, enjoys a long life, possesses self-knowledge and deep understanding, experiences some troublesome happiness in matters related to children, and faces difficult problems. They may engage in political activities.

Venus in the 5th House (Aquarius):

The native possesses the power of self-knowledge, deep knowledge, and foresight. They experience some troubling happiness in matters related to children, have a long life, engage in political activities, and face challenging problems. They may also exhibit some self-centeredness and seek sexual favors.

Venus in the 6th House (Pisces):

The native excels in solving the most difficult problems in their life but may display carelessness. There are some deficiencies in matters of expenditure.

Venus in the 7th House (Aries):

The native effectively manages their daily occupation through special powers. They have a good appearance and handsome features, possess self-awareness, diplomatic skills, and cleverness in accomplishing their tasks. They may experience distress in the family connected with their spouse and have a self-centered approach, seeking sexual favors.

Venus in the 8th House (Taurus):

The native enjoys a long life but experiences some deficiencies in the body. They make whole-hearted efforts to acquire wealth and desire a harmonious family life.

Venus in the 9th House (Gemini):

The native leads a fortunate life without anxieties. They possess a fatalistic and industrious nature but may face some deficiencies in the affection received from siblings. They are highly respectable and clever.

Venus in the 10th House (Cancer):

The native lives a royal life, acquires authority, greatly enjoys comfort and pleasures, faces difficulties in the progress of honor, and achieves progress in business with some challenges. They can be obstinate.

Venus in the 11th House (Leo):

The native gains various kinds of wealth in their life but may experience some laziness in matters of personal gains. They are highly clever, have children, and receive good education.

Venus in the 12th House (Virgo):

The native experiences significant weakness in their body, faces distress and deficiencies in expenditure, and endures sufferings in their daily routine of life.

7. Saturn

Here are the predictions for Saturn in Libra ascendant:

Saturn in the 1st House (Libra):

The native has a very handsome physique and enjoys pleasures. They receive a good education, possess wisdom and influence, are diligent, and pay attention to a big business. They may face troubles with their spouse in domestic affairs due to their speech and intellect.

There may be some deficiencies in the area of sexual pleasures and the relationship with the spouse. They derive much pleasure and happiness from their property and have a sense of self-pride.

Saturn in the 2nd House (Scorpio):

The native gains power and property, places great importance on accumulated cash deposits, experiences happiness due to their intellect, people, and wealth. They improve the situation in their mother's house but may also encounter problems and restrictions related to their mother and children.

Saturn in the 3rd House (Sagittarius):

The native is highly energetic and possesses great intellectual power. They are talkative but not gentle in their speech. They have active and lively children, spend much of their efforts, and face opposition in matters related to their mother.

Saturn in the 4th House (Capricorn):

The native is very happy and pays great attention to seek happiness. They have significant influence in dealing with enemies and gain power over their homeland and property. There is completeness in matters related to children, and they lead a carefree life.

Saturn in the 5th House (Aquarius):

The native receives education and is highly intelligent. They experience spontaneous happiness from their children but feel a deficiency in their relationship with their spouse. Their speech may cause suffering, and they make efforts to increase their wealth. There are some deficiencies in matters of wealth, occupation, and gains. They experience happiness from their mother.

Saturn in the 6th House (Pisces):

The native faces unhappiness in matters related to their mother and children. They experience deficiencies in acquiring happiness and education but find happiness in their age and daily routine. Their speech may be somewhat bitter, and they may have some enmity with their siblings.

Saturn in the 8th House (Aries):

The native feels distress in their relationship with their spouse, experiences a loss in their father's house, faces a loss of domestic peace, but gains happiness from education after overcoming some difficulties in acquiring it. They may experience distress in their daily occupation.

Saturn in the 8th House (Taurus):

The native is a diplomat and thinks about remote things. There are deficiencies in matters of education and children. There may be separation in the relationship with the mother and deficiencies in matters of wealth. They possess some mysterious knowledge.

Saturn in the 9th House (Gemini):

The native is very wise and experiences happiness from destiny. They receive a firm education, have happiness from their children, and are fortunate, happy, and just.

Saturn in the 10th House (Cancer):

The native faces enmity in their relationship with their father but gains happiness from their mother. They gain power in matters related to children but experience deficiencies and mistakes in their relationship with their spouse. They may hurt their spouse with their speech and face some weakness in their occupation. They possess buildings and find happiness in them.

Saturn in the 11th House (Leo):

The native gains heavy gains and happiness and experiences some happiness from their children. They may be worried about their income.

Saturn in the 12th House (Virgo):

The native spends much to seek happiness and derives happiness only through expenditure. They experience deficiencies in their mother country, weakness in intellect and education, face losses in matters related to children, and find little happiness. They face great enmity in connection with their family and

8.Rahu

Here are the predictions for Rahu (Dragon's Head) in Libra ascendant:

Rahu in the 1st House (Libra):

The native accomplishes tasks with great tactics and cleverness. They are cautious and experience physical and mental worries. They may gain some fame but also bear special blows on their body, which makes them nervous.

Rahu in the 2nd House (Scorpio):

There is unhappiness in the area of accumulating wealth and distress in connection with family. They may face severe blows on their wealth and encounter challenges with people.

Rahu in the 3rd House (Sagittarius):

There may be losses in the relationship with siblings. The native may use occult powers but can be somewhat inactive and lazy. They may experience some weakness in their physique.

Rahu in the 4th House (Capricorn):

There are some deficiencies in the means of happiness and weakness in the house of mother. The native may feel restlessness in their residential place and face obstacles related to buildings and properties.

Rahu in the 5th House (Aquarius):

Difficulties arise in acquiring education and there may be troubles in matters related to children.

Rahu in the 6th House (Pisces):

The native achieves victory over difficulties like diseases and defeats enemies. They are careful, alert, and selfish in their pursuits.

Rahu in the 7th House (Aries):

There may be distress in the relationship with the spouse and worries in daily occupation. The native may experience some disorders in their organs.

Rahu in the 8th House (Taurus):

There is distress in life and improper management of daily routine. The native may experience disorders of the stomach, constipation, or issues in the lower part of the stomach. There may also be a loss of hereditary wealth and fatal blows in matters of longevity.

Rahu in the 9th House (Gemini):

The native makes efforts to increase their fortune and speaks extensively about Dharma (righteousness). However, they may experience weakness in matters of destiny.

Rahu in the 10th House (Cancer):

There may be some loss in the relationship with the father and distress in matters related to government, society, and business.

Rahu in the 11th House (Leo):

The native gains a lot, but there may also be some weaknesses or deficiencies in their gains.

Rahu in the 12th House (Virgo):

The native spends a lot and experiences incompleteness in matters of expenditure. They may bear deficiencies in their expenditure-related matters.

9. Ketu

Here are the predictions for Ketu (Dragon's Tail) in Libra ascendant:

Ketu in the 1st House (Libra):

The native may experience some weakness in the body and a sense of incompleteness. They live with pride and bravery, work hard in difficult circumstances, and tend to stay in one place and pursue their work persistently. They can be obstinate in their approach.

Ketu in the 2nd House (Scorpio):

There may be some loss in the house of wealth and family. The native may face sudden losses and work hard to accumulate wealth.

Ketu in the 3rd House (Sagittarius):

The native works very hard and holds some special but incomplete importance in the relationship with siblings. They are influential, hardworking, diligent, cunning, and may exhibit a somewhat violent nature.

Ketu in the 4th House (Capricorn):

There may be a loss of happiness and a restless nature in the house of mother. The native is somewhat clever in their approach.

Ketu in the 5th House (Aquarius):

The native faces significant challenges in acquiring education and experiences distress in matters related to children. They may have some anxieties regarding wisdom and knowledge.

Ketu in the 6th House (Pisces):

The native holds a significant influence over enemies, gains less in the relationship with their grandfather, possesses patience and courage, and makes efforts to overcome diseases. They have a fearless nature.

Ketu in the 7th House (Aries):

There may be loss and distress in the relationship with the spouse. The native experiences anxieties in the family and faces loss and worries in their daily occupation. They encounter hindrances and find both happiness and obstacles in their work.

Ketu in the 8th House (Taurus):

The native may experience restlessness in life and a sense of incompleteness in their daily routine. There may be weakness in hereditary wealth and some stomach disorders.

Ketu in the 9th House (Gemini):

The native experiences happiness based on their destiny but may face defamation. They may have a weakened sense of righteousness (Dharma) and hold less faith in God.

Ketu in the 10th House (Cancer):

There may be a loss in the relationship with the father and financial losses in business and occupation. The native may experience mental anxieties and opposition to the government.

Ketu in the 11th House (Leo):

The native strives for significant strength in their income and achieves substantial gains. However, there may be hindrances in matters related to income.

Ketu in the 12th House (Virgo):

The native spends in a determined manner and works boldly, despite having some weaknesses in expenditure-related matters.

10. Scorpio Ascendant Predictions: Planetary Influences on Scorpio Rising

The Scorpio Ascendant, or rising sign, is known for its intensity, passion, and determination. In this essay, we will explore the various predictions of the planets in relation to the Scorpio Ascendant, focusing on the influence of the Sun in each of the twelve houses.

1. Sun

Sun in the 1st House (Scorpio):

for Scorpio Ascendant

When the Sun is in the first house for Scorpio Ascendant individuals, they are likely to possess a regal and commanding presence. They are highly influential and take great pride in their accomplishments. These individuals are able to assert their authority and get things done with ease. However, they may experience some difficulties in their marital life and may struggle to find a balance between their personal and professional lives. Despite these challenges, they are likely to be successful in business and enjoy a luxurious lifestyle, adorned with beautiful clothing and jewelry.

Sun in the 2nd House (Sagittarius):

for Scorpio Ascendant

With the Sun in the second house, Scorpio Ascendant individuals are likely to accumulate significant wealth through their business ventures and professional endeavors. They may also receive financial support from the government and their community, which further contributes to their prosperity. These individuals are highly respected within their family and may inherit valuable assets from their ancestors. Their hardworking and honorable nature ensures their continued success and financial stability.

Sun in the 3rd House (Capricorn) :

for Scorpio Ascendant

Scorpio Ascendant individuals with the Sun in the third house are incredibly energetic and hardworking. They may experience some rivalry with their siblings or close relatives but are able to overcome these challenges through their perseverance and determination. These individuals are highly respected and considered fortunate by others. They may not always achieve complete success in their endeavors, but their efforts are recognized and appreciated by those around them.

Sun in the 4th House (Aquarius):

for Scorpio Ascendant

When the Sun is in the fourth house, Scorpio Ascendant individuals may experience some obstacles in their professional and personal lives. They may struggle to find complete happiness and satisfaction in their work, and may also face challenges related to property and land ownership. Despite these difficulties, they remain loyal and respectable individuals who are committed to their responsibilities.

Sun in the 5th House (Pisces):

for Scorpio Ascendant

Scorpio Ascendant individuals with the Sun in the fifth house are highly intelligent and possess a deep understanding of business matters. They are able to apply their education and knowledge in practical and strategic ways, which contributes to their success in their professional endeavors. These individuals are likely to have children and enjoy significant gains from their business ventures. They are constantly focused on their personal growth and are not afraid to prioritize their own interests.

Sun in the 6th House (Aries):

for Scorpio Ascendant

With the Sun in the sixth house, Scorpio Ascendant individuals are able to triumph over their adversaries and overcome any obstacles that stand in their way. They may experience some financial difficulties but are able to maintain their composure and remain focused on their goals. These individuals are skilled strategists who are able to build a strong reputation for themselves through their clever tactics and determination.

Sun in the 7th House (Taurus):

for Scorpio Ascendant

Scorpio Ascendant individuals with the Sun in the seventh house may experience some challenges in their professional and personal lives. They may struggle to find complete satisfaction in their work, but are still able to achieve a certain level of success and recognition. In their marital life, they may encounter some conflicts and may have a temperamental spouse. Despite these challenges, they remain intelligent and resourceful individuals who are able to navigate through difficult situations.

Sun in the 8th House (Gemini):

for Scorpio Ascendant

When the Sun is in the eighth house, Scorpio Ascendant individuals may experience a loss in their relationship with their father and may struggle to maintain their self-esteem and sense of self-worth. They may need to travel to foreign countries and face various challenges in order to achieve success and accumulate wealth. Despite these difficulties, they are able to make progress in their personal and professional lives and enjoy a long and fulfilling life.

Sun in the 9th House (Cancer):

for Scorpio Ascendant

Scorpio Ascendant individuals with the Sun in the ninth house are considered to be very fortunate and are deeply committed to their spiritual and religious beliefs. They find great joy in exploring the mysteries of the universe and are able to achieve success in their professional endeavors. They are highly influential individuals who are respected and admired by others.

Sun in the 10th House (Leo):

for Scorpio Ascendant

With the Sun in the 10th House (Leo) for Scorpio Ascendant, you have a strong desire for recognition and success in your career. You possess natural leadership abilities and a need to be in the spotlight. Your ambition and drive propel you towards positions of authority and power. Creative fields, entrepreneurship, or professions that allow you to showcase your talents may be favorable. Remember to balance your intense determination with diplomacy and collaboration for long-term success.

Sun in the 11th House (Virgo):

for Scorpio Ascendant

With the Sun in the 11th House for Scorpio Ascendant, you have a strong desire to make a significant impact within your social circle and community. Your natural charisma and leadership skills attract influential and like-minded individuals, allowing you to form valuable networks and friendships. You thrive in group settings and may excel in team-oriented projects. Your innovative ideas and ability to inspire others can lead to success in areas such as social activism, entrepreneurship, or organizational leadership. Embrace collaboration and harness the power of your network to achieve your goals.

Sun in the 12th House(Venus):

for Scorpio Ascendant

With the Sun in the 12th House for Scorpio Ascendant, you may experience a strong urge for solitude and introspection. Your individuality and self-expression may be hidden or expressed in a more private or behind-the-scenes manner. Spiritual and metaphysical pursuits can be significant in your life, and you may find fulfillment in serving others or engaging in humanitarian activities. Developing a strong inner connection and exploring your subconscious can lead to personal growth and self-discovery.

2.Moon

Moon in the 1st House (Scorpio):

Individuals with Moon in the 1st house in Scorpio may experience mental anxieties and a sense of weakness in their destiny. They work hard in their occupation and take full care of their family. There is a strong mental fascination with their spouse and sexual pleasures. They make progress in their career through the combination of mental power and destiny. However, they may have some incompleteness in practicing righteousness (Dharma).

Moon in the 2nd House (Sagittarius):

This placement indicates good fortune and wealth. These individuals are likely to acquire significant wealth through the power of destiny. They enjoy the pleasures of family life and find success in worldly affairs. Their financial situation improves over time.

Moon in the 3rd House (Capricorn):

Individuals with Moon in the 3rd house in Capricorn are enthusiastic, fortunate, and religious. They have a deep devotion to God and experience unexpected joy through their siblings. They always work with lofty ideas for progress and growth.

Moon in the 4th House (Aquarius):

Having the Moon in the 4th House in Aquarius indicates a unique and unconventional approach to emotions, home, and family life. You possess a strong need for independence and freedom within your domestic sphere. You may have an unconventional or non-traditional family setup or choose to create a chosen family that aligns with your ideals. Your emotional well-being is closely tied to your sense of individuality and the ability to express your authentic self within the home environment. You may also have a deep sense of humanitarianism and may be involved in social causes related to home, family, or community. Your emotional nature may be intellectually oriented, and you seek intellectual stimulation and freedom of thought within your home.

Moon in the 5th House (Pisces):

This placement signifies great fortune and happiness. These individuals excel in their education and intelligence. They are farsighted and enjoy the blessings of children. They have a pleasant and virtuous way of speaking. They also fulfill their religious duties and find happiness in their mother's love and their property.

Moon in the 6th House (Aries):

These individuals may have less faith in Dharma (righteousness) and God. They may face some weaknesses in their destiny and experience increased expenditure. They may encounter opposition from enemies.

Moon in the 7th House (Taurus):

With Moon in the 7th house in Taurus, individuals experience happiness and benefits through their spouse. They also enjoy substantial gains in their occupation or business.

Moon in the 8th House (Gemini):

Individuals with Moon in the 8th house may face mental distress and various troubles. They may have anxieties about increasing their wealth and can be indifferent to justice or injustice when it comes to acquiring wealth. However, they tend to have a good lifespan.

Moon in the 10th House (Cancer):

This placement indicates good fortune and fame. These individuals uphold righteousness (Dharma) in a respectable manner. They receive cooperation from their siblings and have a cheerful disposition.

Moon in the 11th House (Virgo):

Individuals with Moon in the 11th house experience splendid gains due to the power of destiny. They enjoy a carefree attitude towards income and manage their finances well. They make good use of educational opportunities and find happiness through their children. They are fortunate and kind-hearted.

Moon in the 12th House (Libra):

With Moon in the 12th house, individuals may face some weakness in their destiny. However, they receive support from destiny in managing their expenses. They may also find some reconciliation with their enemies and in their maternal grandfather's family.

3.Mars

1st House (Scorpio):

Mars is influential and has a short body. This person may have a fiery and proud personality, and could be prone to health issues related to excess heat. They may face difficulties with buildings and have some restlessness in their home life. They may also experience some occupational challenges, but they are very courageous.

2nd House (Sagittarius):

This person is likely to be rich due to their physical appearance. They work hard to accumulate wealth and may have some conflicts with their children. They may not always follow a moral code.

3rd House (Capricorn):

With Mars in this house, the individual is influential and gains respect by performing great deeds. They have strength in their maternal grandfather's house, and they are successful in overcoming obstacles and defeating enemies. They may experience some challenges in their relationship with their father and siblings, but they are full of self-respect.

4th House (Aquarius):

This placement can bring some loss in the area of motherhood and happiness, but the person is able to acquire gains and honors through their occupation. They may also possess some land.

5th House (Pisces):

Those with Mars in this house tend to be wise and clever, but with a hot temper. They work hard to generate income, but may spend too much. They may experience opposition and worries regarding their children, as well as some physical ailments.

6th House (Aries):

This individual is very brave and has a strong body. They do not fear enemies and gain respect through their willpower. They may face some challenges in the area of morality and experience fatigue in their body.

7th House (Taurus):

With Mars in this house, there may be some conflicts and enmity, but also power and benefits in the area of marriage. The person works diligently in their profession and enjoys sexual pleasure. They may face some troubles and diseases related to their body and organs, but they take special care of their wealth and honor. They may also have some power and influence in the government and society.

8th House (Gemini):

Those with Mars in this house may experience health issues related to the heart, and may live in a foreign place with troubles and struggles. They acquire wealth through hard work and have a strong bond with their siblings. They are not easily insulted.

9th House (Cancer):

This placement can bring a feeling of weakness in destiny and may weaken the person's body and moral code. They may experience worry due to labor and spend too much. They may also have some challenges with their mother, but work hard to acquire land and happiness.

10th House (Leo):

Mars in this house brings great power, physical pleasure, and cleverness. This person secures progress in their father's house and gains honor in government and society. They may face opposition from their mother but have a strong bond with their children. They are also wise, learned, and influential.

11th House (Virgo):

This placement brings a heavy income through physical labor, and the person is influential and performs decent deeds. They may have some troubles related to their children, but are victorious over enemies. They may experience some weakness in their body, but are furious and cautious.

12th House (Libra):

With Mars in this house, the person may experience troubles related to their physique and finances. They may spend money on quarrels and diseases and live in foreign places. They have a strong bond with their siblings and maintain their influence even in a weakened state. They may face unhappiness with their

4. Mercury

Predictions for Mercury in Scorpio Ascendant:

Mercury in the 1st House (Scorpio):

Individual gains and income are indicated. The person tends to have a gentle behavior and a gentle nature. They enjoy a long life and experience occupational success. They take full care of their family and provide for them through their income.

Mercury in the 2nd House (Sagittarius):

This placement suggests success in accumulating wealth, but there may also be some losses. The person may face challenges in accumulating wealth due to their high standard of living. Nevertheless, they enjoy a long life, respect, and prosperity. They have the potential to acquire significant gains.

Mercury in the 3rd House (Capricorn):

Individuals with this placement perform energetic deeds in a gentle manner. They experience a long life and have intimate connections with their brothers and sisters, albeit with some hardships. They may exhibit selfish tactics regarding their moral or spiritual beliefs.

Mercury in the 4th House (Aquarius):

The person acquires income with happiness, despite encountering some obstacles. They enjoy a long life and derive happiness from mysterious or unconventional devices.

Mercury in the 5th House (Pisces):

There may be some weakness in intellect and education with this placement. The person might possess limited education and experience losses or challenges concerning their children. They may feel weak as they age and encounter various sufferings in life. They tend to speak bitterly and maintain secrecy.

Mercury in the 6th House (Aries):

Individuals with this placement often face worries and dependency in acquiring income. They may earn a little through troublesome deeds and struggle to make good use of their daily routine or life. Anxieties and the use of secret schemes may be prevalent.

Mercury in the 7th House (Taurus):

This placement suggests hidden distress alongside happiness in the house of the spouse. After marriage, there is an increase in indirect advantages related to sexual pleasures. Gains in occupation are indicated, but hard work is required.

Mercury in the 8th House (Gemini):

Individuals with this placement enjoy a long life and experience glory and grandeur in their daily routine. They tend to be careless and exhibit both strictness and tenderness in their daily life.

Mercury in the 9th House (Cancer):

Income is indicated through the power of destiny, and hereditary gains are possible. However, there may be a tendency to leave tasks incomplete. The person finds pleasure in their daily routine, enjoys a long life, but may experience some deficiency in fame.

Mercury in the 10th House (Leo):

This placement suggests gaining respect, honor, and hereditary gains. However, there may be distress in the relationship with the father. The person enjoys a long life and engages in influential deeds but may face obstacles in terms of respect, honor, and position.

Mercury in the 11th House (Virgo):

Individuals with this placement enjoy a long life but may experience weakness in intellect and education. There may be distress related to their children, and they may struggle with communication and exhibit rude conversation.

Mercury in the 12th House (Libra):

People with this placement tend to spend excessively and have connections to other places. They may gain prosperity during the later period of life, but there can be weaknesses in the gains. Nervousness, struggles, and diseases may also be present in the house of longevity.

5. Jupiter

Jupiter in the Scorpio Ascendant:

Jupiter in the 1st House:

You possess wisdom, knowledge, and diplomatic skills. You have the potential to accumulate wealth and enjoy a prosperous family life. Your faith in God and love for justice guide your actions.

Jupiter in the 2nd House:

Your intellect and education are instrumental in accumulating wealth. You may receive advantages from the government and society. Children may play a significant role in your life.

Jupiter in the 3rd House:

While you may face challenges with your siblings and education, you maintain a strong religious faith. Your occupation brings substantial gains, and you enjoy the cooperation of your spouse. However, take care of your heart health.

Jupiter in the 4th House:

You are intelligent, respected, and financially stable. Your life is filled with richness and longevity. You may face some difficulties in finding happiness and accumulating wealth, but your mother and father provide support.

Jupiter in the 5th House:

You are highly learned and possess authority in religious and spiritual matters. Children bring joy and prosperity into your life. Your wisdom and knowledge lead to substantial gains, and you are fortunate overall.

Jupiter in the 6th House:

Wealth may come to you with some effort and dependence. You cleverly handle enemies and work diligently to accumulate wealth. However, you may face challenges in matters of education and children.

Jupiter in the 7th House:

Your daily occupation brings wealth, and you engage in respectable work. There may be some weakness in your relationship with siblings, but after marriage, you experience increased wealth and influence. You are cautious in your endeavors.

Jupiter in the 8th House:

You may have limited education and wealth. Challenges with children and restlessness in your heart are present. Hard work is required to earn more wealth, especially through foreign connections. There may be some discontentment regarding happiness, buildings, and your mother. However, you have a long life and a sense of living like a rich person.

Jupiter in the 9th House:

You are fortunate, intelligent, and engage in religious activities. Your children bring honor and joy. Astrological knowledge and a farsighted approach contribute to your wealth. However, you may experience some deficiencies in your relationships with siblings. You possess spiritual wisdom.

Jupiter in the 10th House:

You are highly respectable and earn substantial wealth. Your intellect and business endeavors bring financial strength from the government and society, as well as from your father's house. You pursue a significant occupation and display enthusiasm in your endeavors.

Jupiter in the 11th House:

Your wisdom and education lead to wealth accumulation. You find happiness through your children, although there may be some weaknesses in your relationship with siblings. Pursuing your occupation may come with some uneasiness, but you enjoy domestic gains and overall wealth.

Jupiter in the 12th House:

You may spend a significant amount and face weaknesses in wealth matters. Losses may occur in the realm of children. Education may present challenges, and your mode of communication may not always be understood properly. The house of peace, happiness, and mother may lack fulfillment. However, you maintain friendships with your enemies and live an aristocratic life.

6.Venus

Venus in the Scorpio Ascendant:

Venus in the 1st House:

You attain a good occupation and have a majestic spending style. Careful work and some happiness are found in the realm of your spouse. You spend generously and may face some weaknesses due to your spouse. Your occupation may require traveling, and you possess cleverness and a desire for high-quality pleasures. You manage worldly affairs skillfully and appreciate beauty.

Venus in the 2nd House:

You acquire wealth through your occupation, but there may be some weaknesses and monetary losses in wealth accumulation. You have a strong sexual drive and try to control your expenditures.

Venus in the 3rd House:

You work hard and dedicate your energy to your occupation. Your spouse provides enthusiasm and sexual pleasures. You gain power through your siblings and enjoy cooperation from your spouse in managing expenses. You pay attention to justice within your occupation.

Venus in the 4th House:

You experience some losses and deficiencies in your occupation. Happiness comes from your spouse, but there may be some loss in the house of your mother. You enjoy expenditure and pleasures, but there may be conflicts with your father. You may have some ownership of land and possess a jovial nature.

Venus in the 5th House:

You are clever, educated, and intelligent. You spend generously, but there may be some deficiencies in income. Your wife holds influence, and you have children. Heavy expenditures may cause perplexity, but you strive for a successful occupation.

Venus in the 6th House:

You face opposition from your spouse and experience weaknesses in your occupation. Worries entangle your spending, and domestic obstacles hinder your happiness. There may be deficiencies in sexual pleasures, and you bear extraordinary expenditures on your wife's side. You are very careful and clever.

Venus in the 7th House:

You pursue multiple occupations and work hard. You spend generously to maintain stability in your occupation. You enjoy the pleasure of your wife and family, and your sexual instincts are strong. You pay attention to beauty, charm, and art within your occupation and manage it well. However, there may be some weaknesses in your occupation, and your relationship with your wife is special.

Venus in the 8th House:

There may be some losses in the realm of your spouse. You face difficulties in managing your occupation but handle them well to increase your wealth. Sexual pleasures may be significantly deficient, and you pursue secret strategies.

Venus in the 9th House in Cancer

Having Venus in the 9th House in Cancer indicates a strong emotional and nurturing connection to matters related to higher knowledge, spirituality, and travel. You have a deep appreciation for cultural diversity and may find joy in exploring different belief systems and philosophies. Your values are influenced by your emotional experiences and your desire for a sense of belonging and security. You may have a romanticized view of foreign cultures or long-distance relationships, and may find pleasure in exploring new places or immersing yourself in different traditions. Your love for learning and expanding your horizons is accompanied by a desire for emotional connection and a sense of emotional security in your philosophical and spiritual pursuits. You may find fulfillment in nurturing and supporting others on their spiritual or intellectual journeys.

Venus in the 10th House:

You gain power in your occupation and have the destiny-driven power of expenditure. Happiness from your wife and family is mixed with some weaknesses. You have a conjunction with your siblings, but there may be some weaknesses as well.

Venus in the 11th House:

Your occupation may be weak, and you experience significant weaknesses in income. The advantage of your wife and family is weak, and there may be deficiencies in sexual pleasures. However, you have some advantages in the realm of expenditures and receive children.

Venus in the 12th House:

You may experience the loss of your wife and family. Pleasures of wife and sex are connected to expenditures. You manage to get work done in the realm of enemies.

7.Saturn

Saturn in the Scorpio Ascendant:

Saturn in the 1st House:

You are very energetic and zealous. You gain power from your brothers and sisters and make progress in your occupation. There may be some perplexity in government and big business matters. You have a sharp and pungent nature, and you have a desire for sexual pleasures. You work hard for progress, demonstrating industry and courage.

Saturn in the 2nd House:

You earn income through land and property and take pleasure in accumulating wealth. There may be some restrictions on the happiness of your mother. You have good income and find some happiness in longevity and daily routines. You always strive to increase your wealth and generally feel content.

Saturn in the 3rd House:

You are highly energetic and engage in significant endeavors. You derive happiness from your brothers and sisters. However, you tend to spend excessively. Progress in the realm of children may come a bit later. You have some influence over land and property, and you have a tendency to speak bluntly. You find happiness in other places.

Saturn in the 4th House:

You possess substantial property and experience happiness and strength from land, property, and buildings. You derive happiness from your mother, brothers, and sisters. You may feel restless in the presence of enemies and face some deficiencies in your physical well-being. There may be some deficiencies in the realm of your father.

Saturn in the 5th House:

You have a sharp intellect and receive a good education. There may be some dullness or lack of excitement regarding children. You make progress in your occupation and have a special fascination for sexual pleasures.

Saturn in the 6th House:

There may be a loss in the happiness of your mother, and you may experience enmity from your brothers. Your power may be weak in dealing with certain diseases. You may feel distressed in the presence of enemies and adopt misguided strategies.

Saturn in the 7th House:

You find happiness in your domestic life and own buildings. There is some happiness derived from your spouse and occupation. You have a fascination for sexual pleasures and may experience physical tiredness. You make efforts for the progress of your occupation.

Saturn in the 8th House:

There may be a loss of happiness from others' side, and you may feel restless in your relationships with brothers and sisters. You have a long life and may experience restlessness in the realm of your father. There may be opportunities for travel to foreign countries.

Saturn in the 9th House in (Cancer):

Having Saturn in the 9th House in Cancer suggests a serious and disciplined approach to matters related to higher education, belief systems, and long-distance travel. This placement indicates a need for structure and practicality in your pursuit of knowledge and spiritual growth. You may have a strong sense of responsibility and may feel a need to establish firm foundations in your philosophical or religious beliefs. You may face challenges or limitations in expanding your horizons, and may feel a sense of restriction or duty in regards to long-distance travel or higher education. However, with patience and persistence, you can develop a strong and enduring wisdom that is grounded in emotional depth and personal experience. Your journey of self-discovery and intellectual growth may be slow and steady, but it can ultimately lead to profound personal transformation and a solid understanding of your core beliefs.

Saturn in the 10th House:

You are very energetic and perform admirable deeds. You are considered lucky and achieve significant gains. You receive cooperation from your brothers, and you find happiness in devotion to God and righteousness (Dharma). You may acquire land and buildings.

Saturn in the 11th House:

You comfortably bear heavy income and benefit from the support of your brothers and sisters. Your longevity is increased, and you have advantages related to land and buildings. You work hard to increase your income and experience happiness as a result.

Saturn in the 12th House:

You spend according to your own power and find comfort in spending. You have a fascination for Dharma and devotion to God. You perceive your enemies to be somewhat weak.

8.Rahu

Rahu in the Scorpio Ascendant:

Rahu in the 1st House:

You have an emaciated physique and may experience physical shocks frequently. It is challenging for you to maintain a gentle nature, and you resort to strong tactics to acquire power. However, you are courageous and clever.

Rahu in the 2nd House:

You face distress and losses in wealth, experiencing a shortage of resources. There may be difficulties in your family life, and you may have a tendency to engage in work with devotion.

Rahu in the 3rd House:

You are full of valor, courage, and intelligence. You make progress by employing strong strategies. You may experience conflicts with your siblings but maintain patience despite weaknesses. Sometimes, you may lose courage but ultimately emerge victorious.

Rahu in the 4th House:

There may be some weaknesses in your relationship with your mother, and you may face deficiencies in your happiness. You may encounter obstacles regarding land and experience restlessness due to a quarrelsome family atmosphere.

Rahu in the 5th House:

You are wise but inclined to present selfish ideas. Truthfulness and falsehood may not concern you. You may face troubles with children and encounter difficulties in acquiring education. Your conversational style may not be pleasant, and you tend to be careless. You strongly believe in your own views.

Rahu in the 6th House:

You possess significant influence and achieve victory over your enemies. However, you struggle to maintain gentleness and contentment. You exhibit great patience in accomplishing your tasks, regardless of the troubles or diseases you face. You have a diplomatic nature.

Rahu in the 7th House:

You handle your work carefully and cleverly in relation to your occupation. You employ diligent and mysterious methods in conducting your work. There may be afflictions in your relationship with your spouse, and you are reluctant to reveal your weaknesses. You may experience some worries.

Rahu in the 8th House:

You have grand aspirations in life and exhibit forcefulness and coquetry. You ponder deeply on obscure and mysterious matters. You have a long life ahead of you.

Rahu in the 9th House:

You feel significant concern about your destiny and may be disappointed with your luck. There may be a real deficiency in your connection with God and religion, leading to mental agony.

Rahu in the 10th House:

You experience loss and distress in relation to your father. Obstacles may arise in government and society, and you may not receive the honor you desire. Your business and occupation may cause great botheration, impeding your progress.

Rahu in the 11th House:

You accumulate significant wealth and earn a heavy income. You may not prioritize justice, truthfulness, or falsehood when acquiring wealth and tend to be cautious in your pursuits.

Rahu in the 12th House:

You tend to spend generously and employ clever tactics in your endeavors. You do not worry about expenditure and manage it efficiently, disregarding the troubles associated with acquiring wealth.

9. Ketu

Ketu in the Scorpio Ascendant:

Ketu in the 1st House:

You may experience weakness and wounds in your body. Despite excessive strength, you lack concern for others. You possess a heroic nature but feel a deficiency of knowledge. Your sensual desires are intense, and you face numerous troubles. You tend to be anxious and serious.

Ketu in the 2nd House:

You strive to increase your wealth but face disorder and obstacles in the progress of your family. You may put on a show of aristocracy but encounter significant troubles in acquiring wealth.

Ketu in the 3rd House:

You have a heroic nature, long arms, and a diligent approach. You may face separations but move forward with enthusiasm, even in the face of multiple failures. Eventually, you attain some strong power.

Ketu in the 4th House:

You experience deficiencies in your relationship with your mother, as well as in buildings, property, and happiness. You may face separation from your birthplace.

Ketu in the 5th House:

You are intellectually worried and face hurdles in education. However, you patiently work towards gaining knowledge. There may be distress related to children, and your speech may come across as rude. You have a stubborn nature.

Ketu in the 6th House:

You are very brave and possess a heroic nature. You achieve victory over enemies and face troubles without becoming discouraged. You skillfully and attentively overcome diseases and difficulties, focusing on serving your own selfish interests.

Ketu in the 7th House:

You experience agony in your relationship with your spouse. There may be worries in your occupation, but you work patiently and diligently. You remain composed and active despite facing grave troubles. You may encounter some difficulties within your family but manage them tactfully. You have a strong inclination towards sensual pleasures.

Ketu in the 8th House:

You experience great unhappiness and remain disturbed. There may be weakness in your longevity, and your daily routine may be clumsy. You may encounter issues related to the anus or stomach.

Ketu in the 9th House:

You feel restless about your destiny and experience a weakness in your adherence to Dharma. You adopt strong and advantageous tactics to uplift your fate but may have weak moral principles.

Ketu in the 10th House:

You face weakness and loss in your relationship with your father and encounter hindrances in government and society. There are obstacles in your rise to position or prestige, and you face complexities in business progress. However, you exhibit courage and work patiently.

Ketu in the 11th House:

You earn a heavy income but prioritize serving your own interests over notions of good or bad. You may experience occasional setbacks in your income, but your courage always brings you advantages.

Ketu in the 12th House:

You tend to spend a lot but manage your expenses patiently and tactfully. Sometimes, you may find it challenging to handle your expenditures effectively.

11. Predictions of the Planets with Reference to Sagittarius Ascendant

1. Sun

Predictions of Sun in Sagittarius Ascendant:

Sun in the 1st House:

You are very fortunate and have a handsome appearance. You follow Dharma (righteousness) and exhibit benevolence. You have faith in God and experience success in your occupation. You have influence in matters related to your wife and family. You are influential and renowned.

Sun in the 2nd House:

You acquire wealth with great difficulty and face problems in family matters. Accumulating wealth poses challenges for you. You have a long life and may experience some setbacks in matters of Dharma. You prioritize wealth over moral principles. You lead a civilized life and are fortunate.

Sun in the 3rd House:

You uphold Dharma and work with great courage. However, you may face some weaknesses in your diligence. There may be some deficiencies in your relationship with your brothers and sisters, despite their cooperation. You enjoy fame and good fortune.

Sun in the 5th House:

You are very fortunate and possess land and property. You experience happiness from others and benefit from your father. You have advantages in government-related matters and succeed in business. You engage in virtuous deeds.

Sun in the 6th House:

You face various challenges and obstacles in life. Your destiny may cause distress, and you may struggle to uphold Dharma. You exert influence over opponents and enemies, suppressing calamities and gaining control over diseases. You tend to spend a lot and have a significant influence.

Sun in the 7th House:

You have a beautiful and influential spouse. You experience progress in your occupation and gain respect and fame through your profession. You are honest in your work and enjoy good fortune. You are diligent and hardworking.

Sun in the 8th House:

You may face setbacks in matters related to destiny. The rise of fortune may come late and with great difficulty, possibly from foreign countries. However, you lead a decent and influential life, and your age increases.

Sun in the 9th House:

You are very fortunate and illustrious. You uphold a fiery sense of Dharma but may have less faith in your brothers and sisters.

Sun in the 10th House:

You are extremely fortunate, and the power of destiny brings you great honor and respect. You achieve fame and success in business, benefit from your father, and make progress with the support of the government and society. You adhere to religious formalities, possess influence, seek justice, and may hold an authoritative position.

Sun in the 11th House:

You may experience some deficiencies in matters related to gains. Upholding Dharma may be challenging for you, but you have the power of your children. You face some restrictions and confusion concerning income.

Sun in the 12th House:

You may face setbacks in matters related to destiny and encounter delays in the rise of fortune. You tend to spend a lot and have influence in the house of enemies. Your faith in God may not be strong, and you possess worldly wisdom.

2. Moon

Predictions for Moon in Sagittarius Ascendant:

Moon in the 1st House (Sagittarius):

You are likely to have a long life, but there may be some feelings of physical inadequacy or weakness. You may experience occasional worries related to your occupation, and there could be some confusion or perplexity in your relationship with your spouse.

Moon in the 2nd House (Capricorn):

You have a tendency to live a disciplined and aristocratic life. However, you may face challenges when it comes to accumulating wealth. Family-related losses or difficulties in financial matters are possible. Despite these challenges, you have the strength and perseverance to overcome obstacles and work through difficulties.

Moon in the 3rd House (Aquarius):

You may experience some setbacks or losses in your relationship with your siblings. There could be some obstacles or difficulties in matters related to your Dharma (duty or righteousness). However, you have a resourceful and tactical nature, and you may find joy and contentment in life.

Moon in the 4th House (Pisces):

When the Moon is placed in the 4th House in Pisces, it signifies certain aspects in your life. You may experience some losses or challenges in matters related to your mother. This could indicate difficulties or setbacks in your relationship with your mother or in matters concerning your mother's well-being.

On the positive side, you are likely to have good longevity and enjoy a long life. However, there may be some losses or dissatisfaction in domestic happiness. Your progress, honor, and business endeavors may encounter obstacles or difficulties.

Fortunately, you are generally free from stomach troubles or ailments related to digestion. However, it's important to note that you may have a tendency to spend your time carelessly or without much purpose.

Moon in the 5th House (Aries):

You may face challenges and losses in matters related to children. Difficulties in acquiring education or pursuing intellectual pursuits are possible. Despite these challenges, you carry yourself with grace, dignity, and grandeur in life.

Moon in the 6th House (Taurus):

You may experience weakness or challenges related to expenditure. You may have an influence over your enemies and can fearlessly accomplish your tasks. However, there is a possibility that you may not be modest in your actions.

Moon in the 7th House (Gemini):

Domestic life may bring some troubles or challenges. There may be some hidden difficulties in your relationship with your spouse. You may experience perplexities in your occupation and have a somewhat rigid approach to both your work and your spouse.

Moon in the 8th House (Cancer):

You are likely to have a long life and possess deep knowledge and concentration abilities. You may have certain advantages or inheritances from your family. However, there may be some losses or challenges in matters related to wealth.

Moon in the 9th House (Leo):

You may experience setbacks or losses in matters related to your Dharma or righteousness. However, you have the potential for a good means of livelihood. There may be obstacles and difficulties in matters of fortune and some obstacles from your siblings.

Moon in the 10th House (Virgo):

You may face obstacles in matters related to your father or authority figures. There could be challenges in your career advancement. Difficulties may arise in the house of government, society, and occupation. Your approach may involve following obscure tactics to navigate through these challenges.

Moon in the 11th House (Libra):

You have a long life and may face hindrances in matters related to income and financial gains. There may be some distress regarding your children. Obstacles in the field of education are also possible.

Moon in the 12th House (Scorpio):

You may experience distress and restlessness in various aspects of life. Longevity may be a concern, and there may be confusion or perplexity in matters of expenditure. You may have an influence from enemies or face challenges from them. Your mind may wander frequently, and you may have a narrow-minded approach to life.

3.Mars

Mars in the 1st House (Sagittarius):

When Mars is positioned in the 1st House in Sagittarius, it brings certain characteristics and influences into your life. You have a tendency to travel frequently, and your physical strength may be relatively weaker compared to others. However, you are capable of undertaking high-level tasks and have the ability to manipulate and convince others with your cunning speech. Unfortunately, this may lead to some negative consequences.

There could be a loss of your mother, and your relationship with your wife may involve difficulties and distress. You may experience restlessness in your daily routine and tend to spend money impulsively. Additionally, there may be some challenges or deficiencies in the area of children.

Mars in the 2nd House (Capricorn):

In the 2nd House, Mars indicates a mixture of gains and losses concerning wealth. Your wisdom and intelligence can contribute to accumulating significant wealth, but you may also experience periods of financial loss. It's important to manage your existing wealth wisely and avoid excessive spending.

Mars in the 3rd House (Aquarius):

With Mars in the 3rd House, you may face challenges in your relationships with siblings or encounter losses in their lives. You have a strong influence over your enemies and possess a courageous nature. However, there might be some difficulties in your occupation, and you tend to approach tasks with a conceited mindset.

Mars in the 4th House (Pisces):

This placement suggests the possibility of experiencing the loss of your mother and facing property or building-related losses. Your educational pursuits may encounter some deficiencies, but you manage your expenses carefully. There is also a likelihood of residing in foreign places.

Mars in the 5th House in Aries

Having Mars in the 5th House in Aries indicates a fiery and dynamic energy in matters of creativity, self-expression, romance, and entertainment. You possess a bold and assertive approach to these areas of life. Your passion and enthusiasm drive you to take risks and pursue your creative endeavors with great intensity. You have a strong desire for self-validation and recognition for your talents and may actively seek opportunities to showcase your skills. Your romantic relationships are often passionate and filled with a sense of adventure, as you crave excitement and spontaneity in love. You enjoy competitive activities and may excel in sports or other forms of physical expression. Your energy and enthusiasm can inspire and motivate others, making you a natural leader in creative projects or recreational activities. However, it's important to balance your assertiveness with consideration for others' feelings and avoid being overly impulsive or aggressive in your pursuits.

Mars in the 6th House in Taurus

Mars in the 6th House in Taurus indicates a persistent and determined approach to work and health. You possess a stable and grounded energy, preferring steady progress and a methodical approach. Your work ethic is strong, and you excel in tasks that require patience and attention to detail. Physical well-being is important to you, and you maintain a disciplined approach to health and fitness. However, be mindful of potential stubbornness and resistance to change. You value reliability and responsibility in the workplace, and your problem-solving skills are practical and resourceful. Balancing work and self-care is crucial for maintaining a healthy work-life balance.

Mars in the 7th House (Gemini):

In the 7th House, Mars indicates potential losses in your marital life. There may also be setbacks in your occupation, but you possess the ability to devise unique strategies for increasing your wealth. You may face difficulties with the government and encounter educational deficiencies and physical weaknesses.

Mars in the 8th House (Cancer):

When Mars is in the 8th House, you may experience specific challenges related to your children. Educational deficiencies, financial troubles, and a shorter life span are possible. You tend to employ secrecy, and there may be losses in your relationships with siblings. You exert significant effort in pursuing income and gains, but there might be health issues related to the anus.

Mars in the 9th House in Leo

Having Mars in the 9th House in Leo indicates a bold and passionate approach to matters of higher education, travel, belief systems, and spirituality. You have a strong desire for adventure and self-discovery, and you pursue these areas of life with great enthusiasm and energy. Your drive for personal growth and expansion is fueled by a sense of courage and self-assurance. You may be drawn to leadership roles within educational or philosophical pursuits, and your assertiveness can inspire others to take action. Your actions and beliefs may be intertwined, and you may actively defend and express your views. However, it's important to be mindful of becoming overly dogmatic or domineering in your interactions with others. Balancing your personal drive with respect for different perspectives can lead to powerful and transformative experiences in your spiritual and intellectual journey.

Mars in the 10th House (Leo):

With Mars in the 10th House, you tend to spend money excessively. There may be losses in your destiny and difficulties in your relationship with your mother. Educational deficiencies and challenges with siblings are also indicated. The rise in fortune may occur later in life and from unexpected sources.

Mars in the 11th House (Libra):

In the 11th House, Mars signifies your determination to increase wealth. However, there may be educational deficiencies and challenges in the area of children. You may also encounter enemies or opponents.

Mars in the 12th House (Scorpio):

With Mars in the 12th House, you tend to spend money extravagantly. You may experience significant losses in matters related to children and face challenges in your marital life. Occupational losses and deficiencies in wisdom and education are indicated. Additionally, you may have some influence over your enemies.

4.Mercury

Mercury in the 1st House (Sagittarius):

When Mercury is placed in the 1st House in Sagittarius, it indicates a person who engages in elegant and skillful occupations. You are hardworking but may also have some sinful tendencies. You possess good knowledge of worldly affairs and generally experience satisfactory success in your endeavors. You achieve honor in domestic matters and have an influential wife. However, there may be some loss in sexual pleasure and respect. You may also face deficiencies in your relationship with your father. Overall, you are clever, intelligent, and a good manager.

Mercury in the 2nd House (Capricorn):

In the 2nd House, Mercury signifies the potential to earn significant wealth through business and occupation. You make progress in your professional life and receive substantial wealth from your father. You may have a large family and could experience some constraints or obligations in your relationship with your spouse and family. There is a desire for more sexual pleasures, and you accumulate wealth. Additionally, you may benefit from the government and possess wisdom and cleverness.

Mercury in the 3rd House (Aquarius):

When Mercury is positioned in the 3rd House, you gain power through your relationships with siblings. You make progress in your family life and have notable success in business and occupation. You work diligently and cleverly, and there is a sense of self-conceit. Overall, you are fortunate, wise, and enjoy the advantages of your family and spouse.

Mercury in the 4th House (Pisces):

With Mercury in the 4th House, there may be losses and weaknesses in matters of honor. You may experience restlessness in family affairs and face deficiencies in land and property. There could be some challenges in your occupation, although you may see progress in large-scale business ventures. There may be weaknesses or difficulties from your spouse's side, and while you possess wisdom, it may not be readily apparent.

Mercury in the 5th House (Aries):

This placement suggests the ability to manage a significant business. You are wise and possess knowledge about government and society. You gain advantages from your spouse's side and desire sexual pleasures.

Mercury in the 6th House (Taurus):

In the 6th House, Mercury indicates the possibility of enmity and opposition from your paternal side. You may encounter significant troubles in your business or occupation and exhibit some politeness in dealing with enemies. There may be deficiencies in sexual pleasures.

Mercury in the 7th House (Gemini):

With Mercury in the 7th House, you engage in a dignified occupation and enjoy the pleasures of a happy family. You have a beautiful, influential, and clever spouse, and you dress nicely. Business endeavors are successful, and you derive great satisfaction from sexual pleasures. Additionally, you have a very good relationship with your father-in-law.

Mercury in the 8th House (Cancer):

When Mercury is in the 8th House, you may face losses and perplexity in your business or occupation. There could be challenges in your relationship with your spouse, and you may have work-related connections or opportunities in foreign countries. You strive hard to increase your wealth but may experience deficiencies in sexual pleasures.

Mercury in the 9th House in Leo

Mercury in the 9th House in Leo signifies a communicative and expressive approach to higher knowledge and travel. You possess a natural flair for teaching, writing, and public speaking, captivating others with your creativity and confidence. Your curiosity fuels a love for learning and exploring philosophical and spiritual subjects. Your communication style is charismatic and dramatic, captivating audiences with your storytelling abilities. However, be mindful of being overly attached to your own opinions and remain open to different perspectives. Travel becomes an avenue for intellectual and cultural expansion, enriching your experiences and broadening your horizons.

Mercury in the 10th House (Leo):

In the 10th House, Mercury indicates that you take good care of your moral and ethical values in business and occupation. You have a dutiful and beautiful spouse and receive strong cooperation from your siblings. You also benefit from the government and society.

Mercury in the 11th House (Libra):

With Mercury in the 11th House, you experience significant gains in your business or occupation. You have a beautiful spouse, achieve a high level of education, and enjoy abundant sexual pleasures. You also gain advantages from the government and society.

Mercury in the 12th House (Scorpio):

In the 12th House, Mercury suggests losses in business or occupation and in your father's house. You tend to spend a lot and may experience losses in your relationship with your spouse. You work hard for your occupation but face weaknesses in dealing with the government and society. There may be obstacles to your progress, and you have a somewhat lazy nature. Troubles in the family are also indicated.

5. Jupiter

Jupiter in Sagittarius Ascendant

Jupiter in the 1st House (Sagittarius):

The individual enjoys happiness, honor, and a respectable position. They may have a well-built body and a peaceful nature. They appreciate sweet and delicious food and find happiness in their marriage. They have a comfortable occupation, live in their own place, and find joy in education and following righteous principles. They are fortunate and blessed with children.

Jupiter in the 2nd House (Capricorn):

This placement suggests that the individual is willing to take risks, even to the extent of endangering their life, for the sake of acquiring wealth. They may prioritize wealth above all else and may feel unsatisfied or unhappy in terms of their financial situation. They may face losses related to their mother and experience deficiencies in land and property. Despite these challenges, they are hardworking, engaged in business or occupation, and maintain a respectable status.

Jupiter in the 3rd House (Aquarius):

Individuals with this placement gain financial prosperity and happiness through their spouse or their spouse's family. However, there may be some difficulties or deficiencies in the relationship with their mother and siblings. They enjoy family happiness and are industrious in their pursuits.

Jupiter in the 4th House in (Pisces)

Jupiter in the 4th House in (Pisces) indicates a nurturing and expansive energy within the realm of home, family, and emotions. You have a deep sense of empathy and compassion, creating a warm and inviting atmosphere in your domestic life. Your family connections are often uplifting and supportive, and you may come from a culturally diverse or spiritually inclined background. Your home is a sanctuary where you can explore and express your spiritual beliefs and ideals. You have a natural inclination towards personal growth and may find solace in introspection and inner exploration. Your emotional well-being is closely tied to your spiritual connection, and you may seek transcendence and higher understanding within the comforts of your home.

Jupiter in the 5th House (Arise):

This placement brings happiness through the mother and the possession of lands and buildings. The individual experiences dignity, pleasure, and a long life. They have a place of their own and exhibit energetic qualities.

Jupiter in the 6th House (Taurus):

Individuals with this placement are wise, self-confident, and dignified. They possess a handsome physique and are blessed with illustrious children and wisdom. They have inner knowledge and diplomatic skills. They are fortunate and likely to own property.

Jupiter in the 7th House (Gemini):

Those with Jupiter in the 7th house enjoy a comfortable occupation and have a beautiful and influential spouse. They may experience enmity or conflicts within their siblings' and sisters' families. There may be some possession of landed property, and they have a self-conceited nature.

Jupiter in the 8th House (Cancer):

Individuals with this placement enjoy unique powers, elegance, and splendor in their daily life. However, there may be some weaknesses in terms of wealth. They tend to spend a lot and live in a majestic style, but they may feel a weakness in their social position. They acquire land and property and possess the power of their mother.

Jupiter in the 9th House (Leo):

Those with Jupiter in the 9th house are very fortunate and possess scientific knowledge. They perform religious rituals, have faith in God, and display wisdom and authority in education. They own land and property and find happiness in their children. They may also experience some enmity within their siblings' relationships.

Jupiter in the 10th House (Virgo):

Individuals with this placement comfortably pursue a successful business or occupation. They make progress in their career and attain land and property. They receive honor from the government and society. However, there may be some deficiencies in terms of wealth. They are hardworking and may exhibit an arrogant nature.

Jupiter in the 11th House (Libra):

Those with Jupiter in the 11th house find happiness and enjoyment but may experience some enmity within their siblings' relationships. They have command and authority in education, enjoy the happiness of children, a harmonious relationship with their spouse, and income from their occupation.

Jupiter in the 12th House (Scorpio):

This placement may bring deficiencies in physical attractiveness but an inclination towards spending extravagantly. Despite this, they find splendor in their daily routine and effectively use peace and influence even in the house of their enemies. They have a tendency to travel extensively and may lead a life of adventure and exploration.

6. Venus

Predictions of Venus in Sagittarius Ascendant:

Venus in the 1st House (Sagittarius):

You earn income through physical labor and hard work. There may be some health issues, but you pay great attention to your occupation. Your relationship with your spouse may bring both perplexity and advantage. You have the potential to earn a significant amount of money, suppress your enemies, and have a desire for ornamentation and joy.

Venus in the 2nd House (Capricorn):

You have the ability to accumulate wealth and enjoy financial prosperity. However, there may be occasional losses. Overall, you are respected for your financial prowess.

Venus in the 3rd House (Aquarius):

You experience numerous advantages and a substantial income. There may be both cooperation and antagonism in your relationship with your siblings.

Venus in the 4th House (Pisces):

You enjoy a heavy income and possess land and property. You gain advantages through your mother. You have a desire for delicious food but may experience some deficiency in the relationship with your father.

Venus in the 5th House (Aries):

Your intellectual cleverness brings you significant financial gains. You have permanent means of acquiring wealth and income. You excel in wisdom, education, and cleverness. However, there may be some deficiency or challenges related to children, and you are able to overcome your enemies.

Venus in the 6th House (Taurus):

You may face difficulties in generating income and tend to spend a lot. You are very clever and employ intricate tactics. Your haughtiness and cleverness may be prominent traits.

Venus in the 7th House (Gemini):

You gain advantages in your occupation and experience good cooperation within your wife's house. However, there may be some enmity through your wife's side. You have a strong desire for sexual pleasures, appreciate beauty, and may encounter some health issues related to your spouse. Overall, you experience honor and are highly clever.

Venus in the 8th House (Cancer):

You bear numerous worries regarding gains and income, but you also experience elegance in your daily routine. There may be some deficiencies in financial gains, but you have the ability to overcome your enemies.

Venus in the 9th House (Leo):

You attain gains, but there may be some uneasiness associated with them. Obstacles and troubles may arise in your destiny's progress. Your relationship with your brother is continuous, and you display courage and cleverness. You gain advantages through the garb of Dharma (righteousness).

Venus in the 10th House (Virgo):

There may be distress within your father's house, and you experience weakness in the progress of your business and income. However, you gain advantages in the realm of property.

Venus in the 11th House (Libra):

You achieve a substantial income and make gains through intellectual prowess and strategic tactics. There may be some advantages related to your children, and you even gain from your enemies.

Venus in the 12th House (Scorpio):

You tend to spend a significant amount and face some deficiencies in financial gains. However, you manage to work diligently and cleverly to overcome the difficulties associated with expenses. You employ intricate tactics to solve financial challenges and demonstrate cleverness.

7.Saturn

Predictions of Saturn in Sagittarius Ascendant:

Saturn in the 1st House (Sagittarius):

You are very energetic and industrious. Through diligent work, you increase your wealth. You derive strength from your brothers and sisters. There may be some restlessness in your body. You are capable of conducting a big business and gain power through your wife and father.

Saturn in the 2nd House (Capricorn):

You are wealthy and have the means to acquire land and buildings. There may be some loss in the house of your mother. You enjoy a heavy income but experience restlessness in your daily routine of life.

Saturn in the 3rd House (Aquarius):

You possess limited wisdom in matters related to wealth. Your speech may be bitter and rude. There may be deficiencies in education and in the children's side. You tend to spend a lot and experience uneasiness. Despite challenges, you are industrious and courageous.

Saturn in the 4th House (Pisces):

You experience both happiness and unhappiness in matters of wealth. There may be involvement or influence of a stepmother. Your enemies have a sweet influence on you. You are able to resolve health-related issues. You may feel somewhat physically restless.

Saturn in the 5th House (Aries):

Through hard intellectual labor, you acquire increased wealth. You have anxieties about accumulating wealth. Your speech becomes refined due to your increased wealth. There may be deficiencies in the children's side and in education. However, you improve your occupation and gain special power within your wife's house. Overall, you earn a significant amount.

Saturn in the 6th House (Taurus):

There is weakness in the wealth side, but you oppose your brothers while also receiving their support. You have the ability to suppress your enemies and overcome diseases and difficulties. Some perplexity is present in your daily routine of life. You display bravery, self-conceit, and restlessness.

Saturn in the 7th House (Gemini):

You make progress in your occupation and diligently earn wealth. There may be some weakness in your body. You gain power within your wife's house. However, you do not support Dharma and tend to be passionate.

Saturn in the 8th House (Cancer):

You experience a deficiency of wealth and manpower, which makes you unhappy. There may be losses in wealth and deficiencies in education and intellect.

However, you have a long life and possess secret wisdom.

Saturn in the 9th House (Leo):

You increase your wealth and enjoy a heavy income. You acquire influence within the house of your enemies.

Saturn in the 10th House (Virgo):

You gain dignity in government administration and make significant progress. Your occupation is influential and brings wealth. However, there may be some limitations or restrictions within your wife's house. You exert your full strength for the progress of your occupation and display obstinacy.

Saturn in the 11th House (Libra):

You earn a significant amount and gain power through wealth. There are advantages within your family. However, there may be deficiencies in handsomeness.

Saturn in the 12th House (Scorpio):

You tend to spend a significant amount and possess the power of wealth. You maintain a show of being rich. However, you struggle to uphold Dharma and maintain influence within the house of your enemies through secret tactics.

8. Rahu

Predictions of Rahu (Dragon's Head) in Sagittarius Ascendant:

Rahu in the 1st House (Sagittarius):

You experience physical distress and worries. There may be a deficiency in the handsomeness of your body, and you might face physical blows or risks to your body. You employ tactical strategies to get things done and undertake challenging tasks for your progress. At times, you may have to depend on others.

Rahu in the 2nd House (Capricorn):

You may incur losses in matters of wealth. There could be afflictions within the family. You employ deep tactics to acquire wealth but may experience some unhappiness in this regard.

Rahu in the 3rd House (Aquarius):

You are highly energetic and work with great courage. You achieve success by using clever strategies. There may be some conflicts or arguments within the house of your siblings.

Rahu in the 4th House (Pisces):

You face losses in your mother's house and encounter obstacles to happiness. There may be some deficiencies in relation to land and buildings. Separation from your mother and motherland is possible.

Rahu in the 5th House (Aries):

There are deficiencies in education and in matters related to children. You may adopt a bitter and secretive approach within matters of intellect. While you may reveal the truth, you might not prioritize it.

Rahu in the 6th House (Taurus):

You are influential and capable of suppressing your enemies. You are not deterred by hindrances and troubles, and you prioritize your own self-interest.

Rahu in the 7th House (Gemini):

You work tactfully in your occupation, putting in great effort and devising complex plans for progress. You have an extraordinarily charming spouse and experience heightened sexual pleasures. You are clever and cunning.

Rahu in the 8th House (Cancer):

You face perplexities in life and may experience complaints related to the stomach and anus. Your daily routine is challenging, and you harbor secret anxieties. Traveling to foreign countries brings you happiness.

Rahu in the 9th House (Leo):

You feel anxious about your destiny and encounter hindrances, troubles, and losses in connection with your fate. There may be weaknesses in matters related to Dharma.

Rahu in the 10th House (Virgo):

You employ great tactics for your progress. There is unhappiness in your relationship with your father. You work secretly in business and government affairs, and you worry about social matters.

Rahu in the 11th House (Libra):

You enjoy numerous advantages and work determinedly to increase your income. You employ secret and intricate strategies to gain advantages, without concern for truth or falsehood.

Rahu in the 12th House (Scorpio):

You tend to spend a significant amount and face distress and troubles in your expenditures. You employ various methods to escape from financial worries. You make considerable efforts to establish stability in managing your expenses but struggle to discern between truth and falsehood.

9.Ketu

Predictions of Ketu (Dragon's Tail) in Sagittarius Ascendant:

Ketu in the 1st House (Sagittarius):

You are tall in stature and possess bravery, diligence, and conceit. You may also be superstitious and careless. There is a deficiency in physical handsomeness. You have a sense of greatness and possess the power of concealment and bravery. Selfishness is prominent in your nature.

Ketu in the 2nd House (Capricorn):

You face troubles in matters of wealth and experience losses within the family. Your focus is always on accumulating wealth, and you may resort to occult practices to achieve your goals.

Ketu in the 3rd House (Aquarius):

There are losses in your relationship with siblings. You work hard for your progress and live with great influence.

Ketu in the 4th House (Pisces):

You encounter troubles in the house of your mother and experience separation from her. Restlessness is present in matters of happiness. There is a deficiency in relation to land and buildings. You take risks in pursuit of happiness and eventually find some contentment. You exhibit obstinacy in seeking happiness and possess patience.

Ketu in the 5th House (Aries):

You carry intellectual worries and face troubles related to children. Acquiring education presents many difficulties. Others may have difficulty understanding your perspective. Your speech can be somewhat bitter, and you may disregard truth and modesty. Selfishness and obstinacy are prominent in your nature.

Ketu in the 6th House (Taurus):

You possess a brave nature and have the ability to suppress your enemies. Self-conceit is prominent, and you work hard to gain victory over opponents. You gain control over opponents and diseases. You devise secret schemes and engage in selfish actions.

Ketu in the 7th House (Gemini):

You face significant trouble in your spouse's house and experience dependence in your occupation. Fatigue is common, and you earn a livelihood with great difficulty and strategic tactics. There is a deficiency in sexual pleasures.

Ketu in the 8th House (Cancer):

You face great troubles in life and may experience complaints related to the stomach, lower body, or anus. Daily routines bring worries, and you may come across as rude. However, you possess patience and work diligently.

Ketu in the 9th House (Leo):

You feel worried about your destiny and experience a deficiency in fame. You may lack faith in matters of Dharma.

Ketu in the 10th House (Virgo):

There are deficiencies in your relationship with your father. Worries surround business matters, but you work patiently for progress in your business and occupation.

Ketu in the 11th House (Libra):

You achieve heavy gains and work obstinately to acquire money. You strive for significant advantages.

Ketu in the 12th House (Scorpio):

You tend to spend a significant amount and aim to establish stable power for expenditures. Troubles accompany heavy expenditures, but you exhibit courage in your actions.

12. Predictions of the Planets with Reference to Capricorn Ascendant:

Predictions of Sun in Capricorn Ascendant:

1.sun

Sun in the 1st House (Capricorn):

You may experience physical afflictions and engage in difficult tasks. Diseases like smallpox and syphilis may affect you. Your life span is generally long, but restlessness is present. Calamities may occur in your married life, and there may be confusion in matters of education. You may have a deficiency in charm and complexion. Your nature tends to be haughty, and you possess the power of concealment.

Sun in the 2nd House (Aquarius):

You may experience losses and deficiencies in matters of wealth and separation from family members. Your daily routine is marked by aristocracy and elegance. Your longevity increases, but accumulating wealth may pose challenges.

Sun in the 3rd House (Pisces):

You lead a life of influence and enjoy a long life span. However, your house of fortune and Dharma may suffer. You may face distress in your relationship with siblings.

Sun in the 4th House (Aries):

You have hidden wealth, but there may be some losses in the house of your mother. Your life span is long, but you may face distress in your relationship with your father. Weakness in government and society is possible. You lead a pleasurable daily life but may exhibit some inactivity and hastiness.

Sun in the 5th House (Taurus):

You may experience losses and distress in matters concerning children. There may be weakness in education, and your speech may tend to be bitter. You employ various tactics to earn more wealth.

Sun in the 6th House (Gemini):

You possess great influence and exhibit haughtiness. Your daily life is dignified, and you enjoy a long life span. You defeat your enemies, demonstrate courage, and display patience.

Sun in the 7th House (Cancer):

You may face afflictions in your spouse's side and feel worried about domestic life. Worries may arise in connection with your occupation, and there may be some distress in your sexual life. Your occupation may involve contact with foreign countries, and you may engage in strange and dreadful deeds.

Sun in the 8th House (Leo):

You have a long life span and lead an influential life. However, there may be financial losses and afflictions within your family. You possess the power of secrecy, and you maintain a dignified lifestyle. You may not concern yourself with your future and tend to be haughty and grumble.

Sun in the 9th House (Virgo):

You enjoy a long life span and experience some losses in matters of destiny. Your daily routine is fortunate, but problems may arise in your relationship with your siblings. Your approach to Dharma may be self-centered, and you live as a respectable individual.

Sun in the 10th House (Libra):

There may be losses in your father's house, and weaknesses may be present regarding longevity. You work hard but face worries in business matters.

Restlessness may be present in government-related affairs. You may gain some parental advantages in terms of land and buildings.

Sun in the 11th House (Scorpio):

You have a good life span and lead your daily routine with influence and advantage. There may be losses and calamities concerning children. Worry may arise in matters of education, and you may employ secrecy and bitterness in your conversations.

Sun in the 12th House (Sagittarius):

You may have some deficiencies in the influence of life and experience weakness regarding age. Your expenses may be high, but you maintain influence over your enemies. Difficulties may arise in matters of expenditure, and you may experience complaints in the stomach below

2.Moon

Moon in Capricorn Ascendant

Moon in the 1st House (Capricorn):

Individuals with Moon in the 1st house in Capricorn focus on their occupation with great concentration. However, there may be some deficiency in experiencing beauty and happiness in their married life. They have a strong desire for sexual pleasures and often indulge in them. They tend to have a fair complexion and are known for their diligence and hard work.

Moon in the 2nd House (Aquarius):

Those with Moon in the 2nd house accumulate wealth through their occupation. However, they may face certain limitations and unpleasantness in their family life. They need to be cautious about financial matters and may experience fluctuations in their income.

Moon in the 3rd House (Pisces):

Individuals with this placement work diligently in their occupation. They are likely to have an influential and beautiful spouse. They possess special sexual powers and pay attention to the growth of their wealth. They have a strong bond with their siblings and sisters.

Moon in the 4th House (Aries):

People with Moon in the 4th house enjoy good happiness within their family. They have a beautiful spouse and possess property. They experience sexual pleasures and find joy in their occupation. They are respected in both government and society, and their nature is jovial and happy.

Moon in the 5th House (Taurus):

Individuals with Moon in the 5th house possess good knowledge and skills in their occupation. They are determined and focused in their pursuits. They have a beautiful and wise spouse and are passionate in their approach. However, they may face some deficiencies in terms of income. They are skilled and passionate individuals.

Moon in the 6th House (Gemini):

Those with Moon in the 6th house encounter obstacles in their occupation. They often experience mental perplexity and worries related to their spouse. There may be a deficiency in sexual pleasures, and they tend to spend a significant amount of money to avoid diseases and deal with enemies.

Moon in the 7th House (Cancer):

People with this placement have a very beautiful spouse and enjoy significant sexual pleasures. They pursue a stable and fulfilling occupation and experience contentment in their married life.

Moon in the 8th House (Leo):

Individuals with Moon in the 8th house may face losses in their married life and experience mental affliction due to family matters. They may encounter deficiencies in terms of sexual pleasures and face difficulties in their occupation. They possess secret knowledge or intuition.

Moon in the 9th House (Virgo):

Those with Moon in the 9th house have a fortunate spouse and engage in religious affairs. They are considered fortunate in business and have supportive siblings. They are inclined towards spiritual pursuits and seek knowledge and wisdom.

Moon in the 10th House (Libra):

Individuals with Moon in the 10th house pursue a successful occupation and enjoy respect in their business dealings. They are honored in the government, society, and family. They receive support from their parents and find happiness through their spouse. They have a harmonious family life.

Moon in the 11th House (Scorpio):

Those with Moon in the 11th house may experience restlessness in their married life. They find happiness within their family but have average sexual pleasures. There may be some deficiencies in terms of income. They may possess sharpness in education and intellect but can be prone to anger in conversations. They find satisfaction in the progress of their occupation.

Moon in the 12th House (Sagittarius):

People with Moon in the 12th house may experience losses in their married life. There may be deficiencies in terms of sexual pleasures and weakness in their occupation. They tend to spend a lot and may face perplexity in family matters. However, they are able to work calmly and effectively in the presence of enemies. Despite the challenges, they can find success in their family-related occupations and manage their expenditures wisely.

3.Mars

Predictions of Mars in Capricorn Ascendant:

Mars in the 1st House (Capricorn):

You experience a great deal of happiness and acquire a lot of property and gains. There is a special connection with your mother's house. However, there may be deficiencies in your occupation and from your wife's side. You may also experience a lack of sexual pleasures. You create avenues of happiness through your occupation and sexual pursuits. You tend to be self-conceited and proud.

Mars in the 2nd House (Aquarius):

You gain monetarily and acquire land and property. There is happiness, but there may be some deficiencies in terms of children and education.

Mars in the 3rd House (Pisces):

You possess the power of your siblings and benefit from land and your mother's house. There are advantages in business and occupation, as well as happiness from government and society. You receive honor and prestige and live carefree.

Mars in the 4th House (Aries):

You gain income from land and property but may display idleness in your occupation. There may be deficiencies from your wife, as well as in terms of sexual pleasure. You find happiness through government and society.

Mars in the 5th House (Taurus):

You have advantages through your intellect, receive education, and have children. You are always discussing profitable schemes.

Mars in the 6th House (Gemini):

You gain advantages and income through influential and dependent actions. There may be unhappiness in your mother's house, but you overcome diseases and difficulties. You have faith in Dharma and gain advantages over enemies. You tend to spend a lot.

Mars in the 7th House (Cancer):

You experience losses in your wife's house and deficiencies in your mother's house. There is weakness in connection with your occupation and restlessness in terms of income and domestic happiness. There may also be deficiencies in sexual pleasures.

Mars in the 8th House (Leo):

You gain a lot and experience separation from your mother. There is happiness in terms of longevity and in your daily life. However, there may be unhappiness in domestic pleasures. You work courageously and diligently.

Mars in the 9th House (Virgo):

You are very fortunate and enjoy good fortune. You acquire land and property and find happiness through your mother. You are overjoyed, energetic, and receive support from your siblings.

Mars in the 10th House (Libra):

You gain income through business and occupation. You benefit from the government and receive advantages from your father and education. You perform influential deeds.

Mars in the 11th House (Scorpio):

You experience an increase in income and benefit from your mother's house. There may be conflicts within the family, but you receive some education and have children. You exert influence over enemies and achieve victory over diseases and calamities.

Mars in the 12th House (Sagittarius):

You experience the loss of your mother and motherland. There may be weakness in terms of income and deficiencies in happiness. However, you find happiness through your wife. There are deficiencies in your brother's house, and you tend to spend a lot. You maintain influence within your enemies' house and experience deficiencies in sexual pleasures.

4.Mercury

Predictions of Mercury in Capricorn Ascendant:

Mercury in the 1st House (Capricorn):

You are clever, fortunate, gentle, and influential. You have faith in Dharma and achieve victory over enemies. You may experience some ordinary physical ailments.

You pursue your occupation diligently and have an ordinary liking for sexual pleasures.

Mercury in the 2nd House (Aquarius):

You are very wealthy and fortunate. You benefit from your family, but there may be some deficiencies within the family. You may experience restlessness in acquiring wealth.

Mercury in the 3rd House (Pisces):

You may exhibit idleness and consider destiny to be of great importance. You feel worried due to enemies, but destiny protects you. There may be delays in the rise of your fate.

Mercury in the 4th House (Aries):

You find happiness through the power of destiny. You may acquire happiness through land and buildings. You achieve victory in the enemies' house.

Mercury in the 5th House (Taurus):

You work cleverly and intelligently. You possess good knowledge of Dharma. You have clever and intelligent children. You acquire wealth and exert influence over enemies.

Mercury in the 6th House (Gemini):

You experience weakness in your destiny and often face worries and difficulties in the progress of your destiny. However, you gain control over diseases, enemies, and troubles. You tend to spend a lot.

Mercury in the 7th House (Cancer):

You make progress in your occupation due to your powerful destiny. You have good fortune in the daily management of your occupation. There may be some ordinary afflictions on the wife's side. You perform religious duties because of your wife.

Mercury in the 8th House (Leo):

You have a weak destiny and face weaknesses in terms of Dharma. You employ tactics to increase your wealth. You have a long life and tend to be selfish.

Mercury in the 9th House (Virgo):

You are fortunate and gain great advantages through wisdom. You uphold Dharma but face opposition from your brother. You are very clever.

Mercury in the 10th House (Libra):

You gain influence and pursue Dharma selfishly. You make progress in business and have both strengths and weaknesses in your father's house. You benefit from the government and are honorable and fortunate.

Mercury in the 11th House (Scorpio):

You experience good fortune due to your cleverness. You do not face difficulties in the house of income. You receive a good education and possess intelligence. You gain advantages from the enemies' house and are influential.

Mercury in the 12th House (Sagittarius):

You may experience loss in terms of Dharma. You tend to spend a lot and encounter delays and worries in the rise of your fate.

5. Jupiter

Predictions of Jupiter in Capricorn Ascendant:

Jupiter in the 1st House (Capricorn):

You may bear physical troubles and have an emaciated body. There is a deficiency in expenditure and weakness from the side of brothers and sisters. You may have a deficiency in physical handsomeness but acquire some elegance in your wife's house. You make progress in your occupation and gain strength from the children's side.

Jupiter in the 2nd House (Aquarius):

You experience loss and deficiency in the house of wealth. There may be deficiencies in the relationship with your siblings, and you may not achieve the desired success. Some deficiencies are present in the family.

Jupiter in the 3rd House (Pisces):

You tend to spend a lot. You gain advantages in terms of family and profession. You possess a special desire for sexual pleasures but experience weakness in the brothers' house.

Jupiter in the 4th House (Aries):

You spend in a majestic manner and manage your expenditure comfortably. However, you may experience some loss and weakness in land and property. There are obstacles in acquiring peace and happiness, and you may struggle to control excessive expenditure. You feel somewhat restless.

Jupiter in the 5th House (Taurus):

You manage your expenditure wisely but may have a deficiency in education. There may be some loss in the children's side, and you may have a deficiency in physical handsomeness. You may experience restlessness, but you are clever.

Jupiter in the 6th House (Gemini):

You have worries and dependence related to expenditure. You face opposition from brothers and have a deficiency in accumulating wealth. There are obstacles to your independence, and you employ hidden policies to cause enmity. You have an idle nature.

Jupiter in the 7th House (Cancer):

You work energetically in your line of occupation. You tend to spend a lot and gain special sexual powers and happiness. There may be weakness in your body, but you maintain contact with your brothers and sisters.

Jupiter in the 8th House (Leo):

You have weakness in your strength and energy. You face hindrances in connection with expenditure and tend to spend a lot. You gain from foreign countries but experience weakness in connection with brothers and sisters. There is a deficiency in accumulating wealth. You maintain your daily routine with influence and dignity.

Jupiter in the 9th House (Virgo):

You experience weakness in destiny and Dharma. You receive cooperation from your brother but with some weaknesses. You may not be physically handsome and may face some loss in the children's house.

Jupiter in the 10th House (Libra):

You experience loss in your father's house and bear some deficiencies and losses in your occupation. There may be a lack of success despite your special efforts. You tend to spend a lot and face some monetary deficiencies and losses.

Jupiter in the 11th House (Scorpio):

You gain numerous advantages and benefit from your brothers and sisters, although there may be some deficiencies. You have a beautiful wife and make progress in your occupation.

Jupiter in the 12th House (Sagittarius):

You tend to spend a lot and face some weakness in your mother's side. There is a deficiency in the brothers' house, and you fail to attain grandeur in your daily routine. Despite your efforts, you are unable to decrease expenditure. You may wander frequently and have a restless disposition.

6.Venus

Predictions of Venus in Capricorn Ascendant:

Venus in the 1st House (Capricorn):

You are highly respectable, clever, wise, and engage in noble and high-standard deeds. You pursue a significant occupation and receive honor and advantage from your father. You gain favor from the government and are respected in public. You engage in multiple occupations, enjoy sexual pleasures, find happiness in children, appreciate beauty, and have a great love for astrology.

Venus in the 2nd House (Aquarius):

You accumulate considerable wealth and derive power from your father's house. You earn wealth cleverly through education and intellect and manage a large business. You have good luck and may experience some bondage from the children's side. You benefit from the government and society, acquiring honor and respect in your daily life.

Venus in the 3rd House (Pisces):

You possess influence and a handsome stature. You have brothers and sisters and gain wisdom and education. You benefit in government affairs and may experience some loss in matters of Dharma. You are a good manager.

Venus in the 4th House (Aries):

You receive numerous advantages and manage a substantial business. You find happiness in relationships with parents and children. You gain education and own buildings and property. You benefit from the government and society. You have a taste for beauty and art and are highly respectable.

Venus in the 5th House (Taurus):

You acquire knowledge in various areas, particularly in politics. You receive support from children and gain advantages from the government and society. You appreciate decoration, beauty, and intoxication. You possess wit.

Venus in the 6th House (Gemini):

You may experience enmity from your father's house and encounter some troubles from children. You are influenced by education and may experience dependence. You tend to spend a lot but defeat enemies with secret tactics of wisdom. You gain control over diseases. There may be some opposition from the government and society, but you are very clever.

Venus in the 7th House (Cancer):

You pursue a powerful occupation and draw strength from children. You experience happiness in the family and engage in honorable deeds for the government and society. There may be some deficiencies in business, but you focus on increasing wealth. You employ diplomatic policies and may experience mental worries.

Venus in the 8th House (Leo):

You may experience the loss of your father and have deficiencies in education. You tend to conceal things in your conversations and strive for honor in the government and society. There may be some deficiencies in the progress of your business, but you pay attention to increasing wealth.

Venus in the 9th House (Virgo):

You have some weaknesses in the house of destiny and experience weaknesses from the side of your father. However, you are considered fortunate and receive honor in the government and society. You have brothers and sisters but face some weaknesses in business and occupation.

Venus in the 10th House (Libra):

You gain government and administrative power and may work as a judge. You receive a high-standard education and derive power and happiness from your father and mother. You possess property and pursue a significant occupation. You appreciate beauty and art and communicate with dignity and influence. You are self-conceited, respectable, learned, and industrious.

Venus in the 11th House (Scorpio):

You obtain great advantages from business and benefit from your father and children. You excel in conversation and gain advantages from the government and society. You enjoy easy means of sexual pleasures and grandeur. You are clever and industrious.

Venus in the 12th House (Sagittarius):

You tend to spend a lot and experience the loss of your father and children. There may be deficiencies in education and business, as well as in the government and society. However, you manage your expenses cleverly and exhibit a somewhat inactive and idle nature.

7.Saturn

Saturn in the 1st House (Capricorn)

indicates that you will be very rich, live aristocratically, wear costly dresses, and experience progress from your father's house. You will pursue a big business occupation and may have some deficiencies in your relationships with siblings. However, you will gain name and honor in society, despite facing some opposition within your family.

Saturn in the 2nd House (Aquarius)

suggests that you will accumulate much wealth and may even take risks to acquire it, even at the cost of risking your life. You will experience progress in the family but face weaknesses from others. There may be deficiencies in landed property and the house of happiness, leading to restlessness in your daily routine.

Saturn in the 3rd House (Pisces)

indicates that you will be influential, energetic, and work very hard. However, there may be deficiencies in your relationships with siblings and in your expenditure. Nonetheless, you will hold a strong belief in God.

Saturn in the 4th House (Aries)

suggests restlessness and deficiencies in the house of happiness. You will have influence in the house of enemies and engage in big business ventures. However, there may be a lack of land and property.

Saturn in the 5th House (Taurus)

indicates that you will be very handsome, wise, clever, and learned. You will earn wealth through your wisdom and face some enmity in the house of your spouse. You will have a strong desire for sensual pleasures and pay attention to the progress of your occupation. Additionally, you will be a good manager.

Saturn in the 6th House (Gemini)

suggests that you may face enmity from your father's house and encounter troubles related to children. You will have an influence on education and experience some dependence. There may be hindrances in your expenditure, enmity within your relationships with siblings, and deficiencies in accumulating wealth and physical attractiveness. Nonetheless, you will be clever and cautious in dealing with these challenges.

Saturn in the 7th House (Cancer)

indicates that you will labor hard in your occupation and have a great fascination for your spouse. However, you may develop some enmity within your family and experience uneasiness in your occupation. You will make great efforts for the rise of your destiny, but there may be deficiencies in owning land and buildings.

Saturn in the 8th House (Leo)

suggests that you may live in foreign countries and face troubles in your body. There may be a loss of wealth, but you will gain education and have children. You will have a long life but encounter obstacles in accumulating wealth. Nonetheless, you will exhibit great industriousness.

In the 9th House (Virgo),

Saturn indicates that you will be very fortunate, religious, virtuous, and possess a handsome body. You will seem lucky but have enmity in the house of income. You will have a positive influence over your enemies and opponents, effectively managing diseases. However, there may be some sourness in your relationships with siblings.

Saturn in the 10th House (Libra)

suggests that you will engage in big business ventures with the help of money. You will have a splendid body and wield significant influence. You will gain honor in the government and experience progress in your father's house. There may be deficiencies in your mother's house and enmity within your relationships with your spouse. Worries related to your occupation may arise, but you will enjoy the splendor of sexual pleasure.

In the 11th House (Scorpio),

Saturn indicates that you will earn much wealth and attain fame.In the 11th House (Scorpio), Saturn indicates that you will earn much wealth and attain fame. You will always be busy increasing your money and experience progress in education and wisdom. You will gain power from your children and put forward weighty ideas.

Saturn in the 12th House (Sagittarius)

suggests that you may spend a lot and live in other places. You may have an emaciated body and acquire wealth through sources outside of your immediate surroundings. Excessive expenditure may pose difficulties in increasing your wealth, leading to a constant state of unhappiness.

8.Rahu

Rahu in the 1st House (Capricorn)

suggests that you may experience some physical perplexity and a sense of intoxication. There may be deficiencies in your body, but you cleverly find ways to progress through concealment and manipulation. You become firm and resilient after bearing worries, and you have a tendency to accomplish your goals using gentle and cunning means, regardless of truth or falsehood.

In the 2nd House (Aquarius),

Rahu indicates losses in the realm of wealth. You constantly worry about increasing your wealth and may engage in difficult and challenging actions to achieve financial gain. Sometimes, you may face great calamities in pursuit of wealth, leading to the separation of your family.

Rahu in the 3rd House (Pisces)

signifies great influence and courageous actions. You may experience some loss in the domain of siblings. You employ secret tactics to enhance your influence and display cleverness, caution, and haughtiness in your endeavors.

Rahu in the 4th House (Aries)

brings affliction to your mother and may cause deficiencies in your residential situation. Pleasures and happiness may be lacking, but you receive support from hidden powers or mystical realms.

Rahu in the 5th House (Taurus)

brings distress in matters related to children. You may experience educational deficiencies and have a desire for intoxicants. Your conversations may lack sincerity, as you are indifferent to truth or falsehood.

Rahu in the 6th House (Gemini)

signifies great influence and the ability to defeat enemies. You achieve significant victories through diplomacy, wisdom, and cleverness. You handle tasks carelessly and with pride, exhibiting control over diseases. You tend to be selfish, fearless, and haughty.

Rahu in the 7th House (Cancer)

indicates significant losses in your spouse's domain and deficiencies in sexual pleasures. Obstacles arise in your occupation, and you face mental worries concerning family matters. You may seek unauthorized advantages, being indiscriminate in pursuing sexual pleasures, and your mind may be unstable.

Rahu in the 8th House (Leo)

brings worries and diseases related to the lower abdomen. Your daily routine is filled with agony, and there may be blows to your longevity. Inheritance may be affected, and you may face distress when traveling to foreign countries. You have a desire to increase your wealth.

Rahu in the 9th House (Virgo)

brings anxieties about your life and encounters blows to your destiny. Deficiencies in following righteous paths (Dharma) are observed, but you display cleverness and cunning in your actions.

Rahu in the 10th House (Libra)

brings unhappiness in your father's domain and obstacles in business and progress. After facing worries, you are able to accomplish tasks connected with the government.

Rahu in the 11th House (Scorpio)

indicates significant gains and a relentless pursuit of more wealth. You desire gratuitous wealth and often worry about your income. Selfish tendencies may be present.

Rahu in the 12th House (Sagittarius)

suggests troubles regarding expenditure. You manage your expenses with some shortages, and greed may be a characteristic trait.

9.Ketu

Ketu in the 1st House (Capricorn)

indicates a strong obstinacy in your nature. You may experience wounds and physical worries. Fame and reputation are acquired even if it means disregarding disrepute. Troubles and obstacles do not deter you, and you possess a passionate and self-centered demeanor. You have a tendency to accomplish tasks through secretive means.

In the 2nd House (Aquarius),

Ketu signifies deficiencies in the realm of wealth. You work hard to acquire wealth but often face severe calamities and setbacks in your financial pursuits.

Ketu in the 3rd House (Pisces)

indicates energy and diligence in your actions. However, you may experience losses concerning your siblings and face severe failures. There may be a sense of physical and inner strength deficiency.

Ketu in the 4th House (Aries)

brings a lack of happiness from your mother. There may be separation from your motherland or birthplace, and obstacles may arise regarding buildings and residential places. You gain courage through the use of secret strategies and policies.

Ketu in the 5th House (Taurus)

suggests working with stable wisdom and inner knowledge. However, difficulties may arise in acquiring education, and you may face distress in matters related to children. You employ secretive methods and have little regard for truth or falsehood.

Ketu in the 6th House (Gemini)

indicates causing harm to enemies and overcoming diseases and difficulties. You exhibit fearlessness in your actions.

Ketu in the 7th House (Cancer)

brings loss and obstacles in your spouse's domain. Family life is marked by significant worries, and you may face numerous failures and losses in your occupation. There is a longing for sexual pleasures.

Ketu in the 8th House (Leo)

suggests troubles and disorders in the lower abdomen region. Daily routine is filled with worries, and there may be blows to your longevity. Traveling may also cause distress.

Ketu in the 9th House (Virgo)

brings worries regarding destiny. You may experience internal weakness and face delays in the rise of your fortune. Secret powers may be employed, and fame may be deficient. Neglect of righteous paths (Dharma) may be observed.

Ketu in the 10th House (Libra)

indicates obstacles in your father's domain and worries in business. You exert considerable effort for business progress, but there may be perplexity in dealings with the government. Selfishness and industriousness are notable traits.

Ketu in the 11th House (Scorpio)

suggests gaining numerous advantages and engaging in difficult actions for acquiring wealth. Secret methods are employed to increase wealth, and stability is found in income. Selfish tendencies prevail.

Ketu in the 12th House (Sagittarius)

implies extravagant spending and managing expenditures with great force. Controlling expenses may be challenging, and there is a tendency to have blind faith in others.

13. Predictions of the Planets with Reference to Aquarius Ascendant

1. Sun

Predictions of Sun in Aquarius Ascendant

Sun in the 1st House (Aquarius)

You may get an influential wife and pursue an influential occupation. You may have some weakness in both your body and the power to enjoy sexual pleasures. You give much dignity to your wife but may also have some enmity. You get honor, possess vigor, and may feel unsatisfied even after accomplishing big tasks.

Sun in the 2nd House (Pisces)

You earn wealth through your occupation and may have fascination in the house of your wife. You have some influence in your daily routine of life and do valuable deeds. You possess family.

Sun in the 3rd House (Aries)

You pursue a great business and accomplish daily tasks very influentially. You may get an influential wife and have the dignity of power of brother and family. You may have an excess of sexual pleasures, labor very hard, have weakness in destiny, and deficiency in Dharma.

Sun in the 4th House (Taurus)

You enjoy some happiness from the house of your wife and also from the house of occupation. You pay attention to work regularly for progress.

Sun in the 5th House (Gemini)

You pursue business with the power of intellect and get a wise wife. You get influential and clever progeny, get technical education, talk very influentially, secure intellectual advice from your wife, and are always careful in acquiring gains.

Sun in the 6th House (Cancer)

You get influence from the house of your wife and maintain it. You face some struggle with your wife, bear some hardships in your occupation, gain some influence from the line of your occupation, manage a business, get victory over enemies, and have some bitterness in spending.

Sun in the 7th House (Leo)

You gain influential power from your occupation, experience some distress in your body, maintain great influence on your family, and face some disturbance due to sexual pleasures.

Sun in the 8th House (Virgo)

You may face restlessness and distress in the house of your wife, have deficiency in the side of sexual pleasures, bear hardship in the line of your occupation, get association from foreign countries in your occupation, face some troubles and separation in the house of your family, and have some defects in your organs.

Sun in the 9th House (Libra)

You may experience some weakness in luck and also in the side of your occupation. You may have weakness in rearing Dharma, get the power of brothers and sisters, and have deficiency in the side of sexual pleasures.

Sun in the 10th House (Scorpio)

You pursue your daily occupation with great influence and honor in the line of your occupation. You get power through your wife, get influential wife and sexual pleasures, get honor in government, are a good manager, and have some deficiency in the house of your mother.

Sun in the 11th House (Sagittarius)

You earn much wealth through your daily occupation, gain influence in your occupation, get great honor from your wife and gain much wealth through her. You get the advantage of children and education, and are highly intelligent.

Sun in the 12th House (Capricorn)

You may bear loss in the house of your wife, get loss in occupation, have great deficiency in the side of sexual pleasures, get loss and disturbance in family, have sourness in the house of expenditure, get the support of some other place in the side of sexual pleasures, keep influence in the house of enemy, and have perplexities like diseases and deficiency of cleverness in the worldly affairs.

2. Moon

Predictions of Moon in Aquarius Ascendant

Moon in the 1st House (Aquarius)

You may gain honor through the power of concentration but suffer from physical perplexities and cold. You may experience some mental disorder and struggle with your wife. You use secret policies in your line of occupation.

Moon in the 2nd House (Pisces)

You accumulate wealth but may face some separation in the family. You maintain influence over your enemies and live a majestic life.

Moon in the 3rd House (Aries)

You put forward energetic deeds and gain influence due to the power of concentration. You suppress your enemies but may face opposition from your brother. You take great care about Dharma, work hard, and possess power.

Moon in the 4th House (Taurus)

You do not care for the enemy's side but experience hindrance in peace and happiness. There may be distress in the house of your mother and some influence in the house of land. You may face weakness in business relations with the government and display carelessness.

Moon in the 5th House (Gemini)

You face some distress from the children's side and have some deficiency in education. You think of great strategies to gain wealth and have fluctuating speech.

Moon in the 6th House (Cancer)

You are very careful and cautious in dealing with enemies and achieve victory. You do not care about calamities, spend freely, remain happy and carefree, utilize influence in expenditure, and can be a formidable enemy.

Moon in the 7th House (Leo)

You diligently pursue your occupation but face perplexities of concentration. You experience enmity in the house of your wife and sexual pleasures, suffer distress and bondage in the body, and may face complaints of smallpox in the wife's side. You employ diplomacy in your occupation.

Moon in the 8th House (Virgo)

You bear perplexities in the enemies' side, experience some stomach troubles, strive hard for wealth accumulation, and have a disturbed mind.

Moon in the 9th House (Libra)

You have some anxieties in the house of destiny, maintain influence over your enemies, perform laborious and energetic deeds, face some enmity from brothers and sisters, maintain friendly relations with enemies, and have a peaceful disposition.

Moon in the 10th House (Scorpio)

You experience restlessness in the house of your father, face hardships, incur losses in the way of progress, and encounter blows and shocks in the house of honor and respect from the government. You may feel somewhat restless in the house of enemies and regret past sins.

Moon in the 11th House (Sagittarius)

You gain by suppressing your enemies but experience mental distress and perplexities in the house of receipts and gains. You desire wealth without much effort, face some trouble with progeny, have deficiencies in education, and do not care much about diseases and afflictions.

Moon in the 12th House (Capricorn)

You experience weakness in the house of enemies and in your influence. You employ secret policies in dealing with enemies and face perplexity due to heavy expenditure. You spend money on diseases.

3. Mars

Predictions of Mars in Aquarius Ascendant

Mars in the 1st House (Aquarius)

You make progress due to the vigour of your body, utilizing your good working power and courage. You have a harmonious association with your father and brother in an ordinary manner. There may be uneasiness in the side of your mother, but you achieve progress in your occupation. You earn honor and a good reputation with the government and society. However, you may face some perplexity in your wife's house and have some seminal defects.

Mars in the 2nd House (Pisces)

You acquire respect and receive support from your father. You may experience some bondage with your brother. You make efforts to acquire wealth and pay attention to religious deeds. You gain power in education and have some influence over your children. You strive hard for the progress of your destiny.

Mars in the 3rd House (Aries)

You possess great authority and influence in government and society. You defeat your enemies and have the support of your brother. You are dignified and energetic.

Mars in the 4th House (Taurus)

You receive support from your father and experience the usual happiness of your mother and brother, although there may be some deficiencies. You receive great honor from the government and society. You own buildings and property and maintain influence in the side of your wife. You secure a good income through your deeds and are very influential.

Mars in the 5th House (Gemini)

You possess knowledge of royal education and receive support from your father and brother. You tend to spend a lot and may act hastily. However, you acquire good gains.

Mars in the 6th House (Cancer)

You may feel restless and face opposition with your father and brother. However, you possess hidden power and can overcome your enemies deceitfully. You tend to spend a lot and face hindrances in your position. You gain respect in foreign places.

Mars in the 7th House (Leo)

You pursue your occupation with great respect and honor. You have brothers and sisters and manage affairs smoothly in the government and society. You maintain influence in the house of your wife and are a good administrator.

Mars in the 8th House (Virgo)

You may experience losses in the house of your father and have debilitated relationships with your brothers and sisters. You acquire income through hard labor and face deficiencies in honor and respect. There may be a lack of proper dress.

Mars in the 9th House (Libra)

You are very fortunate and experience progress in business or occupation through destiny and energy. You perform religious formalities and tend to spend a lot. You gain strength in terms of happiness and buildings and receive honor in the government and society.

Mars in the 10th House (Scorpio)

You are very powerful and pursue an independent occupation. You gain great respect in the government and society. You acquire land and buildings and may not pay much attention to your brothers and sisters. You wear rich clothing, acquire administrative education, and become a legal expert.

Mars in the 11th House (Sagittarius)

You acquire a huge income through business occupation and gain much from your father. You enjoy gains from the government and society, and your brother supports you. You exert full power to accumulate wealth, possess keen wisdom, have children, achieve success in the enemies' house, wear good clothes and ornaments, and wield influence.

Mars in the 12th House (Capricorn)

You tend to spend a lot and incur losses in the house of your father. Your contact with your brother may be strange. You experience loss in your business occupation and employ secret power in the house of your enemies. You possess influence in the house of your wife and gain strength in

4. Mercury

Predictions of Mercury in Aquarius Ascendant

Mercury in the 1st House (Aquarius)

You have a long life and live your daily routine majestically. You acquire good education and wisdom. However, you may face some perplexity in relation to your children. There are both friendship and challenges in your marital life. You use shrewdness in business matters.

Mercury in the 2nd House (Pisces)

You may have deficiencies in education and children. There is weakness in accumulating wealth, and you experience loss and distress in your family. You gain wisdom but live a life restricted by narrow perspectives of education and wisdom. You have a stubborn power of intellect and may engage in obstinate discussions.

Mercury in the 3rd House (Aries)

You possess the power of education and intellect. You have children, but also face some distress in that area. Your relationship with your siblings brings both power and challenges. Your longevity is increased, and you speak authoritatively on worldly matters. You utilize intellect and courage in your travels and live a carefree life.

Mercury in the 4th House (Taurus)

Your longevity is increased, and you live your life intelligently and comfortably. However, you may feel uneasiness in your relationship with your mother. There may be some deficiencies in the area of children, and you may experience some loss in properties and lands.

Mercury in the 5th House (Gemini)

You possess great wisdom and education. There may be uneasiness in your relationship with your children. You have a long life and accumulate wealth. You tend to hide things in formal affairs and may experience some mental distress and confusion.

Mercury in the 6th House (Cancer)

You face loss and affliction in various areas of life. There may be distress in your relationship with children and deficiencies in education. You worry intellectually and adopt modesty in your daily routine. You face obstacles and disturbances in life, and may experience stomach complaints.

Mercury in the 7th House (Leo)

You acquire education and have children. You work with wisdom in your occupation and may feel fascination and perplexity in your marital life. You have a good lifespan and engage in worldly and domestic affairs in your daily routine. You receive honor but may face some deficiencies in sexual pleasures.

Mercury in the 8th House (Virgo)

There may be some weakness in education. You have a long lifespan but experience distress in relation to children. You tend to neglect accumulated wealth and possess clever speech.

Mercury in the 9th House (Libra)

You gain advantages from already accumulated wealth. You have a good lifespan and experience good fortune in your daily routine. You have religious knowledge and may feel some anxiety related to destiny. There may be some perplexity in your relationship with siblings. You have children and are very clever.

Mercury in the 10th House (Scorpio)

You acquire worldly knowledge and have children. You have a good lifespan and live your daily routine with great influence. However, you may experience losses in your father's house and face troubles in business and occupation. There may be some worries in relation to the government, and you may feel some perplexity in your relationship with your mother.

Mercury in the 11th House (Sagittarius)

You gain education and enjoy the advantages of children and already accumulated wealth. You benefit from a long lifespan and have a successful daily routine. You are honorable.

Mercury in the 12th House (Capricorn)

You may experience the loss of children and weakness in education. There is weakness in your lifespan, and you tend to spend a lot. You feel restless in your daily routine and maintain a sense of equality in your relationship with enemies.

5. Jupiter

Predictions of Jupiter in Aquarius Ascendant

Jupiter in the 1st House (Aquarius)

indicates income and wealth acquired through diligence. You earn respect and honor for your body and benefit from children and education. Your speech is filled with wisdom and positivity. You experience progress in destiny and gain from your occupation. The house of your spouse brings advantages, and your desires are fulfilled. You have a somewhat dependent nature.

Jupiter in the 2nd House (Pisces)

signifies great wealth and substantial gains. You put whole-hearted effort into accumulating income and hold significant influence over your enemies. You work hard and employ strategies to pursue big business ventures and accumulate wealth. You receive substantial gains from your father's house and earn respect from both the government and society. Your family holds influence and is influential in its own right.

Jupiter in the 3rd House (Aries)

suggests earning wealth through your vigor. You pursue your occupation with great enthusiasm and generate considerable profit in business. You have a beautiful spouse who provides support. Your brothers and sisters also offer assistance. You embrace righteousness and experience gains in various forms, including clothes, ornaments, and wealth. There is a fascination for sexual pleasures within your heart, and you appreciate beauty.

Jupiter in the 4th House (Taurus)

indicates the accumulation of wealth. You enjoy the daily routine of life and make efforts to curtail excessive expenditures. You gain respect and advantages from the government and society. Wealth brings you happiness, and you acquire buildings and property.

Jupiter in the 5th House (Gemini)

suggests great wisdom and educational achievements. You have children and gain wealth through education. Your words hold value, and you enjoy significant gains. You uphold righteousness and maintain dignity.

Jupiter in the 6th House (Cancer)

indicates immense wealth and a tendency to misuse it. You may unexpectedly receive wealth as if it were a gift. However, you tend to spend it in a narrow and inappropriate manner.

Jupiter in the 7th House (Leo)

pursues significant business or occupation leveraging your wealth. You earn substantial wealth through your occupation and accumulate wealth after marriage. You enjoy various advantages and receive strength from your brothers and sisters. A fixed income is sufficient, and you possess cleverness in wealth accumulation.

Jupiter in the 8th House (Virgo)

suggests losses of both people and wealth. You work hard and travel to foreign countries in search of income, but you still do not achieve sufficient earnings. Wealth comes to you sporadically.

Jupiter in the 9th House (Libra)

indicates the acquisition of wealth through the power of destiny. You gain wisdom, education, and cleverness. You have children and possess a self-conceited nature.

Jupiter in the 10th House (Scorpio)

pursues significant business or occupation and earns wealth. You receive much respect and honor from the government and society. You derive strength from your father and support from your mother. You have great influence in the house of enemies.

Jupiter in the 11th House (Sagittarius)

suggests heavy income and success due to your strong determination. You benefit from children and have brothers and sisters. Your wife and father-in-law provide assistance, and you are respected and cheerful.

Jupiter in the 12th House (Capricorn)

indicates losses and deficiencies in wealth. You manage to curtail expenditures and acquire wealth through bribery. You gain influence in the house of enemies but face deficiencies and distress within the family. You receive gains in the form of buildings and lands and experience aristocracy in your daily routine. However, you do not have access to good garments or ornaments.

6.Venus

Predictions of Venus in Aquarius Ascendant

Venus in the 1st House (Aquarius)

signifies great happiness and good luck. You derive happiness from your mother and acquire lands and buildings. You enjoy food, drink, and clothes and uphold righteousness. Divine support and fame are bestowed upon you. You find success in your occupation and experience happiness in your family, although some enmity may be present.

Venus in the 2nd House (Pisces)

indicates the acquisition of significant wealth. You experience happiness and prosperity through the increase of wealth. Your family expands, and you acquire lands and buildings. You accumulate virtue and increase your wealth with the help of destiny. However, there may be some deficiencies in your daily routine, and you may face weaknesses associated with age.

Venus in the 3rd House (Aries)

suggests comfortable progress in destiny. You acquire buildings and property and have supportive brothers and a mother. You possess cleverness and foresight and gain fame. You utilize the strength of justice and value peace.

Venus in the 4th House (Taurus)

indicates the practice of religious formalities. You acquire land and buildings and receive support from your mother. Happiness comes to you through destiny, and you engage in business pursuits. You benefit from your father and gain honor and prestige in society and government.

Venus in the 5th House (Gemini)

suggests the birth of good children. You acquire good education and wisdom and derive power from your mother. You find happiness in owning land and property and may write articles on divine subjects. You possess foresight.

Venus in the 6th House (Cancer)

indicates weaknesses in destiny and opposition from others. You face obstacles to peace and happiness and tend to spend a lot. However, you are able to suppress enemies and provide free medicine for certain diseases. You help alleviate the worries of others.

Venus in the 7th House (Leo)

brings happiness and auspiciousness to your family, although there may be some deficiencies in mutual love. You may experience unhappiness from others but possess strength in terms of land and buildings. You have a good physique and work satisfactorily and truthfully in your occupation.

Venus in the 8th House (Virgo)

suggests significant weaknesses in matters of righteousness. You experience losses in your mother's house and deficiencies in happiness. There may be weaknesses in your land, buildings, and property. Destiny may not favor you initially, and you may feel restless in foreign countries. You strive to earn more money.

Venus in the 9th House (Libra)

indicates great fortune and adherence to righteousness. You gain fame and derive strength from your mother.

You possess the dignity of land, buildings, and property and receive divine assistance. You receive help from your brothers and sisters and exhibit foresight, knowledge, and cleverness.

Venus in the 10th House (Scorpio)

suggests attaining a high position due to destiny. You enjoy authority and benefits from the government and society. You receive support from your parents and derive strength from land and property. You indulge in royal pleasures and demonstrate competence in your business affairs. You value peace and justice.

Venus in the 11th House (Sagittarius)

indicates significant gains through the power of destiny. You receive help from your mother's house and benefit from land. You engage in religious deeds and acquire food, clothes, and ornaments. You receive education and speak modestly, demonstrating foresight, selfishness, and virtue.

Venus in the 12th House (Capricorn)

suggests excessive spending and weaknesses in destiny. You experience the loss of your mother and weaknesses in land, buildings, or your place of residence. There may be deficiencies in happiness.

7. Saturn

Predictions of Saturn in Aquarius Ascendant

Saturn in the 1st House (Aquarius)

indicates a strong willpower and self-respect. You may gain some fame, but you may also experience losses in the house of your siblings. Afflictions and weaknesses may arise in your relationships with your spouse and father. Your occupation, business, and prestige may suffer, and you may face difficulties in dealing with the government and society.

Saturn in the 2nd House (Pisces)

suggests efforts to increase your wealth through your physical abilities. However, there may be occasional losses in your wealth, and you strive to control your expenses. You may receive some benefits from your mother and land.

Saturn in the 3rd House (Aries)

indicates a tendency to easily become tired. You work secretly and may experience physical weakness and have a short stature. There may be deficiencies in your appearance. You tend to spend a lot and try to reduce your expenses. Losses may occur in your relationships with your siblings, and you may follow a narrow and misguided path, resulting in incorrect spending. You may experience both losses and strengths in the areas of education and children.

Saturn in the 4th House (Taurus)

signifies significant influence and spiritual knowledge. You have a handsome physique and enjoy physical luxuries. However, you may experience losses in matters related to your mother, although you receive support from other women. Happiness may be lacking, and there may be deficiencies in your land and buildings. You have a strong influence over your enemies and safeguard your self-pride, but excessive expenditure causes worry.

Saturn in the 5th House (Gemini)

suggests authority, although there may be deficiencies in education. You possess self-knowledge but may face some enmity in your relationship with your spouse. You work diligently in your occupation but may encounter some difficulties.

Saturn in the 6th House (Cancer)

indicates influential actions and dignity, although with some dependence. You work courageously and patiently, but weakness may be present in your relationship with your siblings. You do not concern yourself with enemies and maintain dignity in your daily life. While you try to control expenditure, you are selfish and not particularly kind.

Saturn in the 7th House (Leo)

suggests perplexity in domestic life and deficiencies and enmity in your relationship with your spouse. You may experience worries and losses in your occupation but pay proper attention to Dharma. You may have a short stature.

Saturn in the 8th House (Virgo)

signifies hidden strength and engagement in risky activities. You have a long life but may experience physical concerns. There may be enmity in your relationship with your father, although you gain some strength in relation to your children. Education is also indicated.

Saturn in the 9th House (Libra)

suggests a handsome appearance and good fortune. You work hard to accumulate wealth and have a significant influence in the realm of your enemies. Deficiencies may arise in your relationship with your siblings, and you may spend a lot. However, you are overjoyed and fearless.

Saturn in the 10th House (Scorpio)

indicates influential actions and gaining respect after overcoming many difficulties. You tend to spend a lot and may experience losses in the house of your father. Some enmity may be present in your relationship with your spouse, and weaknesses may arise in your relationship with your mother. Nevertheless, you are highly industrious.

Saturn in the 11th House (Sagittarius)

suggests the potential to earn substantial wealth and gain fame. While you may spend a lot, you make efforts to control your expenses. There may be deficiencies in terms of age and children, as well as some physical weaknesses.

Saturn in the 12th House (Capricorn)

indicates a tendency to spend a lot. Your body may appear emaciated, but you pay attention to and uphold Dharma. You receive honor in foreign places and gain influence in the house of your enemies. However, there may be some losses in your wealth.

8. Rahu

Rahu in the 1st House (Aquarius)

You may experience physical perplexity and face calamities. You tend to use secret tactics and work hard to acquire name and fame. Your mind is always occupied with self-serving motives.

Rahu in the 2nd House (Pisces)

There may be a deficiency in wealth, and you may experience losses in the family. You manage your expenses by taking loans and relying on others for support. You may face fatal blows in matters related to wealth, and restlessness is common for you.

Rahu in the 3rd House (Aries)

You face troubles in your brother's house and work hard to make progress. You use secret devices to serve your own selfishness and remain cautious even when facing severe challenges. You possess great influence and energy.

Rahu in the 4th House (Taurus)

You may experience loss and separation in your mother's house and have a deficiency in happiness. You employ secret tactics to attain permanent happiness and face weakness in managing land and buildings.

Rahu in the 5th House (Gemini)

You possess cleverness and a sharp mind. You tend to deceive others and prioritize personal gains over truth or falsehood. You may face trouble from the side of children.

Rahu in the 6th House (Cancer)

You gain influence in the house of enemies and are able to defeat them. However, you also experience anxiety from the enemies' side. You are cautious and clever in dealing with such situations.

Rahu in the 7th House (Leo)

You may experience losses in your spouse's house and affliction from your spouse. There is weakness in sexual pleasures, and you may face calamities in your professional life. You engage in laborious deeds and unjustifiably benefit in family and occupation matters.

Rahu in the 8th House (Virgo)

You experience a mixture of dignity and troubles in your life. There may be uneasiness in matters related to hereditary property. You may have complaints related to the stomach and lower part of the body.

Rahu in the 9th House (Libra)

You face troubles and hindrances in matters related to destiny. There may be a deficiency in gaining fame, and you tend to manipulate any kind of religious or moral principles for self-serving purposes. You constantly strive to overcome the weaknesses of destiny.

Rahu in the 10th House (Scorpio)

You may experience afflictions in your father's house and encounter many worries in business and occupation. Obstacles arise in deeds connected with government and society, and you face problems in achieving higher positions. You utilize secret devices to acquire all-round progress.

Rahu in the 11th House (Sagittarius)

You gain a small amount of money through secretive policies and plans. There may be a deficiency in apparent income, and you work to alleviate worries related to income.

Rahu in the 12th House (Capricorn)

You tend to have extravagant expenditure and face unhappiness due to excessive spending. Your thoughts revolve around secret matters.

9. Ketu

Ketu's placement in Aquarius Ascendant brings a distinct influence on various aspects of your life. Let's explore the predictions for Ketu in each house:

Ketu in the 1st House (Aquarius)

suggests a feeling of deficiency in your body. You may not prioritize the well-being of others and instead focus on your own determination and individuality.

Ketu in the 2nd House (Pisces)

indicates a deficiency in accumulating wealth. You may experience losses in financial matters and face disturbances and separation within the family. However, you are willing to work hard to acquire wealth.

Ketu in the 3rd House (Aries)

brings great energy and courage. You may encounter distress in your relationship with siblings and possess secret plans. However, you may feel a lack of strength or stamina.

Ketu in the 4th House (Taurus)

signifies some losses in your mother's house. There may be weakness in matters related to land, property, and buildings. Acquiring happiness may feel complicated, but you have the patience to navigate through challenges.

Ketu in the 5th House (Gemini)

indicates achieving goals through the strength of falsehood. You devise secret schemes to accomplish your aims. Education may pose challenges, and there could be afflictions or difficulties related to children. Your memory may also be weak.

Ketu in the 6th House (Cancer)

brings victory in matters related to enemies. You may experience worries and troubles but remain unaffected by your adversaries. You employ secret schemes to suppress and overcome your enemies.

Ketu in the 7th House (Leo)

suggests distress in your spouse's house. Your occupation may also bring worries and potentially significant losses. There may be uneasiness or complications in your sexual relationships, but you possess a strong sexual drive.

Ketu in the 8th House (Virgo)

brings worries in your daily routine. You pay attention to even the most obscure matters and may face unexpected blows in matters related to longevity.

Despite fearful circumstances, you work fearlessly, and your influence remains intact.

Ketu in the 9th House (Libra)

indicates a deficiency in fame and in matters related to destiny. You cleverly utilize your secret powers, but you may struggle to rise in income or fortune. Your understanding of Dharma may not align with traditional norms.

Ketu in the 10th House (Scorpio)

suggests calamities in your father's house and troubles in business matters. You may face concerns in dealings with the government and society. However, you exhibit great patience and rely on secret powers to navigate through challenges. Your courage is hidden but evident in your industriousness.

Ketu in the 11th House (Sagittarius)

signifies substantial monetary gains through your grand and secret powers. You may prioritize personal benefits over ethical considerations. There is a tendency to pursue excessive gains and advantages.

Ketu in the 12th House (Capricorn)

indicates excessive spending and experiencing distress and agony due to financial extravagance. You rely on secret powers but struggle to control your expenditure.

14. Predictions for the placement of the Sun in Pisces Ascendant are as follows:

1. Sun

Predictions of Sun in Pisces Ascendant:

Sun in the 1st House (Pisces):

Experiences influential power and triumph over enemies. However, there may be some physical distress and a sense of bondage. There could be challenges in the spouse's house, as well as some deficiencies in sexual pleasures. Hindrances in occupation are likely, but the individual is highly industrious.

Sun in the 2nd House (Aries):

After significant hard work, there is potential for acquiring substantial wealth. However, there may also be some influence and separation within the family. Restlessness in daily life could be experienced.

Sun in the 3rd House (Taurus):

The individual is diligent and holds a strong regard for righteousness. Opposition from siblings is possible, and there may be some fatigue due to hard work. The person is known for their cleverness and illustriousness.

Sun in the 4th House (Gemini):

There could be distress in the house of parents and losses in lands, buildings, and residential properties. Happiness may be deficient, but respect and honor are gained in society. The individual tends to engage in forceful actions and wields influence.

Sun in the 5th House (Cancer):

There may be some deficiencies in education, and worries and difficulties could arise. The person strives for income and attains victory over enemies, but can come across as rude.

Sun in the 6th House (Leo):

The individual emerges victorious over enemies, gains significant influence, and possesses the power to remove troubles and calamities. There is a constant pressure maintained on adversaries.

Sun in the 7th House (Virgo):

Challenges are faced in the spouse's house, and there may be distress within the family. Hindrances and worries arise in the line of occupation, along with some deficiencies in sexual pleasures.

Sun in the 8th House (Libra):

Restlessness and hindrances are prominent in this placement. Complaints related to stomach disorders below the navel may arise. Work is accomplished in the enemies' domain through diplomatic tactics, but severe calamities can occur at times.

Sun in the 9th House (Scorpio):

Influence is maintained in the enemies' realm, but obstacles may be encountered in the house of destiny. Weakness in matters of righteousness and opposition from siblings are possible.

Sun in the 10th House (Sagittarius):

Through influence and diligence, advantages are gained from the government and society. Grand deeds are performed in the realms of governance and society, although opposition may arise in the father's house. Challenges and distress from the mother's side, obstacles in peace and happiness, as well as hindrances in matters of lands and buildings can be experienced. The person seeks sovereignty and is highly diligent.

Sun in the 11th House (Capricorn):

There may be uneasiness in the house of gains, worries, and problems arising from the children's side. Acquiring education may be deficient. Advantage is gained from the enemies' side, and the individual is known for their cleverness.

Sun in the 12th House (Aquarius):

There may be a sense of weakness in matters of influence. Work is accomplished secretly in the enemies' house. Troubles with siblings are likely, and hindrances may arise in managing expenditures. The person tends to be haughty and easily angered.

2. Moon

Predictions of Moon in Pisces Ascendant:

Moon in the 1st House (Pisces):

The individual possesses an ideal strength of mind, exhibits a unique splendor in education, and has dignified speech. There is grandeur and beauty in the children's side, and satisfaction is derived from the spouse. Success is attained in occupation, and there is a strong inclination towards sexual pleasures. Hidden knowledge is possessed.

Moon in the 2nd House (Aries):

Education is acquired, and wealth is earned through willpower. Happiness is experienced with progress in the family and increase in wealth. Some sense of bondage may be felt regarding children, but overall, the person is considered wealthy and respectable.

Moon in the 3rd House (Taurus):

Reliance is placed on education and intellect. The person gains the power of children and strength from brothers and sisters. There may be a lack of concern for righteousness and less faith in God. Happiness is derived from the mother, and acquisition of buildings and property is possible. Rise in honor within the government and society is observed, and business development occurs.

Moon in the 4th House (Gemini):

Happiness is obtained from children, and good education is achieved. Pleasure is derived from the mother, as well as from land, buildings, and property. A harmonious relationship with the father is maintained, and there is an elevation of honor in government and society. Progress in business is also indicated.

Moon in the 5th House (Cancer):

The individual is wise and learned, presenting convincing ideas. Happiness from children is experienced, and there is a balanced and stable mind. A gentle nature is possessed.

Moon in the 6th House (Leo):

Difficulties and deficiencies in education are faced. Distress may be encountered in the education of children. Work is accomplished through intricate thinking. Restlessness is experienced in the enemies' house, and significant expenditures are incurred.

Moon in the 7th House (Virgo):

Success in occupation is achieved through willpower. An educated and gentle spouse is obtained. There is a strong fascination for sexual pleasures, and the person is clever and of a happy disposition.

Moon in the 8th House (Libra):

There may be deficiencies in education and health issues in the children's side. Wealth is acquired through significant labor, and elegance is maintained in the daily routine. Progress in the family is attained.

Moon in the 9th House (Scorpio):

Weakness in education and intellect is experienced. Loss and distress may be encountered in the children's side. Attitude towards brothers and sisters is favorable, but there is a tendency to devise schemes for progress through improper means.

Moon in the 10th House (Sagittarius):

Great ability in education is displayed. Progress is gained from the father's house, and there is respect and honor in government and societal matters. Happiness is derived from the mother, and some strength is gained in lands and buildings. The person communicates in an authoritative manner.

Moon in the 11th House (Capricorn):

Good education is acquired, and wealth is earned. Some hindrances may be faced in the realm of income. Children are obtained, and there is a consistent focus on gains.

Moon in the 12th House (Aquarius):

Loss is experienced in the children's house, and there may be defects in the eyes. Weakness is observed in education, along with a poor memory and restlessness. Significant expenditures are incurred, and there is worry regarding finances. Influence is gained in the enemies' domain, and there is a slight tendency towards fear and an unstable mind.

3.Mars

Predictions of Mars in Pisces Ascendant:

Mars in the 1st House (Pisces):

The individual acquires wealth through destiny, adheres to Dharma (righteousness), and is considered fortunate. Ownership of lands, buildings, and happiness derived from the mother is indicated. Good fortune is obtained from the wife's side, and there is an aristocratic lifestyle. Pleasures are enjoyed within the family.

Mars in the 2nd House (Aries):

The person is rich and fortunate, with wealth influenced by destiny. However, there may be some deficiencies and restlessness in the children's side. Education and wisdom may be lacking, but an aristocratic lifestyle is maintained. Faith in God is present, and fame is attained.

Mars in the 3rd House (Taurus):

Dharma is emphasized, and advantages are gained from the government and society. Benefits are received from the father's house, and strength is derived from siblings. Influence is attained in the realm of enemies.

Mars in the 4th House (Gemini):

Ownership of buildings and property is indicated, along with the accumulation of wealth. There is a significant income, fulfillment of religious obligations, and cooperation from the mother. Good luck is obtained from the wife's house, and success is achieved in business and occupation. Overall, the individual is very fortunate.

Mars in the 5th House (Cancer):

Distress may be experienced concerning children, and there may be a deficiency in education. Accumulating wealth might be challenging, and weaknesses may be present in matters of Dharma. Significant expenditures are incurred, and there is no enjoyment derived from the house of expenditure.

Mars in the 6th House (Leo):

Success is attained through challenging means, and victory is achieved through intricate tactics. There is victory in the realm of enemies, but some enmity may arise in matters of expenditure and opposition from the family.

Mars in the 7th House (Virgo):

Occupational progress is experienced through good fortune. Wealth is earned, and there is financial advantage through the wife's good luck, although it may cause unrest in the relationship. The person engages in a large-scale business and gains advantages from the government and society. Cooperation is received from the father. Sexual pleasures are enjoyed, and there is a strong emphasis on wealth, with significant effort exerted to accumulate it.

Mars in the 8th House (Libra):

There may be some weakness in matters of destiny, and some loss of wealth is experienced. Obstacles are encountered in accumulating wealth, but substantial income is gained from foreign sources. Good fortune is observed in the daily routine of life, and some enmity may arise with siblings.

Mars in the 9th House (Scorpio):

The individual is considered fortunate and religious, earning wealth through the power of destiny. Pleasures are derived from the family, although some enmity may exist with siblings. Possession of land and buildings is indicated, and assistance is received from the mother. Influence is attained.

Mars in the 10th House (Sagittarius):

The person is highly influential, commanding great honor and respect. Advantages are enjoyed from the government and society, and the occupation is pursued on a large scale. Communication may be somewhat harsh. Deficiencies may be present in the children's side and in education. Ownership of land and buildings is obtained, and religious obligations are observed.

Mars in the 11th House (Capricorn):

Numerous monetary advantages are gained, and wealth is accumulated unexpectedly. Gracious and grand advantages are obtained, although there may be deficiencies in education and in the children's side. Influence is gained in the realm of enemies, and the person naturally escapes troubles. Family happiness is experienced, and attention is given to increasing wealth.

Mars in the 12th House (Aquarius):

Significant wealth losses are indicated, along with weakness in matters of destiny. The person may spend a lot due to helplessness, and the relationship with siblings is ordinary. Progress is made in daily occupation, and good luck is found in the wife's house. Losses may occur within the family, and there may be a lack of financial discipline.

4.Mercury

Mercury in the 1st House (Pisces):

Has a slender body, experiences some lack of happiness from the mother, faces deficiencies in properties and possessions, encounters challenges in the spouse's house, achieves occupational progress through physical labor, and indulges in sexual affairs without justification.

Mercury in the 2nd House (Aries):

Earns wealth through a respectable occupation, gains strength in properties and possessions, faces some restrictions on family happiness, encounters limitations from the spouse's side, experiences deficiencies in sexual pleasures, and finds happiness in the daily routine of life.

Mercury in the 3rd House (Taurus):

Achieves success in occupation, derives strength from the mother, gains power from properties, siblings, and the spouse, lives comfortably, and enjoys sexual pleasures.

Mercury in the 4th House (Gemini):

Gains strength from properties and possessions, experiences immense family happiness, finds great joy from the mother, achieves occupational success, and benefits from the government and society.

Mercury in the 5th House (Cancer):

Pursues occupation comfortably, manages family affairs well, enjoys the happiness of the spouse and children, indulges in excess sexual pleasures, and derives satisfaction from properties and possessions, although there may be some physical weaknesses.

Mercury in the 6th House (Leo):

Experiences separation in the mother's house, encounters conflicts from the spouse's side, faces weaknesses in properties and possessions, encounters troubles in the occupation, manages the enemy's house peacefully, and tends to spend extravagantly.

Mercury in the 7th House (Virgo):

Attracts a beautiful spouse, pursues influential occupation with success and happiness, gains respect in the mother's house, indulges in excessive happiness and sexual pleasures, and enjoys properties and possessions.

Mercury in the 8th House (Libra):

Experiences losses in the mother's and spouse's house, faces deficiencies in properties and possessions, encounters a lack of happiness, manages affairs through occupation, receives support from foreign countries, enjoys a long life, and finds happiness in the daily routine of life.

Mercury in the 9th House (Scorpio):

Enjoys good fortune within the family, receives affection from the mother, gains increased wealth through the spouse, achieves success in the daily occupation, has a religious spouse, finds happiness with siblings, and possesses properties and possessions.

Mercury in the 10th House (Sagittarius):

Experiences royal pleasures and happiness, gains prestige through the spouse, enjoys domestic happiness, possesses power in properties and possessions, pursues a significant occupation, benefits from the government and society, lives in a well-decorated house, and conducts noble deeds.

Mercury in the 11th House (Capricorn):

Earns substantial gains and income comfortably through the occupation, benefits from properties and possessions, receives advantages from the spouse, enjoys sexual pleasures, gains happiness from children and the mother, achieves success in education, and communicates eloquently.

Mercury in the 12th House (Aquarius):

Experiences some losses in the mother's and spouse's house, faces deficiencies in properties and possessions, encounters limitations in occupation and lacks happiness and comforts, has deficiencies in sexual pleasures, spends extensively through foreign contacts in the pursuit of the occupation, and accomplishes tasks diplomatically in the enemies' house.

5.Jupiter

Jupiter in the 1st House (Pisces):

Gains dignity and engages in noble deeds, possesses a combination of worldly and divine qualities, has a strong physique, receives support from the father, attains a good education, possesses special power related to children, enjoys honor in government and society, is respected in the spouse's family, lives with majesty, and holds great self-esteem.

Jupiter in the 2nd House (Aries):

Obtains strength from the wealth inherited from the father, earns abundant wealth, manages a significant occupation, commands great respect in government and society, enjoys dignity in wealth and family matters, wields influence in the domain of enemies, overcomes difficulties and obstacles, and exerts considerable influence.

Jupiter in the 3rd House (Taurus):

Achieves progress through hard work and ancestral deeds, receives support from the government and society, faces some opposition from siblings, experiences a deficiency in income, upholds righteousness, gains dignity in the chosen occupation, enjoys magnificence in marriage, possesses influence and finds pleasure within the family, exhibits a stubborn nature, and exerts influence.

Jupiter in the 4th House (Gemini):

Leads a comfortable life, possesses strength through land and properties, exerts great influence within the family, experiences parental happiness, pursues the chosen occupation joyfully through personal determination, lives with authority and sovereignty, enjoys a long life, and faces some enmity within the domain of expenditures.

Jupiter in the 5th House (Cancer):

Obtains significant wisdom and knowledge, possesses extensive learning, excels as an influential orator, gains strength from the father and children, possesses a handsome physique, strongly upholds righteousness, experiences a deficiency in income, exhibits self-conceit, enjoys fame, and possesses foresight.

Jupiter in the 6th House (Leo):

Performs influential deeds, albeit with some dependency, faces opposition from the father's side, accumulates wealth, benefits from the government and society, experiences a unique combination of dependence and independence, endeavors to heal others' wounds even when personally facing perplexities.

Jupiter in the 7th House (Virgo):

Possesses a handsome physique, achieves occupational progress through physical labor and determination, earns respect in the chosen occupation, finds happiness within the spouse's family, enjoys sexual pleasures, experiences some deficiency in income, and faces some enmity with siblings.

Jupiter in the 8th House (Libra):

Gains respect through majestic work, faces distress from the father's side, possesses a lean body, encounters obstacles in progress, experiences dissatisfaction from the government and society, faces concerns within the domain of expenditures, maintains some dignity in daily life routines.

Jupiter in the 9th House (Scorpio):

Enjoys great fortune, is religious and just, receives advantages from the government, society, and father, possesses a handsome body, enhances willpower and divine power, maintains purity in the heart, benefits from children, communicates eloquently, values self-respect, places less importance on siblings, and possesses influence and extensive knowledge.

Jupiter in the 10th House (Sagittarius):

Engages in significant business pursuits, shares equal responsibilities with the father in the business, receives great honor and respect from the government and society, accumulates increased wealth, finds happiness from the mother and land, and wields influence within the domain of enemies.

Jupiter in the 11th House (Capricorn):

Exhibits laziness and encounters some deficiencies and distress in income-related matters, experiences weaknesses in financial gains associated with the father, possesses some strength through children, gains respect in the chosen occupation, and is talkative.

Jupiter in the 12th House (Aquarius):

Experiences loss within the father's domain, possesses a lean body, feels restless, manages government and societal affairs despite enduring significant losses, faces weaknesses in honor and business, encounters deficiencies within the domain of expenditures, spends frivolously, and wields influence within the realm of enemies.

6. Venus

Venus in the 1st House (Pisces):

You have a tall stature and are known for your diligence and energy. You enjoy an increased lifespan and live life majestically. However, there may be some deficiencies in your relationship with your spouse and in your diurnal occupation.

Venus in the 2nd House (Aries):

You may experience some bondage in your relationship with your siblings. Despite this, you find aristocracy in your daily routine and have a long lifespan. You have the ability to acquire wealth through diplomatic means, although there may be some losses in your existing wealth.

Venus in the 3rd House (Taurus):

You may face troubles with your siblings, but you take pride in your daily routine. Your lifespan is favorable, and you have a fearless and influential nature. However, you may occasionally compromise on righteous behavior.

Venus in the 4th House (Gemini):

You may experience some loss in your relationship with your mother, but you find happiness through your siblings. Your lifespan is long, and you take pleasure in your daily routine. Finding happiness may be challenging, and your relationship with your father may be unhappy. However, you find some happiness in foreign countries and possess cleverness and honor.

Venus in the 5th House (Cancer):

You may face distress in relation to your children, but you find pleasure in your daily routine. Your lifespan is long, and you have affection for your siblings despite some deficiencies.

Venus in the 6th House (Leo):

You may feel restless in your life and face opposition from your siblings. You depend somewhat on others, and you may be prone to stomach diseases.

Venus in the 7th House (Virgo):

You experience worries in your daily routine due to family and spouse. There may be some loss in your relationship with your spouse, and you face great calamities and worries in your occupation. You may experience the loss of siblings but gain benefits in matters of longevity. Your sexual pleasures may not bring you much happiness, but you possess secret cleverness and courage.

Venus in the 8th House (Libra):

You enjoy an increased lifespan and find great happiness in your daily routine. However, you may experience some loss of energy and face the loss of siblings. You strive hard to acquire wealth and possess some farsightedness.

Venus in the 9th House (Scorpio):

You find great joy in your daily routine through destiny, although there may be some deficiencies in fame. You demonstrate cleverness in your actions.

Venus in the 10th House (Sagittarius):

You may experience some losses in matters related to your father, but you gain strength from your siblings. You enjoy elegance in your age and live your daily routine influentially. You make great efforts to progress in matters of happiness and land, earning honor in government and society through clever and difficult tasks. You are courageous in your endeavors.

Venus in the 11th House (Capricorn):

You enjoy a long life and benefit from your siblings. You find pleasure in your daily routine but may experience some agony in relation to your children. There may be some deficiencies in education, and you may feel uneasy in matters of income.

Venus in the 12th House (Aquarius):

You may experience restlessness in your life and encounter losses in matters of age. Restlessness from your siblings may also be present. You tend to spend liberally but possess the strength to earn a livelihood. You have the ability to overcome enemies and calamities.

7. Saturn

Saturn in the 1st House (Pisces):

You may appear physically weak internally but maintain a good external appearance. You face opposition from your father and have both friendly and weak relationships with your siblings. There may be losses in your marriage, and you work hard in your occupation. However, you may encounter hindrances in dealing with the government and society.

Saturn in the 2nd House (Aries):

You experience weakness in accumulating wealth and suffer heavy losses in matters of wealth. There may be some losses in your relationship with your mother. However, you find joy in your diurnal occupation and daily routine. There may be some deficiencies in your family life.

Saturn in the 3rd House (Taurus):

You are highly energetic but tend to spend more than you earn. You may experience some losses through your siblings and face deficiencies in education. Losses in the realm of children are possible, and there may be some loss in matters of righteousness and fame. You may also have physical strength weaknesses.

Saturn in the 4th House (Gemini):

You experience both losses and gains in various aspects of life. You balance your expenditures but may face weaknesses in your residence. You hold influence in the house of enemies and may experience losses in land. However, you possess courage.

Saturn in the 5th House (Cancer):

You face losses in matters related to children and experience mixed results in education. Weaknesses may be present in the accumulation of wealth, and separation in the family is possible. There are both losses and gains in your occupation and in your relationship with your spouse. You tend to speak selfishly.

Saturn in the 6th House (Leo):

You gain strength from managing expenses and gains. You handle affairs courageously and maintain influence in your diurnal occupation and daily routine. There may be a weak connection with your siblings.

Saturn in the 7th House (Virgo):

You experience both losses and gains in matters of expenditure. Anxiety may be present in matters of righteousness, and there may be deficiencies in happiness due to income and expenditure.

Saturn in the 8th House (Libra):

You lead a happy life and spend your income in a dignified manner. You enjoy a long lifespan but may face weaknesses in accumulating wealth. There may be some enmity with your father, and you experience both losses and gains in matters related to children.

Saturn in the 9th House (Scorpio):

You gain substantial income through destiny but need to work hard for it. You hold great influence over enemies and tend to be self-focused.

Saturn in the 10th House (Sagittarius):

You experience losses in matters related to your father and tend to spend excessively. Dealing with excessive expenditures and weaknesses in connection with the government and society may be challenging. There may be losses in your business occupation and mixed results in matters of happiness, mother, and spouse. Your success in your diurnal occupation may be ordinary.

Saturn in the 11th House (Capricorn):

You gain significant monetary benefits and experience great happiness in your daily routine. However, there may be perplexities in matters of income and expenditure. Worries may arise in matters related to children, and there may be weaknesses in education. You tend to be self-focused.

Saturn in the 12th House (Aquarius):

You tend to spend more than you earn and face weaknesses in matters of wealth. Restlessness may be present within the family, and you may feel anxious about destiny. However, you maintain influence over enemies, overcome difficulties, and genuinely wish well for others.

8.Rahu

Rahu in the 1st House (Pisces):

You may experience physical anxieties and deficiencies. There could be occasional blows to the body. You have a clever and cautious approach to getting things done, employing secretive tactics. You are hardworking and diligent.

Rahu in the 2nd House (Aries):

You may face financial losses and distress. Family matters may also cause difficulties. Progress comes after struggling and taking risks. You utilize secret powers and work hard to acquire wealth.

Rahu in the 3rd House (Taurus):

You achieve success through energetic efforts and hard work. There may be some worries related to your brothers. You may resort to unfair means at times. You are clever and carefree in your approach.

Rahu in the 4th House (Gemini):

You encounter obstacles in your pursuit of happiness. You may own properties and experience vanity regarding your mother. Hindrances may arise in finding your true place or establishing a stable foundation.

Rahu in the 5th House (Cancer):

Challenges arise in matters concerning children. There may be deficiencies in education, and you might experience mental and intellectual concerns. You tackle difficult problems with wisdom and willpower.

Rahu in the 6th House (Leo):

You face obstacles from enemies but manage to overcome them. Hard work, cleverness, and patience lead to victory in difficult circumstances and calamities. You tend to disregard illnesses. Selfishness and courage are prominent traits.

Rahu in the 7th House (Virgo):

You work diligently for the progress of your occupation. Troubles may arise in your married life, but you find stability and happiness after facing worries within the family. There may be deep calamities related to your work.

Rahu in the 8th House (Libra):

You experience concerns in your daily routine. Health issues below the stomach might arise. Despite numerous difficulties, you gain stability in your daily life. There may be severe setbacks in matters of longevity, and obstacles in traveling to foreign countries.

Rahu in the 9th House (Scorpio):

You face hindrances in matters of destiny and incur losses in matters of righteousness. Sudden blows of fate may be encountered, and there may be deficiencies in fame.

Rahu in the 10th House (Sagittarius):

There may be losses in the house of your father, as well as restlessness in societal and governmental affairs.

You may follow a path of deterioration and face setbacks in matters of honor and prestige.

Rahu in the 11th House (Capricorn):

You strive to acquire profits beyond your capacity and tend to accumulate more wealth. You desire to obtain wealth without putting in much effort. Worries may arise in matters of gains, but you may not prioritize the benefits.

Rahu in the 12th House (Aquarius):

You tend to spend excessively and experience confusion in matters of expenditure. You cleverly accomplish your goals through secretive means and the assistance of others in your occupation. Nervousness may be felt in matters of expenditure.

9. Ketu

Ketu in the 1st House (Pisces):

You may experience fatal blows to your body and encounter dangers. There may be deficiencies in your physical appearance, and you might feel bound and dependent. You tend to utilize your strength secretly.

Ketu in the 2nd House (Aries):

You face great difficulties in matters of wealth and suffer from the pain of lacking it. There may be distress in your family and a strong inclination to work hard and increase your wealth. Restlessness may be present.

Ketu in the 3rd House (Taurus):

You are bold and work diligently. Restlessness may arise in your relationship with your siblings. You possess immense physical strength and courage. Severe calamities may be encountered, but you work patiently and believe nothing is impossible.

Ketu in the 4th House (Gemini):

You experience the loss and separation of your mother. There is a significant deficiency in matters of happiness and home. You may live in a small house and face troubles with neighbors and colleagues. You come into contact with people from lower social classes and experience losses in buildings and property. You rely on secret powers to seek happiness.

Ketu in the 5th House (Cancer):

You face severe calamities in matters related to children. There may be deficiencies in education, and you experience mental anxieties from a young age. However, after overcoming significant obstacles, you may gain stable power in education, although others may struggle to understand your ideas.

Ketu in the 6th House (Leo):

You disrupt the plans of your enemies and opponents. You work diligently and patiently, despite disturbances caused by enemies. You achieve victory over troubles and difficulties and possess secret strength. However, you tend to be selfish and obstinate.

Ketu in the 7th House (Virgo):

There may be restlessness in your marital life. You experience unique sexual pleasures and work hard in your diurnal occupation. There is internal stability in your occupation.

Ketu in the 8th House (Libra):

You may experience restlessness in your daily routine. Stomach disorders are possible, and there may be setbacks related to age. You follow stable principles but can be obstinate.

Ketu in the 9th House (Scorpio):

You face severe anxiety in matters related to destiny. There may be losses in matters of righteousness and a strong effort to increase your income and fortune. You progress using secretive methods and may experience deficiencies in fame and reliance on God. Restlessness may be present.

Ketu in the 10th House (Sagittarius):

You achieve progress in government and societal affairs through hard work. However, your relationship with your father may not be favorable. You work fearlessly and courageously, utilizing secret powers to accomplish great deeds. You strive hard to gain honor, prestige, and success in your occupation, often opposing your father.

Ketu in the 11th House (Capricorn):

You put forth great effort to acquire wealth and ultimately succeed in gaining more. Your courageous work leads to the accumulation of wealth, utilizing your secret strength. However, you may face troubles and deficiencies in generating income.

Ketu in the 12th House (Aquarius):

You encounter difficulties in matters of expenditure and manage your expenses through hard work. Severe troubles may arise, but you ultimately succeed due to your secret strength.

15. Basics (Terminology) of the 9 Planets

Nine planets in astrology and their friendship, neutrality, and enmity:

Here is a list of the nine planets in astrology and their friendship, neutrality, and enmity with other planets:
1. Sun:
   - Friends: Moon, Mars, Jupiter
   - Neutral: Mercury, Venus, Saturn
   - Enemies: None
2. Moon:
   - Friends: Sun, Mercury
   - Neutral: Venus
   - Enemies: Mars, Jupiter
3. Mars:
   - Friends: Sun, Moon, Jupiter
   - Neutral: Venus, Saturn
   - Enemies: Mercury
4. Mercury:
   - Friends: Venus, Saturn
   - Neutral: Mars
   - Enemies: Jupiter, Moon
5. Jupiter:
   - Friends: Sun, Moon, Mars
   - Neutral: Saturn
   - Enemies: Mercury, Venus

6. Venus:
   - Friends: Mercury, Saturn
   - Neutral: Mars
   - Enemies: Jupiter, Sun, Moon
7. Saturn:
   - Friends: Mercury, Venus
   - Neutral: None
   - Enemies: Sun, Moon, Mars, Jupiter
8. Rahu (North Node of the Moon):
   - Friends: None
   - Neutral: All planets
   - Enemies: None
9. Ketu (South Node of the Moon):
   - Friends: None
   - Neutral: All planets
   - Enemies: None

Please note that Rahu and Ketu are considered shadowy planets in Vedic astrology and have different characteristics compared to the traditional planets. The friendship, neutrality, and enmity relationships mentioned above are based on general astrological principles and may vary in specific astrological charts or interpretations.

Basics :

1. Planet: In astrology, a planet refers to a celestial body that has an influence on human lives and represents different qualities, energies, and aspects of life.

2. Luminary: The luminaries in astrology are the Sun and the Moon. They are considered the most important celestial bodies and have a significant influence on a person's character, vitality, and emotions.

3. Inner Planets: The inner planets include Mercury, Venus, Earth (not considered in astrology), and Mars. They are closer to the Sun and have relatively faster orbits.

4. Outer Planets: The outer planets include Jupiter, Saturn, Uranus, Neptune, and Pluto. They are located farther from the Sun and have longer orbital periods.

5. Personal Planets: The personal planets are the Sun, Moon, Mercury, Venus, and Mars. They are considered to have a more direct influence on an individual's personality, behavior, and personal life.

6. Social Planets: The social planets are Jupiter and Saturn. They represent broader social influences, growth, expansion, responsibility, and structure in a person's life.

7. Transpersonal Planets: The transpersonal planets are Uranus, Neptune, and Pluto. They represent generational influences, transformation, spirituality, and deeper psychological aspects.

8. Retrograde: Retrograde motion is an apparent backward motion of a planet as observed from Earth. It is believed to intensify and internalize the energies of the planet, often associated with reviewing, revising, and introspection.

9. Exaltation: Exaltation is a position where a planet is believed to be in its strongest and most favorable state, expressing its energies positively. Each planet has a specific sign of exaltation.

10. Debilitation: Debilitation is a position where a planet is believed to be in its weakest state, expressing its energies with challenges or difficulties. Each planet has a specific sign of debilitation.

These are just a few basic terms related to the planets in astrology. There are many more concepts and terminology associated with planetary aspects, houses, dignities, and interactions.

The main planetary aspects along with brief explanations and examples:

1. Conjunction: When two planets are in close proximity (within a few degrees) in the same sign, it creates a conjunction. This aspect intensifies the energy of the involved planets and combines their qualities. For example, a Sun-Mercury conjunction can enhance communication skills and intellectual pursuits.

2. Opposition: When two planets are approximately 180 degrees apart, it forms an opposition. This aspect represents a polarity or tension between the energies of the involved planets. For instance, a Mars-Pluto opposition can manifest as power struggles and conflicts of control.

3. Trine: When two planets are approximately 120 degrees apart, they form a trine aspect. This aspect indicates harmony, ease, and flow of energy between the planets. A Venus-Jupiter trine can bring luck, optimism, and an abundance of love and pleasure.

4. Square: When two planets are approximately 90 degrees apart, they form a square aspect. This aspect represents challenges, friction, and a need for growth and adjustment. An example is a Mercury-Saturn square, which can bring difficulties in communication and a tendency towards pessimism.

5. Sextile: When two planets are approximately 60 degrees apart, they form a sextile aspect. This aspect signifies opportunities, cooperation, and easy communication between the planets. A Moon-Neptune sextile can enhance intuition, sensitivity, and artistic abilities.

6. Quincunx: When two planets are approximately 150 degrees apart, they form a quincunx aspect. This aspect indicates a need for adjustment and adaptation between the energies of the involved planets. A Venus-Pluto quincunx can bring challenges in relationships and a need for transformation in matters of love and intimacy.

7. Semi-Sextile: When two planets are approximately 30 degrees apart, they form a semi-sextile aspect. This aspect represents minor opportunities for growth and adjustment. For example, a Mars-Uranus semi-sextile

can bring sporadic bursts of energy and the need to find a balance between impulsiveness and stability.

These are the main aspects used in astrology to analyze the relationship between planets in a birth chart. Each aspect adds its own unique flavor and influence to an individual's personality and life experiences. It's important to consider the overall pattern of aspects in a birth chart to gain a comprehensive understanding of the individual's astrological profile.

The dignities of planets :

In astrology, the dignities of planets refer to the strength or power that a planet possesses in a particular sign of the zodiac. These dignities determine how well a planet can express its energies and fulfill its potential in a specific sign. Here are the main dignities of planets:

1. Rulership (Domicile): Each planet has a sign that it rules, where it is considered to be in its highest dignity. When a planet is in its ruling sign, it operates with strength, ease, and natural expression. For example, Mars rules Aries and is considered dignified when placed in that sign.

2. Exaltation: Exaltation is another form of high dignity for a planet. It represents a sign in which a planet is believed to express its energy at its best. When a planet is exalted, it is powerful and can bring positive outcomes. For instance, Jupiter is exalted in Cancer,

indicating its heightened influence when placed in that sign.

3. Detriment: The sign opposite to a planet's ruling sign is its detriment. When a planet is in its detriment, it may face challenges or difficulties in expressing its energies effectively. For example, Mars is in detriment in Libra, suggesting that its assertive nature may struggle to find balance and harmony in that sign.

4. Fall: The fall represents the sign where a planet is believed to be least comfortable or weakened. When a planet is in its fall, it may struggle to manifest its qualities in a positive way. For instance, Venus is said to be in fall in Virgo, indicating potential challenges in expressing its harmonious and aesthetic nature in that sign.

5. Triplicity: Triplicity dignities divide the zodiac signs into groups of three, with each group associated with a specific element (fire, earth, air, and water). Each planet rules a particular triplicity in each element. This dignity adds a layer of influence and significance to a planet's expression in a specific sign.

6. Terms (Bounds): The zodiac signs are further divided into smaller sections called terms or bounds, and each planet rules specific degrees within these sections. These bounds provide additional nuances and variations in a planet's expression within a sign.

Understanding the dignities of planets helps astrologers assess the overall strength and potential of a planet in a birth chart. It provides insights into how a planet may influence various areas of life, its ability to navigate challenges, and its overall impact on the individual's personality and experiences.

What is Dasha system?

In Vedic astrology, Dasha is a system used to analyze and predict the major periods of a person's life based on the position of planets in their birth chart. Dasha refers to the main period or major planetary period, while Antardasha, Pratantardasha, and Sukshma Dasha refer to sub-periods within the main period. Here's an explanation of each:

1. Dasha: Dasha is the primary period or major planetary period in Vedic astrology. It represents a specific time period during which a particular planet holds significant influence over a person's life. The length of each Dasha period varies based on the system used, such as Vimshottari Dasha, which is the most commonly used system and spans a total of 120 years.

2. Antardasha: Antardasha, also known as sub-period or bhukti, is a sub-period within the Dasha period. Each Dasha period is divided into multiple Antardasha periods, with each Antardasha corresponding to a specific planet. For example, during the Dasha of a particular planet, an Antardasha of another planet occurs, influencing the overall experiences and events in a person's life.

3. Pratantardasha: Pratantardasha is a further division of the Antardasha period. It represents even smaller sub-periods within the Antardasha. It delves deeper into the influence of the sub-period planet and its impact on the individual's life during that specific time.

4. Sukshma Dasha: Sukshma Dasha, also known as sub-sub-period or pratyantar-dasha, is an even more detailed division of time within the Pratantardasha. It offers a more precise analysis of the planetary influence during a specific duration within the sub-period.

Let's consider an example to understand the concept of Dasha, Antardasha, Pratantardasha, and Sukshma Dasha.

Suppose a person has the Vimshottari Dasha system, which is based on a cycle of 120 years and uses the placement of the Moon as the primary determinant for the Dasha periods. Let's say the person's Moon is in the sign of Aries.

1. Dasha: The main period or Dasha is determined by the position of the Moon. In this case, the person's Moon is in Aries, so the Dasha period associated with the Moon begins.

2. Antardasha: Within the Moon Dasha, there will be sub-periods or Antardashas associated with other planets. For example, during the Moon Dasha, the person may experience an Antardasha of Jupiter. This means that for a specific duration within the Moon Dasha, the influence of Jupiter becomes prominent, and the person may experience events related to Jupiter's

significations such as expansion, growth, spirituality, or wisdom.

3. Pratantardasha: Within the Antardasha of Jupiter, there will be further divisions called Pratantardasha. Let's say during the Jupiter Antardasha, there is a Pratantardasha of Venus. This signifies a more specific time period within the Jupiter Antardasha where the influence of Venus becomes more prominent. The person may experience events related to love, relationships, beauty, creativity, or material comforts associated with Venus.

4. Sukshma Dasha: Finally, within the Pratantardasha of Venus, there will be Sukshma Dasha or sub-sub-periods. These represent even smaller divisions of time. Let's say during the Venus Pratantardasha, there is a Sukshma Dasha of Mars. This indicates a precise duration within the Venus Pratantardasha where the influence of Mars is heightened. The person may experience events related to energy, assertiveness, passion, or conflicts associated with Mars.

These successive divisions of time in the Dasha system help astrologers provide more accurate predictions and interpretations of a person's life events. By analyzing the planetary periods and their sub-periods, astrologers gain insights into the timing of various experiences, achievements, challenges, and transitions in an individual's life.

What is Nakshtras?

In Vedic astrology, Nakshatra refers to the lunar mansions or star constellations through which the Moon passes during its monthly journey around the Earth. The term "Nakshatra" is derived from Sanskrit and translates to "that which does not decay" or "fixed star."

The Moon is considered a significant celestial body in astrology, and its placement in a particular Nakshatra at the time of a person's birth is believed to influence their personality traits, tendencies, and life experiences. There are a total of 27 Nakshatras, each occupying a span of 13 degrees and 20 minutes along the ecliptic.

Each Nakshatra is associated with specific qualities, symbolism, ruling deity, ruling planet, and planetary aspects. These factors contribute to the unique energy and attributes associated with each Nakshatra.

In Vedic astrology, the Nakshatra placement of the Moon is considered significant for understanding a person's emotional nature, mindset, instincts, and overall life path. It provides additional insights into the individual's strengths, weaknesses, and areas of focus.

Astrologers often consider the Nakshatra along with other factors such as the placement of other planets, aspects, and house positions to provide a comprehensive analysis of a person's birth chart and make predictions about various aspects of their life, including career, relationships, health, and spiritual growth.

The Nakshatra system is a fundamental component of Vedic astrology and plays a crucial role in understanding and interpreting the influences of celestial bodies on an individual's life.

Here are the names of the 27 Nakshatras in Vedic astrology along with their ruling deities and a brief description of their qualities and influences:

1. Ashwini - Ruled by the Ashvins, the divine physicians. It signifies energy, swiftness, and the ability to initiate new beginnings.

2. Bharani - Ruled by Yama, the god of death. It represents transformation, restraint, and the power to overcome obstacles.

3. Krittika - Ruled by Agni, the fire god. It symbolizes determination, purification, and the ability to burn away negativity.

4. Rohini - Ruled by Brahma, the creator. It signifies fertility, beauty, nourishment, and creative expression.

5. Mrigashira - Ruled by Soma, the moon god. It represents curiosity, flexibility, and the pursuit of truth.

6. Ardra - Ruled by Rudra, the god of storms. It signifies turbulence, transformation, and the power to cleanse and purify.

7. Punarvasu - Ruled by Aditi, the mother of gods. It represents renewal, abundance, and the ability to regain strength and resources.

8. Pushya - Ruled by Brihaspati, the guru of gods. It signifies nourishment, wisdom, and the ability to provide guidance and support.

9. Ashlesha - Ruled by Naga, the serpent deity. It represents hidden knowledge, intuition, and the power of transformation through self-awareness.

10. Magha - Ruled by Pitris, the ancestors. It signifies royalty, power, and the ability to honor and respect tradition.

11. Purva Phalguni - Ruled by Bhaga, the god of marital bliss. It represents romance, creativity, and the pursuit of pleasure and enjoyment.

12. Uttara Phalguni - Ruled by Aryaman, the god of contracts. It signifies social connections, friendship, and the ability to build strong alliances.

13. Hasta - Ruled by Savitar, the Sun god. It represents skill, dexterity, and the power to manifest and create with one's hands.

14. Chitra - Ruled by Vishvakarma, the celestial architect. It signifies beauty, artistry, and the ability to manifest one's unique vision.

15. Swati - Ruled by Vayu, the wind god. It represents independence, freedom, and the ability to navigate through change and transformation.

16. Vishakha - Ruled by Indra and Agni, the gods of lightning and fire. It signifies determination, focus, and the power to achieve goals.

17. Anuradha - Ruled by Mitra, the god of friendship. It represents loyalty, harmony, and the ability to form deep connections and partnerships.

18. Jyeshtha - Ruled by Indra, the king of gods. It signifies authority, wisdom, and the power to lead and govern.

19. Mula - Ruled by Nirrti, the goddess of destruction. It represents introspection, spiritual growth, and the ability to release attachments.

20. Purva Ashadha - Ruled by Apah, the god of water. It signifies determination, ambition, and the power to overcome obstacles to achieve success.

21. Uttara Ashadha - Ruled by Vishvadevas, the universal gods. It represents strength, perseverance, and the ability to overcome challenges.

22. Shravana - Ruled by Vishnu, the preserver god. It signifies learning, wisdom, and the ability to listen and understand deeply.

23. Dhanishta (or Shravishtha) - Ruled by Vasus, the eight elemental deities. It represents wealth, abundance, and the ability to achieve fame and recognition through hard work and dedication.

24. Shatabhisha - Ruled by Varuna, the god of cosmic waters. It signifies healing, transformation, and the ability to bring about change and renewal.

25. Purva Bhadrapada - Ruled by Ajaikapada, the one-footed goat. It represents spirituality, mystical experiences, and the ability to transcend limitations.

26. Uttara Bhadrapada - Ruled by Ahir Budhnya, the serpent of the deep sea. It signifies compassion, spiritual wisdom, and the ability to navigate the depths of emotions.

27. Revati - Ruled by Pushan, the nurturer of flocks. It represents nurturing, protection, and the ability to care for others with love and compassion.

Each Nakshatra carries its unique energies and qualities that influence various aspects of life, including personality traits, career choices, relationships, and spiritual development. The Nakshatras are considered an essential component in Vedic astrology, providing deeper insights into a person's character and life path based on the positioning of planets within these Nakshatras in their birth chart.

What is Nakshatra-Charan?

In Vedic astrology, Nakshatra Charan refers to the divisions or sub-parts within a Nakshatra (birth star). Each Nakshatra is further divided into four equal parts called Charans, resulting in a total of 108 Charans in the 27 Nakshatras.

The Charans are used to determine the precise position of the Moon within a Nakshatra. Each Charan spans a specific range of degrees within the Nakshatra. By analyzing the Charan placement of the Moon, astrologers can derive more detailed insights about an individual's characteristics, traits, and potential life events associated with that particular Nakshatra.

The Charans of each Nakshatra have their specific ruling deity, symbol, and qualities, which further influence the interpretation and significance of the Nakshatra in an individual's birth chart. The Charans can provide additional information about the strengths, weaknesses, and specific traits associated with the placement of the Moon in a particular Nakshatra.

It's important to note that the Charan of a Nakshatra is not the same as the Pada or quarter of a Nakshatra. The Pada divides the Nakshatra into four unequal parts, whereas the Charan divides it into four equal parts.

To determine the Charan of the Moon in a birth chart, astrologers use specialized software or ephemeris, which provide the precise position of the Moon within the Nakshatra and its corresponding Charan. This information is then incorporated into the overall analysis of the birth chart to gain deeper insights into an individual's personality, behavior, and life events associated with the Nakshatra.

Here are the details of the ruling deity, symbol, and qualities associated with each Charan of the Nakshatras along with an example:

1st Charan:
- Ruling Deity: Varuna
- Symbol: A bed
- Qualities: Spiritual, intuitive, sensitive

Example: If someone's Moon is in the 1st Charan of the Nakshatra Ashwini, they may possess spiritual inclinations, intuitive abilities, and a sensitive nature.

2nd Charan:
- Ruling Deity: Yama
- Symbol: A serpent
- Qualities: Dynamic, energetic, ambitious

Example: If someone's Moon is in the 2nd Charan of the Nakshatra Bharani, they may exhibit dynamic and energetic qualities, with a strong drive towards achieving their ambitions.

3rd Charan:
- Ruling Deity: Agni
- Symbol: A chariot
- Qualities: Active, fiery, enthusiastic

Example: If someone's Moon is in the 3rd Charan of the Nakshatra Krittika, they may possess an active and fiery temperament, along with a strong enthusiasm for life.

4th Charan:
- Ruling Deity: Prajapati
- Symbol: A cot or a hammock
- Qualities: Creative, nurturing, protective

Example: If someone's Moon is in the 4th Charan of the Nakshatra Rohini, they may have a creative and nurturing disposition, showing a protective nature towards loved ones.

Please note that these are general characteristics associated with the Charans, and a complete analysis of an individual's birth chart is necessary to understand the overall impact and nuances of the Moon's placement within a specific Charan of a Nakshatra.

Nakshatras along with their ruling deity, symbol, and qualities:

Here are the Nakshatras along with their ruling deity, symbol, and qualities associated with each Charan, along with an example:

1. Ashwini:
    - Ruling Deity: Ashwini Kumaras
    - Symbol: Horse's head
    - Qualities: Swift, energetic, independent

    Example: If someone's Moon is in the 1st Charan of Ashwini Nakshatra, they may possess a swift and independent nature, with high levels of energy.

2. Bharani:
    - Ruling Deity: Yama
    - Symbol: Yoni (Female reproductive organ)
    - Qualities: Fierce, determined, passionate

    Example: If someone's Moon is in the 2nd Charan of Bharani Nakshatra, they may exhibit a fierce and determined nature, driven by their passions.

3. Krittika:
    - Ruling Deity: Agni
    - Symbol: Razor or flame

- Qualities: Fiery, sharp, transformative

  Example: If someone's Moon is in the 3rd Charan of Krittika Nakshatra, they may possess a fiery and sharp temperament, with the ability to bring about transformation.

  4. Rohini:
  - Ruling Deity: Brahma
  - Symbol: Chariot or ox cart
  - Qualities: Nurturing, creative, abundant

  Example: If someone's Moon is in the 4th Charan of Rohini Nakshatra, they may have a nurturing and creative disposition, with a natural abundance in their life.

  5. Mrigashira:
  - Ruling Deity: Soma
  - Symbol: Deer's head
  - Qualities: Gentle, curious, sensual

  6. Ardra:
  - Ruling Deity: Rudra
  - Symbol: Teardrop or human head
  - Qualities: Intense, transformative, volatile

  7. Punarvasu:
  - Ruling Deity: Aditi
  - Symbol: Bow and quiver of arrows
  - Qualities: Nurturing, abundant, generous

  8. Pushya:
  - Ruling Deity: Brihaspati (Jupiter)
  - Symbol: Cow's udder or lotus

- Qualities: Nurturing, caring, spiritual
9. Ashlesha:
   - Ruling Deity: Nagas (Serpents)
   - Symbol: Coiled snake
   - Qualities: Mysterious, secretive, transformative
10. Magha:
    - Ruling Deity: Pitris (Ancestors)
    - Symbol: Royal throne or palanquin
    - Qualities: Regal, authoritative, ambitious
11. Purva Phalguni:
    - Ruling Deity: Bhaga
    - Symbol: Front legs of a bed or hammock
    - Qualities: Romantic, creative, luxurious
12. Uttara Phalguni:
    - Ruling Deity: Aryaman
    - Symbol: Back legs of a bed or hammock
    - Qualities: Noble, generous, ambitious
13. Hasta:
    - Ruling Deity: Savitar
    - Symbol: Hand or closed fist
    - Qualities: Skilled, crafty, analytical
14. Chitra:
    - Ruling Deity: Tvastar (Vishwakarma)
    - Symbol: Bright jewel or pearl
    - Qualities: Artistic, stylish, charismatic
15. Swati:
    - Ruling Deity: Vayu (Wind)
    - Symbol: Shoot of plant or coral

- Qualities: Independent, balanced, diplomatic
16. Vishakha:
    - Ruling Deity: Indra and Agni
    - Symbol: Archway or triumphal gate
    - Qualities: Ambitious, goal-oriented, disciplined
17. Anuradha:
    - Ruling Deity: Mitra
    - Symbol: Lotus flower or umbrella
    - Qualities: Determined, loyal, diplomatic
18. Jyeshtha:
    - Ruling Deity: Indra
    - Symbol: Earring or talisman
    - Qualities: Wise, authoritative, intuitive
19. Mula:
    - Ruling Deity: Nirriti
    - Symbol: Root or bunch of roots tied together
    - Qualities: Transformative, intense, philosophical
20. Purva Ashadha:
    - Ruling Deity: Apah (Water Deity)
    - Symbol: Fan or winnowing basket
    - Qualities: Determined, adventurous, ambitious
21. Uttara Ashadha:
    - Ruling Deity: Vishvadevas (Universal Gods)
    - Symbol: Elephant tusk or planks of a bed
    - Qualities: Courageous, determined, ambitious
22. Shravana:
    - Ruling Deity: Vishnu
    - Symbol: Ear or three footprints

- Qualities: Studious, focused, attentive
23. Dhanishta:
   - Ruling Deity: Vasus (Eight Elemental Gods)
   - Symbol: Drum or flute
   - Qualities: Creative, artistic, sociable
24. Shatabhisha:
   - Ruling Deity: Varuna
   - Symbol: Empty circle or 100 physicians
   - Qualities: Independent, unconventional, mystical
25. Purva Bhadrapada:
   - Ruling Deity: Ajaikapada (One-footed Goat)
   - Symbol: Front legs of a funeral cot or a sword
   - Qualities: Spiritual, introspective, humanitarian
26. Uttara Bhadrapada:
   - Ruling Deity: Ahirbudhnya (Serpent of the Deep)
   - Symbol: Back legs of a funeral cot or twins in a swing
   - Qualities: Wise, intuitive, mystical
27. Revati:
   - Ruling Deity: Pushan
   - Symbol: Fish or a pair of fish swimming in opposite directions
   - Qualities: Compassionate, nurturing, imaginative

These are the Nakshatras and their associated Charans. Each Nakshatra and Charan combination has its unique qualities and influences on an individual's personality and life events.

27 Nakshatras along with the corresponding Rashis and Padas:

Here is a table listing all 27 Nakshatras along with the corresponding Rashis and Padas:

Nakshatra	Rashi (Zodiac Sign)	Pada 1	Pada 2	Pada 3	Pada 4
Ashwini	Aries (Mesha)	Aries	Aries	Aries	Aries
Bharani	Aries (Mesha)	Aries	Aries	Aries	Taurus
Krittika	Aries (Mesha)	Taurus	Taurus	Taurus	Taurus
Rohini	Taurus (Vrishabha)	Taurus	Taurus	Taurus	Gemini
Mrigashirsha	Taurus (Vrishabha)	Gemini	Gemini	Gemini	Gemini
Ardra	Gemini (Mithuna)	Gemini	Gemini	Gemini	Cancer
Punarvasu	Gemini (Mithuna)	Cancer	Cancer	Cancer	Cancer
Pushya	Cancer (Karka)	Cancer	Cancer	Cancer	Leo
Ashlesha	Cancer (Karka)	Leo	Leo	Leo	Leo

Magha	Leo (Simha)	Leo	Leo	Leo	Virgo
Purva Phalguni	Leo (Simha)	Virgo	Virgo	Virgo	Virgo
Uttara Phalguni	Leo (Simha)	Virgo	Virgo	Virgo	Libra
Hasta	Virgo (Kanya)	Virgo	Virgo	Virgo	Libra
Chitra	Virgo (Kanya)	Libra	Libra	Libra	Libra
Swati	Libra (Tula)	Libra	Libra	Libra	Scorpio
Vishakha	Libra (Tula)	Scorpio	Scorpio	Scorpio	Scorpio
Anuradha	Scorpio (Vrishchika)	Scorpio	Scorpio	Scorpio	Sagittarius
Jyeshtha	Scorpio (Vrishchika)	Sagittarius	Sagittarius	Sagittarius	Sagittarius
Mula	Sagittarius (Dhanu)	Sagittarius	Sagittarius	Sagittarius	Capricorn
Purva Ashadha	Sagittarius (Dhanu)	Capricorn	Capricorn	Capricorn	Capricorn
Uttara Ashadha	Sagittarius (Dhanu)	Capricorn	Capricorn	Capricorn	Aquarius
Shravana	Capricorn (Makara)	Capricorn	Capricorn	Capricorn	Aquarius
Dhanishta	Capricorn (Makara)	Aquarius	Aquarius	Aquarius	Aquarius

| Shatabhisha | Aquarius (Kumbha) | Aquarius| Aquarius| Aquarius| Pisces |
| Purva Bhadrapada | Aquarius (Kumbha) | Pisces | Pisces | Pisces | Pisces

What is Yogas?

In astrology, there are numerous yogas that are formed by the placement and interactions of planets in a birth chart. These yogas indicate specific combinations of planetary energies and can have various effects on an individual's life. The number of yogas is vast, and it would be impractical to list all of them. However, I will mention a few prominent yogas:

1. Raj Yoga: This is one of the most significant yogas and indicates a combination of planets that bestows wealth, power, and success. It is formed when the lords of the 9th and 10th houses are in conjunction or mutual aspect.

2. Gaja Kesari Yoga: This yoga occurs when Jupiter is in a Kendra (1st, 4th, 7th, or 10th house) from the Moon. It signifies wisdom, intelligence, fame, and good fortune.

3. Viparita Raja Yoga: This yoga is formed by the placement of malefic planets (Saturn, Mars, or Rahu) in the 6th, 8th, or 12th house from the Ascendant. It indicates success and victory over adversaries after initial struggles and challenges.

4. Budha Aditya Yoga: This yoga occurs when the Sun and Mercury are in conjunction. It signifies

intelligence, communication skills, and success in areas related to commerce, writing, and speaking.

5. Chandra-Mangal Yoga: This yoga is formed by the conjunction of the Moon and Mars. It indicates courage, vitality, assertiveness, and leadership qualities.

Few combinations of Yogas

1. Raj Yoga: Formed by the conjunction or mutual aspect of the lords of the 9th and 10th houses.

2. Gaja Kesari Yoga: Jupiter in a Kendra (1st, 4th, 7th, or 10th house) from the Moon.

3. Viparita Raja Yoga: Malefic planets (Saturn, Mars, or Rahu) in the 6th, 8th, or 12th house from the Ascendant.

4. Neechabhanga Raja Yoga: Cancellation of debilitation of a planet through specific conditions.

5. Budha Aditya Yoga: Conjunction of the Sun and Mercury.

6. Chandra-Mangal Yoga: Conjunction of the Moon and Mars.

7. Pancha Mahapurusha Yoga: Formation of five great combinations named after the five planets Mars, Mercury, Jupiter, Venus, and Saturn.

8. Malavya Yoga: Venus in its own or exalted sign in a Kendra (1st, 4th, 7th, or 10th house).

9. Ruchaka Yoga: Mars in its own sign in a Kendra.

10. Hamsa Yoga: Jupiter in a Kendra in its own or exalted sign.

11. Bhadra Yoga: Mercury in a Kendra in its own or exalted sign.

12. Shasha Yoga: Saturn in a Kendra in its own or exalted sign.

13. Saraswati Yoga: Venus, Mercury, and Jupiter in Kendras.

14. Vosi Yoga: Benefic planets in the 12th house from the Moon.

15. Kemadruma Yoga: Moon without any planets in the 2nd or 12th house from it.

16. Nanda Yoga: Ascendant lord in an odd sign and Moon in an even sign or vice versa.

17. Parvata Yoga: Benefic planets in Kendras and malefic planets in Panaparas.

18. Dhan Yoga: Combination of planets indicating wealth and financial prosperity.

19. Maha Bhagya Yoga: Benefic planets in the 9th and 10th houses.

20. Parijat Yoga: Venus conjunct or aspected by the Moon.

21. Vasumati Yoga: Four or more planets in their own or exalted signs.

22. Shakti Yoga: Strong placement of Mars and Venus in the birth chart.

23. Surya-Mangal Yoga: Conjunction of the Sun and Mars.

24. Chandra-Budha Yoga: Conjunction of the Moon and Mercury.

25. Chandra-Venus Yoga: Conjunction of the Moon and Venus.

26. Chandra-Jupiter Yoga: Conjunction of the Moon and Jupiter.

27. Chandra-Saturn Yoga: Conjunction of the Moon and Saturn.

28. Gouri Yoga: Venus in the 10th house.

29. Mridanga Yoga: Benefic planets in the 2nd, 5th, 9th, and 11th houses.

30. Paasa Yoga: A planet positioned alone in a house.

31. Shubha Kartari Yoga: Benefic planets flanking a house.

32. Papa Kartari Yoga: Malefic planets flanking a house.

33. Naga Dosha Yoga: Rahu or Ketu in the 1st or 5th house.

34. Aakriti Yoga: Planets occupying consecutive houses.

35. Arishta Yoga: Malefic planets in the 6th, 8th, or 12th house from the Ascendant.

36. Ravi Yoga: The Sun in its own or exalted sign in a Kendra or Trikona house.

37. Shukra Yoga: Venus in its own or exalted sign in a Kendra or Trikona house.

38. Brahma Yoga: Benefic planets in the 1st, 4th, 7th, or 10th house from the Moon.

39. Vishnu Yoga: Benefic planets in the 1st, 4th, 7th, or 10th house from the Ascendant.

40. Rudra Yoga: Malefic planets in the 1st, 4th, 7th, or 10th house from the Moon.

41. Adhi Yoga: Benefic planets in the 6th, 7th, and 8th houses from the Ascendant.

42. Kedar Yoga: Benefic planets in the 4th, 8th, and 12th houses from the Ascendant.

43. Dala Yoga: A combination of planets forming a pattern resembling a flag.

44. Gada Yoga: A combination of planets forming a pattern resembling a mace.

45. Dhwaja Yoga: A combination of planets forming a pattern resembling a flagpole.

46. Kamala Yoga: A combination of planets forming a pattern resembling a lotus.

47. Sarpa Yoga: Rahu or Ketu in conjunction with other planets.

48. Budha-Adhi Yoga: Mercury in the 6th, 7th, or 8th house from the Moon.

49. Raja Sambandha Yoga: Benefic planets in the 1st and 7th houses from the Ascendant.

50. Vasi Yoga: A benefic planet in the 12th house from the Ascendant.

These are just a few examples of the many yoga formations in astrology. Each yoga carries its own significance and can influence various areas of life such as wealth, career, relationships, and spiritual growth. The exact impact of a yoga in an individual's chart depends on the overall planetary placements and their interaction with other factors in the birth chart.

What is Karan?

In Vedic astrology, a Karana is a half of a Tithi, which is a lunar day. The word "Karana" translates to "cause" or "half" in Sanskrit. Karanas are used to determine auspicious and inauspicious timings for various activities, such as starting a new venture, performing rituals, or making important decisions.

There are a total of 11 Karanas, which are as follows:

1. Bava
2. Balava
3. Kaulava
4. Taitila
5. Gara
6. Vanija
7. Vishti
8. Shakuni
9. Chatushpada
10. Naga
11. Kimstughna

Here are examples of each Karana along with their associated activities:

1. Bava Karana: Appropriate for all auspicious ceremonies, marriages, starting new ventures, and religious rituals.

2. Balava Karana: Suitable for buying or selling property, construction activities, and important business meetings.

3. Kaulava Karana: Favorable for traveling, engaging in physical activities, and making important decisions.

4. Taitila Karana: Not considered favorable for important events, ceremonies, or starting new ventures.

5. Gara Karana: Suitable for religious activities, spiritual practices, meditation, and seeking divine blessings.

6. Vanija Karana: Favorable for business transactions, negotiations, signing contracts, and financial matters.

7. Vishti Karana: Inauspicious for most activities, not recommended for starting new ventures or important events.

8. Shakuni Karana: Favorable for intellectual pursuits, studying, learning, teaching, and artistic activities.

9. Chatushpada Karana: Suitable for agricultural activities, gardening, working with animals, and land-related matters.

10. Naga Karana: Considered inauspicious, not recommended for starting new ventures or important events.

11. Kimstughna Karana: Favorable for acquiring knowledge, participating in intellectual discussions, and seeking guidance from mentors.

Each Karana has a specific influence and is associated with certain activities. Some Karanas are considered favorable for starting new endeavors, while others are deemed less auspicious. The Karana for a particular day is determined by the position of the Moon in relation to the Sun.

Astrologers consider Karanas while selecting suitable dates and times for important events or activities. The choice of a favorable Karana is believed to enhance the chances of success and positive outcomes. It is an additional factor to consider alongside other astrological elements in creating a harmonious and auspicious environment.

What is Tithi?

In Vedic astrology, a Tithi is a lunar day or the phase of the Moon. It is one of the important elements considered in determining auspicious or inauspicious timings for various events and activities. Tithis are calculated based on the position of the Moon relative to the Sun.

There are a total of 30 Tithis in a lunar month, which corresponds to the time it takes for the Moon to complete one revolution around the Earth. Each Tithi has a specific name and is associated with certain qualities and energies.

The Tithis are classified into two halves: the Shukla Paksha (waxing phase) and the Krishna Paksha (waning phase). The Shukla Paksha starts from the New Moon (Amavasya) and ends on the Full Moon (Purnima), while the Krishna Paksha starts from the Full Moon and ends on the next New Moon.

Each Tithi has its own significance and is believed to influence different aspects of life. They are also associated with various deities, planetary influences, and recommended activities. For example, certain Tithis may be considered auspicious for starting new ventures, performing religious ceremonies, or undertaking spiritual practices, while others may be considered inauspicious for such activities.

Understanding the Tithi and its qualities can help in determining favorable timings for important events, ceremonies, and activities based on the principles of Vedic astrology.

Here are the names of the 30 Tithis in the lunar month according to Vedic astrology:

1. Pratipada
2. Dwitiya
3. Tritiya
4. Chaturthi
5. Panchami
6. Shashthi
7. Saptami
8. Ashtami
9. Navami
10. Dashami
11. Ekadashi
12. Dwadashi

13. Trayodashi
14. Chaturdashi
15. Purnima (Full Moon)
16. Pratipada
17. Dwitiya
18. Tritiya
19. Chaturthi
20. Panchami
21. Shashthi
22. Saptami
23. Ashtami
24. Navami
25. Dashami
26. Ekadashi
27. Dwadashi
28. Trayodashi
29. Chaturdashi
30. Amavasya (New Moon)

These names represent each specific day of the lunar month and are used in astrological calculations and interpretations to determine the influences and energies associated with each Tithi.

What is Mahendra?

In Vedic astrology, Mahendra is one of the eight Kutas (factors) used to assess the compatibility and harmony between two individuals in the context of marriage and long-term relationships. Mahendra Kuta represents the progeny or the potential for having children in a relationship.

Mahendra Kuta is determined based on the Nakshatra (lunar constellation) of the Moon in the birth charts of the couple. If the Nakshatra of the Moon of one person falls in the 4th, 7th, 10th, 13th, 16th, 19th, 22nd, or 25th Nakshatra from the other person's Moon Nakshatra, it forms a Mahendra Dosha or Mahendra Kuta.

Mahendra Dosha is considered inauspicious as it indicates potential challenges in procreation or having children. However, if the Mahendra Dosha is canceled by other favorable factors in the couple's birth charts, it may not have a significant impact on their ability to have children.

In general, a higher Mahendra score indicates better compatibility and potential for a successful and harmonious relationship in terms of progeny. It is one of the factors considered in assessing overall compatibility along with other Kutas such as Varna, Vashya, Tara, Yoni, Graha Maitri, Gana, Bhakoot, and Nadi.

Let's consider an example to understand Mahendra in astrology:

Suppose we have two individuals, Person A and Person B, and we want to assess their compatibility using Mahendra Kuta.

Person A's Moon Nakshatra is Rohini (4th Nakshatra) and Person B's Moon Nakshatra is Uttarashada (21st Nakshatra).

To determine if Mahendra Dosha is present, we check if Person A's Moon Nakshatra falls in the 4th, 7th, 10th, 13th, 16th, 19th, 22nd, or 25th Nakshatra from Person B's Moon Nakshatra.

In this case, Rohini (4th Nakshatra) falls in the 21st Nakshatra (Uttarashada) for Person B. Since it falls within the allowed range, a Mahendra Dosha is formed.

The presence of Mahendra Dosha suggests potential challenges or obstacles related to progeny or having children in this relationship. However, it's important to consider other compatibility factors and the overall strength of the birth charts to determine the impact of Mahendra Dosha.

Please note that this is a simplified example, and in a real-life analysis, the complete birth charts of both individuals would be considered, including other Kutas and factors, for a comprehensive assessment of compatibility.

What is Varna?

In Vedic astrology, Varna refers to the social class of an individual based on their Moon sign or Ascendant (Lagna). It is one of the important factors considered in assessing the overall personality, traits, and inclinations of a person.

Varna is divided into four main categories:

1. Brahmin Varna: Associated with intellectual pursuits, knowledge, wisdom, and spirituality.

Individuals with Brahmin Varna are often inclined towards teaching, research, philosophy, or spiritual practices.

2. Kshatriya Varna: Associated with leadership, power, courage, and a sense of duty. Those with Kshatriya Varna may excel in professions related to defense, administration, politics, or any field that requires authority and protection.

3. Vaishya Varna: Associated with business, commerce, entrepreneurship, and financial matters. Individuals with Vaishya Varna are often inclined towards trade, finance, business management, or any profession that involves financial dealings.

4. Shudra Varna: Associated with service, labor, and practical skills. Those with Shudra Varna are usually inclined towards manual labor, service-oriented professions, or jobs that require practical skills.

It's important to note that in astrology, Varna is not directly linked to an individual's birth into a particular caste or social class in society. It is instead a classification based on the qualities and inclinations associated with the Moon sign or Ascendant.

The Varna of an individual is determined by the placement of the Moon sign or Ascendant in the birth chart. It provides insights into the inherent nature and tendencies of a person and can be used as a basis for understanding their potential inclinations and career choices.

Determining the Varna

associated with the Lagna (Ascendant) in Vedic astrology involves considering the natural qualities, ruling planets, and characteristics of the sign in which the Lagna falls. Here is a general guideline to help you determine the Varna associated with different Lagna signs:

1. Brahmin Varna:
   - Lagna in Cancer, Scorpio, or Pisces: These signs are associated with sensitivity, intuition, spirituality, and a deep understanding of emotions.
2. Kshatriya Varna:
   - Lagna in Aries, Leo, or Sagittarius: These signs are associated with courage, leadership, ambition, and a sense of adventure.
3. Vaishya Varna:
   - Lagna in Taurus, Libra, or Capricorn: These signs are associated with practicality, materialism, business acumen, and a focus on finances.
4. Shudra Varna:
   - Lagna in Gemini, Virgo, or Aquarius: These signs are associated with intellectual curiosity, adaptability, communication skills, and a practical approach to life.

It's important to note that this classification is based on general associations and should be taken as a broad guideline rather than a definitive determination. Additionally, the determination of Varna is not solely based on the Lagna but considers the entire birth chart, including the positions of other planets and their influences.

What is Vashya?

In Vedic astrology, Vashya refers to the influence or dominance that one planet has over another planet when they are in conjunction or aspecting each other. It is a significant factor in determining compatibility and the nature of relationships between individuals.

Vashya is categorized into five types based on the nature of the planetary pairs:

1. Chatushpada Vashya: This occurs when the male planet (Sun, Mars, or Jupiter) is in conjunction with a female planet (Moon, Venus, or Mercury). The male planet has dominance or control over the female planet. This Vashya indicates a harmonious and supportive relationship.

2. Dwipada Vashya: This occurs when two male planets or two female planets are in conjunction. Both planets have equal dominance or control over each other. This Vashya indicates a balanced and cooperative relationship.

3. Chatushpada Virodha Vashya: This occurs when a male planet is in conjunction with a neutral planet (Saturn) or vice versa. The male planet dominates the neutral planet, but the neutral planet resists or opposes

the dominance. This Vashya indicates a conflicting or challenging relationship.

4. Chatushpada Prakriti Vashya: This occurs when two neutral planets are in conjunction. No planet has dominance or control over the other. This Vashya indicates a neutral and somewhat indifferent relationship.

5. Dwipada Virodha Vashya: This occurs when a male planet is in conjunction with a female planet, but the female planet resists or opposes the dominance of the male planet. This Vashya indicates a challenging or conflicting relationship.

Vashya is considered an important factor in assessing compatibility between individuals, especially in the context of marriage and partnerships. It provides insights into the power dynamics and mutual influence between planets, which can affect the dynamics of a relationship.

How to Determine Vashya?

Here is a Vashya table that shows the Vashya for each combination of Moon signs:

	Aries	Taurus	Gemini
Aries	Chatushpad	Manav	Manav
Taurus	Vanchar	Chatushpad	Jalchar

| Gemini| Vanchar | Jalchar | Chatushpad |

```
------------------------------------
| | Cancer | Leo | Virgo |
------------------------------------
| Cancer| Jalchar | Manav | Keet |
------------------------------------
| Leo | Vanchar | Chatushpad | Manav |
------------------------------------
| Virgo | Jalchar | Vanchar | Chatushpad |
------------------------------------
```
```
------------------------------------
| | Libra | Scorpio | Sagittarius |
------------------------------------
| Libra | Jalchar | Manav | Keet |
------------------------------------
| Scorpio | Jalchar | Jalchar | Manav |
------------------------------------
| Sagittarius | Jalchar | Jalchar | Vanchar |
------------------------------------
```
```
------------------------------------
| | Capricorn | Aquarius | Pisces |
```

| Capricorn | Keet | Vanchar | Jalchar |

| Aquarius | Vanchar | Keet | Manav |

| Pisces | Jalchar | Vanchar | Chatushpad |

...

In this table, each cell represents the Vashya between two Moon signs. The Vashya names are as follows:
- Chatushpad: Favorable and harmonious Vashya.
- Manav: Good Vashya, indicating compatibility.
- Vanchar: Average Vashya, indicating moderate compatibility.
- Jalchar: Incompatible Vashya, indicating challenges in understanding each other.
- Keet: Inimical Vashya, indicating significant differences and potential conflicts.

To determine the Vashya between two individuals, locate their respective Moon signs in the table and find the corresponding Vashya in the intersecting cell.

What is Yoni?

In Vedic astrology, Yoni refers to the sexual and instinctual compatibility between two individuals based on their Moon signs. It represents the primal energy and natural instincts associated with intimate relationships. Yoni is derived from the Sanskrit word for "female reproductive organ" and symbolizes the concept of sexual compatibility and attraction.

There are 14 Yonis, each associated with a particular animal or creature. These Yonis are categorized into different groups based on their characteristics. The Yoni of an individual is determined by their Moon sign.

The Yoni groups and their corresponding animals or creatures are as follows:

1. Ashwa (Horse)
2. Gaja (Elephant)
3. Mesha (Ram)
4. Sarpa (Serpent)
5. Shwana (Dog)
6. Marjara (Cat)
7. Mushaka (Mouse)
8. Gau (Cow)
9. Mahisha (Buffalo)
10. Vyaghra (Tiger)
11. Mriga (Deer)
12. Vanara (Monkey)
13. Nakula (Mongoose)
14. Simha (Lion)

The compatibility of Yonis is determined by the nature of the animals or creatures they represent. Yonis that belong to the same group are considered compatible, while those from different groups may face challenges or conflicts in their intimate relationship.

Assessing Yoni compatibility can provide insights into the sexual dynamics, attraction, and instinctual compatibility between individuals based on their Moon signs. However, it is important to note that Yoni is just one factor among many in astrology, and a comprehensive analysis considers other aspects for a more accurate assessment of compatibility.

How to Determine Yoni?

To determine the Yoni of an individual, you need to know their Moon sign. The Moon sign is the zodiac sign in which the Moon was located at the time of their birth. Once you have identified the Moon sign, you can find the corresponding Yoni.

Here is a list of the Moon signs and their corresponding Yonis:

1. Aries (Mesha) - Mesha Yoni (Ram)
2. Taurus (Vrishabha) - Gau Yoni (Cow)
3. Gemini (Mithuna) - Shwana Yoni (Dog)
4. Cancer (Karka) - Marjara Yoni (Cat)
5. Leo (Simha) - Vyaghra Yoni (Tiger)
6. Virgo (Kanya) - Mushaka Yoni (Mouse)
7. Libra (Tula) - Sarpa Yoni (Serpent)
8. Scorpio (Vrishchika) - Nakula Yoni (Mongoose)
9. Sagittarius (Dhanu) - Mahisha Yoni (Buffalo)
10. Capricorn (Makara) - Vanara Yoni (Monkey)
11. Aquarius (Kumbha) - Gaja Yoni (Elephant)
12. Pisces (Meena) - Simha Yoni (Lion)

To determine someone's Yoni, you need to know their exact date, time, and place of birth. Using this information, you can calculate their Moon sign. You can refer to an astrological birth chart or consult with an astrologer to find the Moon sign and corresponding Yoni for an individual.

Remember, Yoni compatibility is just one aspect of assessing compatibility in relationships. It is always advisable to consider other factors and aspects of astrology for a comprehensive understanding of compatibility.

What is Gan ?

In Vedic astrology, Gan is one of the factors considered for assessing compatibility between two individuals. It is derived from the Moon sign of a person and is categorized into three types: Deva (Divine), Manushya (Human), and Rakshasa (Demon).

Here is a breakdown of each Gan:

1. Deva Gan: If the Moon sign of a person falls under the following signs: Aries, Leo, Sagittarius, Gemini, Libra, or Aquarius, they belong to the Deva Gan. Individuals with Deva Gan are considered kind-hearted, generous, spiritual, and inclined towards serving others. They are usually compatible with individuals from all three Ganas.

2. Manushya Gan: If the Moon sign of a person falls under the following signs: Taurus, Virgo, Capricorn,

Cancer, Scorpio, or Pisces, they belong to the Manushya Gan. Individuals with Manushya Gan are considered balanced, practical, and have a mix of human qualities. They can have compatible relationships with individuals from all three Ganas.

3. Rakshasa Gan: If the Moon sign of a person falls under the following signs: Aries, Leo, Sagittarius, Gemini, Libra, or Aquarius, they belong to the Rakshasa Gan. Individuals with Rakshasa Gan are considered passionate, strong-willed, and assertive. They may have a more challenging compatibility with individuals from other Ganas, but can have a strong connection with someone from the same Gan.

The Gan of two individuals is compared to assess their compatibility in terms of temperament, behavior, and overall compatibility. It is one of the many factors considered in Vedic astrology for determining the potential harmony between two people.

What is Nadi ?

In Vedic astrology, Nadi is one of the eight aspects considered for assessing compatibility and potential issues in a relationship between two individuals. It is based on the assessment of the Nakshatra (birth star) of the Moon in the individual's horoscope.

Nadi is divided into three categories: Adi (beginning), Madhya (middle), and Antya (end). The Nadi category of both individuals is compared to determine their Nadi

Dosha, which indicates potential challenges or incompatibilities in the relationship.

Here is a breakdown of the three Nadi categories:

1. Adi Nadi: If the Nakshatra of the Moon falls in the following groups: Ashwini, Ashlesha, Magha, Jyeshtha, Moola, or Revati, it is considered Adi Nadi. Individuals with Adi Nadi are believed to have a dominant, energetic, and fiery nature.

2. Madhya Nadi: If the Nakshatra of the Moon falls in the following groups: Bharani, Pushya, Purva Phalguni, Anuradha, Uttara Ashadha, or Uttara Bhadrapada, it is considered Madhya Nadi. Individuals with Madhya Nadi are believed to have a balanced, stable, and practical nature.

3. Antya Nadi: If the Nakshatra of the Moon falls in the following groups: Krittika, Ardra, Punarvasu, Vishakha, Purva Ashadha, or Purva Bhadrapada, it is considered Antya Nadi. Individuals with Antya Nadi are believed to have a sensitive, emotional, and intuitive nature.

When assessing compatibility, it is generally recommended that individuals with the same Nadi should not enter into a marriage or long-term relationship. This is known as Nadi Dosha, and it is believed to bring challenges, health issues, and disharmony in the relationship. However, if other factors in the horoscope indicate strong compatibility and support, the negative effects of Nadi Dosha can be mitigated.

What is Dosha?

Dosha, in the context of astrology, refers to an affliction or imbalance caused by the unfavorable positioning or influence of planets in a person's birth chart. Doshas are believed to indicate potential challenges, obstacles, or negative influences in various aspects of life. They are seen as imbalances that need to be addressed and balanced for overall well-being.

In Vedic astrology, three main doshas are considered: Vata Dosha, Pitta Dosha, and Kapha Dosha. These doshas are associated with the elements of air, fire, and earth, respectively. Each dosha represents specific qualities and characteristics, and an imbalance in any of the doshas can lead to physical, mental, or emotional disturbances.

Doshas are analyzed through the planetary positions, aspects, and combinations in a person's birth chart. Astrologers assess the strength and placement of planets to identify doshas and their potential effects. Remedies such as gemstone therapy, mantra chanting, ritual worship, and lifestyle modifications are suggested to mitigate the negative impacts of doshas and restore balance in the individual's life.

It is important to note that doshas are not necessarily negative or purely detrimental. They serve as indicators of potential challenges and imbalances, and their presence provides an opportunity for self-awareness, personal growth, and the implementation of appropriate remedies to harmonize the energies and overcome difficulties.

What is Tatva?

In astrology, Tatva refers to the five elements or fundamental principles that make up the physical and energetic aspects of the universe. These elements are considered essential building blocks and are associated with different qualities and characteristics. The five Tatvas are:

1. Prithvi (Earth): Prithvi represents the element of Earth and is associated with stability, materiality, groundedness, and practicality.

2. Ap (Water): Ap represents the element of Water and is associated with emotions, sensitivity, intuition, adaptability, and fluidity.

3. Tejas (Fire): Tejas represents the element of Fire and is associated with passion, creativity, vitality, transformation, and inspiration.

4. Vayu (Air): Vayu represents the element of Air and is associated with movement, communication, intellect, ideas, and flexibility.

5. Akasha (Ether): Akasha represents the element of Ether or Space and is associated with expansion,

consciousness, connectivity, spirituality, and infinite potential.

Each of these elements has its own unique qualities, and their presence in a person's birth chart can influence their temperament, behavior, and overall energetic makeup. Understanding the Tatvas can provide insights into how the elements manifest in different areas of life and influence various aspects of an individual's personality and experiences.

In astrology, each Tatva is associated with certain qualities and characteristics, and their compatibility is determined by their inherent nature and relationship with each other. Generally, Tatvas that share similar qualities tend to be more compatible, while those with contrasting qualities may experience challenges or require adjustments. Here is a general overview of the compatibility between the Tatvas:

1. Prithvi (Earth): Prithvi is compatible with itself and with Ap (Water). Earth provides stability and grounding, while Water adds emotional depth and sensitivity.

2. Ap (Water): Ap is compatible with itself and with Prithvi (Earth). Water brings emotional flow and adaptability, while Earth provides stability and practicality.

3. Tejas (Fire): Tejas is compatible with itself and with Vayu (Air). Fire brings passion and inspiration, while Air fuels intellectual pursuits and communication.

4. Vayu (Air): Vayu is compatible with itself and with Tejas (Fire). Air promotes ideas and flexibility, while Fire adds energy and enthusiasm.

5. Akasha (Ether): Akasha, being the subtlest element, is compatible with all other Tatvas. It provides the space for the manifestation and interaction of the other elements.

It's important to note that compatibility in astrology is a complex matter and involves many factors beyond just the Tatvas. The placement of planets, individual birth charts, and specific astrological aspects also play significant roles in determining compatibility. Consulting with an experienced astrologer can provide more accurate and personalized insights into compatibility based on your unique birth chart.

12 Rashis specific names and corresponding alphabets:

In Vedic astrology, the 12 Rashis (Zodiac signs) are associated with specific names and corresponding alphabets. Here is a list of the Rashis along with their names and the associated initial alphabets:

1. Aries (Mesha Rashi) - अ (A)

2. Taurus (Vrishabha Rashi) - इ (I)

3. Gemini (Mithuna Rashi) - उ (U)

4. Cancer (Karka Rashi) - ए (E)

5. Leo (Simha Rashi) - अ (A)

6. Virgo (Kanya Rashi) - ए (E)

7. Libra (Tula Rashi) - र (R)

8. Scorpio (Vrishchika Rashi) - त (T)

9. Sagittarius (Dhanu Rashi) - य (Y)

10. Capricorn (Makara Rashi) - भ (Bh)

11. Aquarius (Kumbha Rashi) - ग (Ga)

12. Pisces (Meena Rashi) - द (Da)

These initial alphabets are used in various astrological practices such as naming newborns, selecting auspicious dates, and analyzing the influence of planets based on the Rashi. However, it's important to remember that the entire birth chart should be taken into consideration for accurate analysis and predictions in astrology.

here is a table showing the association of each alphabet with the corresponding Rashis:

Rashi	Alphabets
Aries	चू, चे, चो, ला, ली, लू, ले, लो, अ, ला
Taurus	इ, उ, ए, ओ, वा, वी, यू, वे, वो
Gemini	का, की, कु, के, को, घ, ङा, ङी, ङू, ङे, ङो
Cancer	ही, हू, हे, हो, डा, डी, डू, डे, डो
Leo	मा, मी, मू, मे, मो, टा, टी, टू, टे, टो
Virgo	पा, पी, पू, ष, ण, ठ, पे, पो
Libra	रा, री, रु, रे, रो, ता, ती, तू, ते, तो
Scorpio	ना, नी, नू, ने, नो, या, यी, यू, ये, यो
Sagittarius	भा, धा, फा, ढा, भी, भू, धी, धू, फी, फू, ढी, ढू
Capricorn	ख, ज, खा, जा, खी, खू, खे, खो, जी, जू, जे, जो
Aquarius	गु, गे, गो, सा, सी, सू, से, सो, दा, दी, दू, दे
Pisces	थ, झ, ञ, दो, चा, ची, चू, थी, थू, दी, दू

What is Paya?

In astrology, Paya refers to the concept of "foot" or "step" and is associated with the positioning of the Moon in a person's birth chart. Paya is used to determine the auspiciousness or inauspiciousness of the Moon in terms of its influence on various aspects of life.

There are two types of Paya based on the placement of the Moon:

1. Chara (Movable) Paya: When the Moon is placed in the 1st, 2nd, 3rd, 4th, 5th, 7th, 8th, 9th, 10th, 11th, and 12th houses from the natal Moon sign, it is considered to be in Chara Paya. This is generally considered favorable as it signifies progress, growth, and positive outcomes.

2. Sthira (Fixed) Paya: When the Moon is placed in the 6th house from the natal Moon sign, it is considered to be in Sthira Paya. This is considered less favorable as it may bring challenges, delays, and obstacles in various areas of life.

The determination of Paya helps in understanding the overall strength and impact of the Moon in a person's chart. It is often considered along with other factors in astrology to assess the potential outcomes and influences in an individual's life.

In Vedic astrology, there are three types of Payas or categories based on the placement of the Moon in the birth chart. These are:

1. Gold Paya (Sona Paya): When the Moon is placed in the 1st, 5th, or 9th house from the natal Moon sign, it is considered to be in Gold Paya. This placement is considered highly auspicious and is associated with positive outcomes, success, abundance, and prosperity.

2. Silver Paya (Chandi Paya): When the Moon is placed in the 2nd, 6th, or 10th house from the natal Moon sign, it is considered to be in Silver Paya. This placement is also considered favorable and indicates stability, financial gains, and career success.

3. Copper Paya (Tamra Paya): When the Moon is placed in the 3rd, 7th, or 11th house from the natal Moon sign, it is considered to be in Copper Paya. This placement is generally considered favorable and is associated with good communication skills, intelligence, courage, and success in endeavors related to networking and social interaction.

The classification of Payas is based on the Moon's placement from the natal Moon sign, and it is believed to influence various aspects of an individual's life. However, it's important to remember that the interpretation of the Moon's placement and its impact should be considered in conjunction with other planetary positions and aspects in the birth chart for a comprehensive analysis.

What is Navamsha ?

Navamsha, also known as Navamsa or D-9, is a divisional chart in Vedic astrology that divides each sign of the zodiac into nine equal parts. It is derived from dividing the 30-degree span of a sign into nine divisions of 3 degrees and 20 minutes each.

Navamsha chart is considered significant for analyzing the finer details of a person's life, particularly in relation to marriage, partnerships, and spiritual matters. It provides insights into the strengths and weaknesses of planets in the chart, as well as their influences on specific areas of life.

Some key points about Navamsha chart:

1. Marriage Analysis: Navamsha chart is extensively used for analyzing marriage and marital relationships. It provides information about the nature and compatibility of the spouse, marital harmony, and potential challenges in the marriage.

2. Planetary Strength: Navamsha chart helps in assessing the strength of planets and their significations. It can reveal if a planet gains strength or weakness in the divisional chart, which can impact its influence in specific areas of life.

3. Dasha Analysis: Navamsha chart is used in conjunction with the main birth chart (Rashi chart) for determining the timing and results of planetary periods (dashas). The positioning of planets in Navamsha can modify the outcomes predicted by the Rashi chart.

4. Spiritual Matters: Navamsha chart is also studied for understanding one's spiritual inclinations, spiritual growth, and the potential for spiritual practices or experiences.

Interpreting the Navamsha chart requires a good understanding of the principles of Vedic astrology and the specific combinations, aspects, and influences of planets in this divisional chart. It is often analyzed alongside the Rashi chart to provide a more comprehensive picture of an individual's life.

How to determine navamsha chart?

To determine the Navamsha chart, also known as Navamsa or D-9 chart, you need the exact birth details of an individual, including the date, time, and place of birth. Here are the steps to calculate the Navamsha chart:

1. Obtain the Birth Chart (Rashi Chart): Start by obtaining the birth chart, which is also known as the Rashi chart. It is a graphical representation of the positions of planets at the time of birth.

2. Determine the Ascendant: Identify the Ascendant, also known as the Lagna, in the birth chart. It represents the sign that was rising on the eastern horizon at the time of birth.

3. Calculate the Navamsha Sign: Find the Navamsha sign for each planet by dividing the degree of the planet by 3 and adding the quotient to the original sign. For example, if a planet is in Aries at 15 degrees in the birth chart, divide 15 by 3, which equals 5. Add 5 to Aries, which gives you Leo as the Navamsha sign for that planet.

4. Determine the Navamsha Positions: Once you have calculated the Navamsha sign for each planet, note down their positions in the Navamsha chart. The Navamsha

chart will have 12 houses, each representing different areas of life, just like the birth chart.

5. Interpret the Navamsha Chart: Analyze the positions of planets in the Navamsha chart to gain insights into various aspects of life, including marriage, relationships, spiritual inclinations, and potential strengths and weaknesses of planets.

Analyzing the Navamsha chart for each planet:

Analyzing the Navamsha chart for each planet can provide valuable insights into specific areas of life and their influence on relationships, career, and spiritual growth. Here is a brief overview of how the Navamsha chart can be interpreted for each planet:

1. Sun in Navamsha Chart: The position of the Sun in the Navamsha chart reveals insights into one's individuality, self-expression, and leadership qualities within relationships and partnerships.

2. Moon in Navamsha Chart: The placement of the Moon in the Navamsha chart signifies emotional harmony, nurturing qualities, and the deep emotional bond within relationships.

3. Mars in Navamsha Chart: Mars in the Navamsha chart reflects one's energy, drive, and assertiveness in relationships, as well as the potential for conflicts and challenges within partnerships.

4. Mercury in Navamsha Chart: Mercury's position in the Navamsha chart indicates communication style, intellectual compatibility, and the ability to express oneself effectively within relationships.

5. Jupiter in Navamsha Chart: Jupiter in the Navamsha chart represents growth, wisdom, and spiritual inclinations within partnerships, as well as the potential for mutual expansion and shared beliefs.

6. Venus in Navamsha Chart: Venus in the Navamsha chart highlights romantic inclinations, sensual connections, and the overall harmony and compatibility within relationships.

7. Saturn in Navamsha Chart: Saturn's placement in the Navamsha chart indicates commitment, responsibility, and the potential challenges and lessons within partnerships.

8. Rahu (North Node) in Navamsha Chart: Rahu in the Navamsha chart signifies desires, ambitions, and the potential for intense and transformative experiences within relationships.

9. Ketu (South Node) in Navamsha Chart: Ketu in the Navamsha chart represents past-life connections, spiritual growth, and the potential for detachment and unconventional experiences within partnerships.

The analysis of each planet in the Navamsha chart requires a thorough examination of their placements, aspects, conjunctions, and other astrological factors. It's essential to consider the interactions between the

Navamsha and the birth chart to gain a comprehensive understanding of the individual's life experiences and relationships.

Please note that this is a general overview, and a complete analysis of the Navamsha chart for each planet requires a deeper examination of the individual's birth chart and specific planetary configurations. Consulting an experienced astrologer is recommended for a more personalized and accurate interpretation of the Navamsha chart.

Transit in astrology:

Transit, in astrology, refers to the movement of planets through the zodiac signs in real-time. It involves the current positions of planets in relation to an individual's birth chart or a specific point of reference. Transits are significant because they reflect the ongoing influences and energies that affect an individual's life at a given time.

When a planet transits a particular sign or aspect of the birth chart, it activates and interacts with the energies represented by that sign or house. The transiting planet can stimulate certain areas of life, bring forth opportunities or challenges, and trigger various experiences or events.

For example, if the transiting Jupiter enters the sign of Sagittarius and forms a conjunction with an individual's natal Sun, it may bring opportunities for growth, expansion, and increased self-confidence. This transit could manifest as favorable circumstances, new beginnings, or a sense of purpose and optimism in the person's life.

Transits are used in predictive astrology to forecast future events and understand the timing of specific developments in a person's life. Astrologers analyze the transits of the planets to interpret how they interact with the individual's natal chart, considering factors such as aspects (angular relationships between planets), house placements, and the nature of the transiting planet and the sign it occupies.

It's important to note that transits are not isolated events but part of an ongoing astrological context. The combined influences of multiple transits and their interactions with the natal chart paint a more comprehensive picture of the current energies and potential life events.

To accurately interpret transits and their effects, astrologers consider the specific planetary configurations, the overall themes in the birth chart, and the individual's unique circumstances and personal growth journey.

What is Bhav Chalit Chart?

The Bhava Chalit Chart is a supplementary chart in Vedic astrology that is used to determine the house placements of planets. It is an alternative method of house division, different from the traditional birth chart or Rashi chart, which uses the Ascendant (Lagna) as the starting point for house placements.

In the Bhava Chalit Chart, the division of houses is based on the actual degrees of the Ascendant and the cusps of each house. It takes into account the unequal sizes of the houses in the birth chart and adjusts them according to the degrees of the Ascendant. This chart provides a more accurate representation of the house placements and helps in understanding the specific areas of life that the planets influence.

To create the Bhava Chalit Chart, the degrees of the Ascendant and the cusps of each house are noted. Then, the planets' positions are compared with these degrees to determine their house placements in the Bhava Chalit Chart. The resulting chart shows the modified positions of the planets based on this calculation.

The Bhava Chalit Chart is primarily used for fine-tuning the interpretation of planetary influences in different areas of life. It can reveal additional insights about the specific houses and their significations in a person's life. By comparing the positions of planets in the Rashi chart and the Bhava Chalit Chart, astrologers gain a more comprehensive understanding of how the planets manifest their effects in different life domains.

It's important to note that the Bhava Chalit Chart is not used in all astrological traditions or by all astrologers. Some astrologers prefer to focus solely on the Rashi chart for their interpretations, while others utilize both charts for a more detailed analysis. The decision to use the Bhava Chalit Chart is based on individual astrologer's preferences and the specific astrological system being followed.

Rudraksha beads And Zodiac Signs:

Rudraksha beads are sacred seeds derived from the Rudraksha tree (botanical name: Elaeocarpus ganitrus). They hold significant spiritual and astrological importance in Hinduism and are believed to possess various healing and protective properties. Each Rudraksha bead is associated with a specific ruling planet and is said to resonate with the energies of that planet.

In astrology, the connection between Rudraksha beads and the 12 Rashis (Zodiac signs) is often considered in determining which Rudraksha is suitable for an individual based on their Rashi. The correlation between Rudraksha and Rashis is believed to enhance positive energies, balance planetary influences, and promote overall well-being.

Let's explore the Rudraksha beads associated with each Rashi:

1. Aries (Mesha Rashi):

Rudraksha: 3 Mukhi Rudraksha

Benefits: Enhances courage, self-confidence, and leadership qualities.

2. Taurus (Vrishabha Rashi):
Rudraksha: 6 Mukhi Rudraksha
Benefits: Promotes abundance, wealth, and material prosperity.

3. Gemini (Mithuna Rashi):
Rudraksha: 4 Mukhi Rudraksha
Benefits: Enhances communication skills, intelligence, and creativity.

4. Cancer (Karka Rashi):
Rudraksha: 2 Mukhi Rudraksha
Benefits: Nurtures emotional well-being, enhances relationships, and brings harmony.

5. Leo (Simha Rashi):
Rudraksha: 1 Mukhi Rudraksha (rare and highly revered) or 12 Mukhi Rudraksha
Benefits: Enhances leadership qualities, confidence, and spiritual growth.

6. Virgo (Kanya Rashi):
Rudraksha: 5 Mukhi Rudraksha
Benefits: Promotes good health, intellect, and spiritual growth.

7. Libra (Tula Rashi):
Rudraksha: 6 Mukhi Rudraksha
Benefits: Brings balance, harmony, and success in relationships.

8. Scorpio (Vrishchika Rashi):
Rudraksha: 9 Mukhi Rudraksha

Benefits: Offers protection, removes obstacles, and promotes spiritual growth.

9. Sagittarius (Dhanu Rashi):

Rudraksha: 12 Mukhi Rudraksha

Benefits: Enhances wisdom, intuition, and spiritual knowledge.

10. Capricorn (Makara Rashi):

Rudraksha: 10 Mukhi Rudraksha

Benefits: Promotes success, prosperity, and removes negative energies.

11. Aquarius (Kumbha Rashi):

Rudraksha: 11 Mukhi Rudraksha

Benefits: Enhances creativity, intellectual pursuits, and spiritual growth.

12. Pisces (Meena Rashi):

Rudraksha: 14 Mukhi Rudraksha

Benefits: Facilitates spiritual growth, brings peace, and protects against negative energies.

It's important to note that while these associations between Rudraksha and Rashis are commonly followed, individual consultations with an experienced astrologer or spiritual guide are recommended to determine the most suitable Rudraksha.

List of Nakshatras along with their corresponding Rudraksha beads:

Here is a list of Nakshatras along with their corresponding Rudraksha beads and their associated benefits:

1. Ashwini Nakshatra:

   Rudraksha: 1 Mukhi Rudraksha

   Benefits: Enhances leadership qualities, boosts self-confidence, and promotes spiritual growth.

2. Bharani Nakshatra:

   Rudraksha: 2 Mukhi Rudraksha

   Benefits: Promotes emotional well-being, brings harmony in relationships, and enhances creativity.

3. Krittika Nakshatra:

   Rudraksha: 3 Mukhi Rudraksha

   Benefits: Boosts courage, improves focus and concentration, and brings success in endeavors.

4. Rohini Nakshatra:

   Rudraksha: 4 Mukhi Rudraksha

   Benefits: Enhances communication skills, brings abundance and prosperity, and promotes self-expression.

5. Mrigashirsha Nakshatra:

   Rudraksha: 5 Mukhi Rudraksha

   Benefits: Promotes good health, brings balance, and enhances spiritual growth.

6. Ardra Nakshatra:

   Rudraksha: 6 Mukhi Rudraksha

Benefits: Enhances intellect, brings harmony, and removes obstacles.

7. Punarvasu Nakshatra:

Rudraksha: 7 Mukhi Rudraksha

Benefits: Brings luck and fortune, promotes abundance, and protects against negative energies.

8. Pushya Nakshatra:

Rudraksha: 8 Mukhi Rudraksha

Benefits: Enhances wealth and prosperity, brings success in business endeavors, and offers protection.

9. Ashlesha Nakshatra:

Rudraksha: 9 Mukhi Rudraksha

Benefits: Removes obstacles and negativity, promotes spiritual growth, and brings emotional stability.

10. Magha Nakshatra:

Rudraksha: 10 Mukhi Rudraksha

Benefits: Enhances authority and leadership qualities, brings success in career and endeavors.

11. Purva Phalguni Nakshatra:

Rudraksha: 11 Mukhi Rudraksha

Benefits: Promotes love and harmony, enhances creativity and artistic abilities, and brings prosperity.

12. Uttara Phalguni Nakshatra:

Rudraksha: 12 Mukhi Rudraksha

Benefits: Enhances confidence and charisma, brings success and recognition, and promotes spiritual growth.

13. Hasta Nakshatra:

Rudraksha: 13 Mukhi Rudraksha

Benefits: Enhances intuition and psychic abilities, brings protection and blessings, and promotes spiritual evolution.

14. Chitra Nakshatra:

Rudraksha: 14 Mukhi Rudraksha

Benefits: Enhances charm and charisma, brings success in endeavors, and offers protection against negative energies.

15. Swati Nakshatra:

Rudraksha: 15 Mukhi Rudraksha

Benefits: Promotes clarity of thought, brings wisdom and spiritual growth, and offers protection.

16. Vishakha Nakshatra:

Rudraksha: 16 Mukhi Rudraksha

Benefits: Enhances communication skills, brings success in relationships and partnerships, and offers protection.

17. Anuradha Nakshatra:

Rudraksha: 17 Mukhi Rudraksha

Benefits: Brings prosperity and success in endeavors, enhances leadership qualities, and promotes spiritual growth.

18. Jyeshtha Nakshatra:

Rudraksha: 18 Mukhi Rudraksha

Benefits: enhance leadership qualities, boost self-confidence, and attract success in various endeavours.

19. Mula Nakshatra:

Rudraksha: 19 Mukhi Rudraksha

Benefits: Enhances spiritual knowledge, brings protection from negative energies, and promotes self-realization.

20. Purva Ashadha Nakshatra:

Rudraksha: 20 Mukhi Rudraksha

Benefits: Enhances leadership qualities, brings success in endeavors, and promotes spiritual growth.

21. Uttara Ashadha Nakshatra:

Rudraksha: 21 Mukhi Rudraksha

Benefits: Enhances wisdom and knowledge, promotes success and recognition, and offers protection.

22. Shravana Nakshatra:

Rudraksha: 22 Mukhi Rudraksha

Benefits: Enhances spiritual growth, brings protection and blessings, and promotes success in endeavors.

23. Dhanishta Nakshatra:

Rudraksha: 23 Mukhi Rudraksha

Benefits: Enhances abundance and prosperity, brings success in career and endeavors, and offers protection.

24. Shatabhisha Nakshatra:

Rudraksha: 24 Mukhi Rudraksha

Benefits: Enhances intuition and psychic abilities, brings protection and blessings, and promotes spiritual evolution.

25. Purva Bhadrapada Nakshatra:

Rudraksha: 25 Mukhi Rudraksha

Benefits: Enhances spiritual growth and knowledge, brings protection and blessings, and promotes success.

26. Uttara Bhadrapada Nakshatra:

Rudraksha: 26 Mukhi Rudraksha

Benefits: Enhances spiritual awareness, brings protection and blessings, and promotes self-realization.

27. Revati Nakshatra:

Rudraksha: 27 Mukhi Rudraksha

Benefits: Enhances spiritual growth and knowledge, brings protection and blessings, and promotes success and prosperity.

Please note that these associations between Rudraksha beads and Nakshatras are based on traditional beliefs and practices. Individual consultations with an experienced astrologer or spiritual guide are recommended for personalized guidance and selection of the most suitable Rudraksha based on your specific needs and circumstances.

Gemstones with specific Rashis (zodiac signs):

Gemstones are often associated with specific Rashis (zodiac signs) in astrology. Here is a list of gemstones commonly recommended for each Rashi:

1. Aries (Mesha):
   - Gemstone: Red Coral (Moonga)

- Benefits: Enhances courage, vitality, and leadership qualities.

2. Taurus (Vrishabha):
   - Gemstone: Diamond (Heera)
   - Benefits: Promotes luxury, material wealth, and harmonious relationships.

3. Gemini (Mithuna):
   - Gemstone: Emerald (Panna)
   - Benefits: Enhances intellect, communication skills, and business success.

4. Cancer (Karka):
   - Gemstone: Pearl (Moti)
   - Benefits: Promotes emotional healing, intuition, and domestic harmony.

5. Leo (Simha):
   - Gemstone: Ruby (Manik)
   - Benefits: Enhances confidence, creativity, and leadership abilities.

6. Virgo (Kanya):
   - Gemstone: Emerald (Panna)
   - Benefits: Promotes analytical thinking, communication, and healing abilities.

7. Libra (Tula):
   - Gemstone: Diamond (Heera)
   - Benefits: Enhances beauty, charm, and harmonious relationships.

8. Scorpio (Vrishchika):
   - Gemstone: Red Coral (Moonga)

- Benefits: Promotes courage, passion, and protection from negative energies.

9. Sagittarius (Dhanu):
   - Gemstone: Yellow Sapphire (Pukhraj)
   - Benefits: Enhances wisdom, prosperity, and spiritual growth.

10. Capricorn (Makara):
    - Gemstone: Blue Sapphire (Neelam)
    - Benefits: Promotes discipline, focus, and success in professional endeavors.

11. Aquarius (Kumbha):
    - Gemstone: Blue Sapphire (Neelam)
    - Benefits: Enhances intuition, intellectual abilities, and spiritual growth.

12. Pisces (Meena):
    - Gemstone: Yellow Sapphire (Pukhraj)
    - Benefits: Promotes compassion, spiritual growth, and material prosperity.

It's important to note that wearing gemstones should be done after consulting with a knowledgeable astrologer who can assess your birth chart and recommend the most suitable gemstone based on your individual planetary positions and energies. Gemstones can have a powerful impact on an individual's life, so it's crucial to seek professional guidance before wearing them.

Gemstones with specific Nakshatras (lunar constellations):

Gemstones are also associated with specific Nakshatras (lunar constellations) in astrology. Here is a list of gemstones commonly recommended for each Nakshatra:

1. Ashwini Nakshatra:
   - Gemstone: Ketu's Gem (Cat's Eye)
   - Benefits: Provides protection, spiritual growth, and intuition.
2. Bharani Nakshatra:
   - Gemstone: Venus' Gem (Diamond)
   - Benefits: Enhances beauty, charm, and material prosperity.
3. Krittika Nakshatra:
   - Gemstone: Sun's Gem (Ruby)
   - Benefits: Promotes leadership, confidence, and vitality.
4. Rohini Nakshatra:
   - Gemstone: Moon's Gem (Pearl)
   - Benefits: Enhances emotional healing, intuition, and nurturing qualities.
5. Mrigashirsha Nakshatra:
   - Gemstone: Mars' Gem (Red Coral)
   - Benefits: Promotes courage, energy, and passion.
6. Ardra Nakshatra:
   - Gemstone: Rahu's Gem (Hessonite)

- Benefits: Provides protection, spiritual growth, and clarity of thought.

7. Punarvasu Nakshatra:
    - Gemstone: Jupiter's Gem (Yellow Sapphire)
    - Benefits: Enhances wisdom, knowledge, and spiritual growth.

8. Pushya Nakshatra:
    - Gemstone: Saturn's Gem (Blue Sapphire)
    - Benefits: Promotes discipline, focus, and karmic balance.

9. Ashlesha Nakshatra:
    - Gemstone: Mercury's Gem (Emerald)
    - Benefits: Enhances intellect, communication skills, and business success.

10. Magha Nakshatra:
    - Gemstone: Ketu's Gem (Cat's Eye)
    - Benefits: Provides protection, spiritual growth, and intuition.

11. Purva Phalguni Nakshatra:
    - Gemstone: Venus' Gem (Diamond)
    - Benefits: Enhances beauty, charm, and material prosperity.

12. Uttara Phalguni Nakshatra:
    - Gemstone: Sun's Gem (Ruby)
    - Benefits: Promotes leadership, confidence, and vitality.

13. Hasta Nakshatra:
    - Gemstone: Moon's Gem (Pearl)

- Benefits: Enhances emotional healing, intuition, and nurturing qualities.

14. Chitra Nakshatra:
   - Gemstone: Mars' Gem (Red Coral)
   - Benefits: Promotes courage, energy, and passion.

15. Swati Nakshatra:
   - Gemstone: Rahu's Gem (Hessonite)
   - Benefits: Provides protection, spiritual growth, and clarity of thought.

16. Vishakha Nakshatra:
   - Gemstone: Jupiter's Gem (Yellow Sapphire)
   - Benefits: Enhances wisdom, knowledge, and spiritual growth.

17. Anuradha Nakshatra:
   - Gemstone: Saturn's Gem (Blue Sapphire)
   - Benefits: Promotes discipline, focus, and karmic balance.

18. Jyeshtha Nakshatra:
   - Gemstone: Mercury's Gem (Emerald)
   - Benefits: Enhances intellect, communication skills, and business success.

19. Moola Nakshatra:
   - Gemstone: Ketu's Gem (Cat's Eye)
   - Benefits: Provides protection, spiritual growth, and intuition.

20. Purva Ashadha Nakshatra:
   - Gemstone: Venus' Gem (Diamond)

- Benefits: Enhances beauty, charm, and material prosperity.

21. Uttarashada Nakshatra:
   - Gemstone: Sun's Gem (Ruby)
   - Benefits: Enhances vitality, leadership qualities, and success.

Sure! Here is the continuation of gemstones with Nakshatras:

22. Shravana Nakshatra:
   - Gemstone: Moon's Gem (Pearl)
   - Benefits: Enhances emotional healing, intuition, and nurturing qualities.

23. Dhanishta Nakshatra:
   - Gemstone: Mars' Gem (Red Coral)
   - Benefits: Promotes courage, energy, and passion.

24. Shatabhisha Nakshatra:
   - Gemstone: Rahu's Gem (Hessonite)
   - Benefits: Provides protection, spiritual growth, and clarity of thought.

25. Purva Bhadrapada Nakshatra:
   - Gemstone: Jupiter's Gem (Yellow Sapphire)
   - Benefits: Enhances wisdom, knowledge, and spiritual growth.

26. Uttara Bhadrapada Nakshatra:
   - Gemstone: Saturn's Gem (Blue Sapphire)
   - Benefits: Promotes discipline, focus, and karmic balance.

27. Revati Nakshatra:

- Gemstone: Mercury's Gem (Emerald)
- Benefits: Enhances intellect, communication skills, and business success.

It's important to note that while these gemstones are associated with specific Nakshatras, individual birth chart analysis and consultation with a qualified astrologer is recommended for personalized gemstone recommendations. The suitability and effectiveness of a gemstone may vary based on an individual's unique astrological factors and planetary placements.

Doshas in Astrology:

In Vedic astrology, there are several doshas that are considered when analyzing a person's birth chart. These doshas indicate certain imbalances or afflictions that can affect different areas of life. Here are some of the commonly known doshas:

1. Mangal Dosha (Manglik Dosha): Associated with the placement of Mars in specific houses or in conjunction with certain planets. It is believed to impact marital relationships.

2. Kaal Sarp Dosha: Occurs when all planets are situated between Rahu and Ketu, forming a specific alignment. It is associated with obstacles and challenges in various aspects of life.

3. Pitra Dosha: Related to ancestral lineage and can occur when there are unresolved ancestral issues or if

offerings and rituals for ancestors have been neglected. It may impact familial harmony and success.

4. Shani Dosha (Shani Sade Sati): Associated with the planet Saturn and its transit over the natal moon. It is believed to bring challenges and lessons related to discipline, hard work, and responsibilities.

5. Nadi Dosha: Occurs when the Nadi (pulse) of both partners in a marriage match, indicating potential health issues and conflicts in the relationship.

6. Bhakoot Dosha: Related to the moon signs of the couple and their compatibility. It can indicate challenges in emotional bonding and harmony.

7. Grahana Dosha: Associated with the occurrence of solar or lunar eclipses during specific periods. It is believed to bring inauspicious influences and may require specific remedies.

8. Kemadruma Dosha: Occurs when there are no planets on either side of the moon in the birth chart. It is associated with emotional challenges and instability.

9. Chandra-Mangal Dosha: Pertains to the placement of the moon and Mars in conjunction or opposition, indicating potential conflicts and temperamental issues.

It's important to note that the impact and severity of these doshas can vary based on various factors, such as the overall strength of the birth chart, the influence of other planets, and individual circumstances. A qualified astrologer can provide detailed insights and remedies based on the specific doshas present in a person's chart.

Var (weekday) association for each planet:

In Vedic astrology, the concept of "Var" refers to the weekday association of each planet. Each planet is assigned a specific day of the week, and this association is considered significant in interpreting planetary influences and determining auspicious or inauspicious times for various activities. Here is the Var (weekday) association for each planet:

1. Sun (Surya): Sunday (Ravivar)
2. Moon (Chandra): Monday (Somvar)
3. Mars (Mangal): Tuesday (Mangalvar)
4. Mercury (Budha): Wednesday (Budhvar)
5. Jupiter (Brihaspati): Thursday (Guruvar)
6. Venus (Shukra): Friday (Shukravar)
7. Saturn (Shani): Saturday (Shanivar)

These associations are considered while determining the favorable and unfavorable days for specific activities, such as performing rituals, starting new ventures, or wearing gemstones. The day associated with a particular planet is believed to enhance or align with the energy and qualities represented by that planet.

It's worth mentioning that in some regional or individual astrological traditions, there might be slight variations in the Var associations for certain planets. However, the above-mentioned associations are widely accepted and followed in Vedic astrology.

Numerical associations for the planets:

In Vedic astrology, each planet is associated with a numerical value. These numerical values are used in various calculations and astrological interpretations. Here are the numerical associations for the planets:
1. Sun (Surya): 1
2. Moon (Chandra): 2
3. Mars (Mangal): 9
4. Mercury (Budha): 5
5. Jupiter (Brihaspati): 3
6. Venus (Shukra): 6
7. Saturn (Shani): 8
8. Rahu (North Node of the Moon): 4
9. Ketu (South Node of the Moon): 7

These numerical associations play a role in determining planetary strengths, compatibility between planets, and various other astrological calculations. They are also used in the process of assigning numerical values to letters in the study of numerology and the calculation of birth charts.

Associations of planets with body parts:

In Vedic astrology, each planet is associated with specific body parts. These associations are based on the energies and influences that the planets represent. Here are the traditional associations of planets with body parts:

1. Sun (Surya): Heart, eyes, head, spine, and vitality.

2. Moon (Chandra): Mind, emotions, chest, breasts, and digestive system.

3. Mars (Mangal): Muscles, head, blood, and energy levels.

4. Mercury (Budha): Nervous system, speech, hands, arms, and skin.

5. Jupiter (Brihaspati): Liver, thighs, hips, and fat metabolism.

6. Venus (Shukra): Reproductive system, kidneys, throat, and hormonal balance.

7. Saturn (Shani): Bones, teeth, knees, joints, and aging process.

8. Rahu (North Node of the Moon): Undesirable effects on body parts associated with other planets.

9. Ketu (South Node of the Moon): Undesirable effects on body parts associated with other planets.

It's important to note that these associations are general in nature and may vary in different astrological traditions or interpretations. Additionally, other factors in the birth chart, such as the Ascendant and planetary aspects, can also influence the health and well-being of specific body parts.

Associations of planets with directions:

In Vedic astrology, each planet is associated with specific directions. These directional associations are based on the energies and influences that the planets represent. Here are the traditional associations of planets with directions:
1. Sun (Surya): East
2. Moon (Chandra): North-West
3. Mars (Mangal): South
4. Mercury (Budha): North
5. Jupiter (Brihaspati): North-East
6. Venus (Shukra): South-East
7. Saturn (Shani): West
8. Rahu (North Node of the Moon): South-West
9. Ketu (South Node of the Moon): South

These directional associations can be used in various astrological practices, such as Vastu Shastra (Indian system of architecture) or determining the placement of planetary influences in a horoscope. It's important to note that these associations are traditional and may vary in different astrological systems or interpretations.

Associations of planets with animals:

In astrology, planets are sometimes associated with animals based on their symbolic meanings and characteristics. These associations can vary across different cultural and astrological traditions. Here are some common associations of planets with animals:

1. Sun: Lion - The Sun is often associated with the majestic and powerful lion, representing leadership, courage, and vitality.

2. Moon: Rabbit - The Moon is associated with the gentle and intuitive nature of the rabbit, symbolizing sensitivity, nurturing, and emotional depth.

3. Mars: Ram - Mars is often associated with the energetic and assertive qualities of the ram, representing courage, ambition, and strength.

4. Mercury: Monkey - Mercury's association with the quick-witted and clever monkey reflects its qualities of intelligence, agility, and adaptability.

5. Jupiter: Elephant - Jupiter's association with the wise and benevolent elephant symbolizes wisdom, abundance, and good fortune.

6. Venus: Dove - Venus is associated with the peaceful and harmonious nature of the dove, representing love, beauty, and gentleness.

7. Saturn: Crow - Saturn's association with the crow represents its qualities of discipline, patience, and wisdom.

8. Rahu (North Node of the Moon): Serpent/Dragon - Rahu's association with the serpent or dragon reflects its mysterious and transformative nature.

9. Ketu (South Node of the Moon): Eagle - Ketu's association with the eagle represents its qualities of spirituality, detachment, and keen insight.

These associations serve as symbolic representations and can be used to gain insights into the planetary energies and their effects in astrology. However, it's important to note that these associations may vary in different astrological systems and interpretations.

Associations of planets with flowers:

In astrology, planets are sometimes associated with flowers based on their symbolic meanings and qualities. These associations can vary across different cultural and astrological traditions. Here are some common associations of planets with flowers:

1. Sun: Sunflower - The Sun is associated with the vibrant and radiant sunflower, symbolizing warmth, vitality, and power.

2. Moon: Lotus - The Moon is often associated with the delicate and ethereal lotus flower, representing purity, intuition, and emotional depth.

3. Mars: Red Rose - Mars is associated with the passionate and fiery red rose, symbolizing love, desire, and courage.

4. Mercury: Lily - Mercury's association with the graceful and elegant lily reflects its qualities of intellect, communication, and beauty.

5. Jupiter: Jasmine - Jupiter's association with the fragrant jasmine flower represents its qualities of abundance, wisdom, and spirituality.

6. Venus: Rose - Venus is often associated with the beautiful and romantic rose, symbolizing love, beauty, and grace.

7. Saturn: Black Orchid - Saturn's association with the mysterious and rare black orchid represents its qualities of discipline, perseverance, and depth.

8. Rahu (North Node of the Moon): Blue Water Lily - Rahu's association with the exotic and enchanting blue water lily reflects its mystical and transformative nature.

9. Ketu (South Node of the Moon): White Chrysanthemum - Ketu's association with the serene and pure white chrysanthemum represents its qualities of spirituality, detachment, and transcendence.

These associations provide symbolic connections between the planets and the qualities associated with each flower. However, it's important to note that these associations may vary in different astrological systems and interpretations.

Associations of planets with plants:

In astrology, planets are sometimes associated with plants based on their symbolic meanings and characteristics. These associations can vary across different astrological traditions and interpretations. Here are some common associations of planets with plants:

1. Sun: Sunflower - The Sun is associated with the vibrant and radiant sunflower, symbolizing warmth, energy, and vitality.

2. Moon: White Jasmine - The Moon is often associated with the delicate and fragrant white jasmine, representing sensitivity, intuition, and emotional nourishment.

3. Mars: Red Aloe Vera - Mars is associated with the resilient and healing red aloe vera plant, symbolizing strength, courage, and vitality.

4. Mercury: Green Herbs (such as mint, parsley, or dill) - Mercury's association with green herbs reflects its qualities of communication, intellect, adaptability, and versatility.

5. Jupiter: Oak Tree - Jupiter is associated with the majestic and expansive oak tree, symbolizing growth, abundance, wisdom, and spiritual strength.

6. Venus: Rose - Venus is often associated with the beautiful and romantic rose, representing love, beauty, harmony, and sensual pleasures.

7. Saturn: Cypress Tree - Saturn's association with the tall and enduring cypress tree represents its qualities of discipline, endurance, stability, and maturity.

8. Rahu (North Node of the Moon): Cannabis - Rahu's association with cannabis represents its transformative and illusionary nature, associated with altered states of consciousness and seeking higher knowledge.

9. Ketu (South Node of the Moon): Neem Tree - Ketu's association with the neem tree reflects its purifying and transformative qualities, often associated with spiritual growth and healing.

These associations provide symbolic connections between the planets and the qualities associated with each plant. However, it's important to note that these associations may vary in different astrological systems and interpretations.

Associations of planets with colors:

In astrology, planets are often associated with specific colors based on their energetic qualities and symbolism. These associations can vary across different astrological traditions and interpretations. Here are some common associations of planets with colors:

1. Sun: Gold, Orange, Yellow - The Sun is associated with bright and vibrant colors symbolizing warmth, vitality, and energy.

2. Moon: White, Silver - The Moon is often associated with soft and luminous colors representing purity, intuition, and emotional sensitivity.

3. Mars: Red - Mars is associated with the bold and fiery color red, symbolizing energy, passion, and courage.

4. Mercury: Green, Yellow - Mercury's associations include the lively and versatile colors green and yellow, representing communication, intellect, and adaptability.

5. Jupiter: Yellow, Sky Blue - Jupiter is associated with expansive and optimistic colors like yellow and sky blue, symbolizing wisdom, abundance, and growth.

6. Venus: Green, Pink - Venus is often associated with the harmonious and gentle colors green and pink, representing love, beauty, and artistic expression.

7. Saturn: Black, Dark Blue - Saturn's associations include the solemn and grounding colors black and dark blue, symbolizing discipline, structure, and wisdom.

8. Rahu (North Node of the Moon): Smoky Grey, Black - Rahu is associated with smoky grey and black, representing illusion, mystery, and transformation.

9. Ketu (South Node of the Moon): Brown, Ash Grey - Ketu's associations include earthy colors like brown and ash grey, symbolizing spirituality, detachment, and inner transformation.

These color associations provide symbolic connections between the planets and the energetic qualities represented by each color. However, it's important to note that these associations may vary in different astrological systems and interpretations.

Associations of planets with sounds:

In astrology, planets are often associated with specific sounds or vibrations that resonate with their energetic qualities. These sound associations can vary across different astrological traditions and interpretations. Here are some common associations of planets with sounds:

1. Sun: "Ah" - The Sun is associated with the sound "Ah," which represents vitality, life force, and creative energy.

2. Moon: "Aum" or "Ch" - The Moon is often associated with the sound "Aum" or "Ch," which symbolizes the cosmic sound and the rhythm of life.

3. Mars: "K" or "Ksh" - Mars is associated with the sounds "K" or "Ksh," representing strength, assertion, and courage.

4. Mercury: "H" or "Th" - Mercury's associations include the sounds "H" or "Th," symbolizing communication, intellect, and mental agility.

5. Jupiter: "G" or "Dh" - Jupiter is associated with the sounds "G" or "Dh," representing expansion, abundance, and spiritual wisdom.

6. Venus: "Sh" - Venus is often associated with the sound "Sh," symbolizing love, beauty, and harmony.

7. Saturn: "S" or "Sh" - Saturn's associations include the sounds "S" or "Sh," representing discipline, structure, and karmic lessons.

8. Rahu (North Node of the Moon): "Th" or "Ph" - Rahu is associated with the sounds "Th" or "Ph," symbolizing illusions, mystery, and transformative experiences.

9. Ketu (South Node of the Moon): "Ch" or "Ksh" - Ketu's associations include the sounds "Ch" or "Ksh," representing spiritual liberation, detachment, and inner transformation.

These sound associations provide a way to connect with the energetic qualities of the planets and create harmonious vibrations. However, it's important to note that these associations may vary in different astrological systems and interpretations.

Mantras associated with each planet:

In astrology and spiritual practices, specific mantras are often associated with each planet. Chanting these mantras is believed to invoke the energy and blessings of the respective planet. Here are some commonly used mantras associated with each planet:

1. Sun: "Om Suryaya Namaha" - This mantra is dedicated to the Sun, representing divine light, energy, and vitality.

2. Moon: "Om Chandraya Namaha" - This mantra is associated with the Moon, symbolizing emotional well-being, intuition, and nourishment.

3. Mars: "Om Mangalaya Namaha" or "Om Angarakaya Namaha" - These mantras are chanted to invoke the energy of Mars, representing courage, strength, and determination.

4. Mercury: "Om Budhaya Namaha" - This mantra is associated with Mercury, symbolizing intelligence, communication, and mental clarity.

5. Jupiter: "Om Gurave Namaha" - This mantra is dedicated to Jupiter, representing wisdom, abundance, and spiritual growth.

6. Venus: "Om Shukraya Namaha" - This mantra is chanted to invoke the energy of Venus, symbolizing love, beauty, and harmony.

7. Saturn: "Om Shanaischaraya Namaha" - This mantra is associated with Saturn, representing discipline, patience, and karmic lessons.

8. Rahu (North Node of the Moon): "Om Rahave Namaha" - This mantra is chanted to invoke the energy of Rahu, symbolizing transformation, spiritual growth, and overcoming challenges.

9. Ketu (South Node of the Moon): "Om Ketave Namaha" - This mantra is associated with Ketu, representing spiritual liberation, inner transformation, and letting go of attachments.

Chanting these mantras with devotion and intention is believed to align oneself with the qualities and blessings of the respective planet. It is recommended to learn the pronunciation and correct intonation of the mantras from a knowledgeable source to derive their full benefits.

how to chant mantras effectively:

Chanting mantras is a powerful practice for invoking specific energies and achieving various spiritual and personal goals. Here are some general guidelines on how to chant mantras effectively:

1. Find a Quiet and Sacred Space: Choose a peaceful and clean environment where you can sit comfortably

and focus without distractions. Create a sacred atmosphere by lighting incense or candles, if desired.

2. Proper Posture: Sit in a comfortable position, with your spine straight and relaxed. You can sit on a cushion or chair, whichever is most comfortable for you.

3. Set an Intention: Before starting the mantra, set a clear intention for your practice. It could be for healing, peace, spiritual growth, or any other specific purpose.

4. Relax and Center Yourself: Take a few deep breaths to calm your mind and relax your body. Let go of any tension or stress.

5. Begin with Pranayama: You can start your mantra chanting practice with a few rounds of deep breathing or pranayama exercises to further calm the mind and prepare for the chanting.

6. Focus on the Mantra: Begin chanting the mantra with full concentration and devotion. Repeat it aloud or silently, depending on your preference. Use a mala (prayer beads) to help keep count if desired.

7. Pronunciation and Rhythm: Pay attention to the correct pronunciation of the mantra. If you are unsure, it is recommended to learn from a knowledgeable teacher or use audio recordings to guide you. Chant the mantra with a steady rhythm and flow.

8. Engage the Mind: As you chant, try to immerse yourself fully in the sound and meaning of the mantra. Visualize the energy and qualities associated with it. Let the vibrations of the mantra resonate within you.

9. Maintain Focus and Devotion: Keep your focus on the mantra, allowing any distractions or thoughts to gently fade away. Maintain a sense of devotion and surrender to the practice.

10. Duration and Frequency: Start with a manageable duration, such as 5-10 minutes, and gradually increase it over time. You can practice chanting mantras daily or as often as you feel called to do so.

11. Closing the Practice: After completing your chanting session, take a few moments to sit in silence, absorbing the energy and vibrations generated by the practice. Offer gratitude for the experience.

Remember, the essence of mantra chanting lies not only in the repetition of words but in the intention, devotion, and connection you bring to the practice. It is a personal and sacred journey, so approach it with an open heart and sincere dedication.

The significance of 108:

In astrology and various spiritual traditions, the number 108 holds special significance. Here are a few interpretations of the significance of 108:

1. Spiritual Significance: The number 108 is considered sacred and divine in many spiritual practices. It is believed to represent the wholeness of existence, encompassing the divine, the universe, and the individual. Each digit in 108 has symbolic meaning: 1 represents the supreme consciousness, 0 represents

emptiness or completeness, and 8 represents infinity or eternity.

2. Astronomical Significance: There are several astronomical connections to the number 108. For example, the distance between the Earth and the Sun is about 108 times the diameter of the Sun. The average distance between the Earth and the Moon is approximately 108 times the diameter of the Moon.

3. Sacred Beads: In various spiritual traditions, especially in Hinduism and Buddhism, prayer or meditation malas (beads) often consist of 108 beads. The repetition of mantras or prayers using these beads is believed to help purify the mind and connect with the divine.

4. Energy Centers: According to some interpretations of yoga and Ayurveda, there are 108 energy channels, or nadis, converging to form the heart chakra. Chanting mantras or performing specific practices 108 times is believed to activate and balance these energy centers.

5. Time and Space: The number 108 is also associated with time and space. In ancient Indian cosmology, it is believed that there are 108 stages on the journey of the soul. Additionally, the number 108 is seen as the product of 12 (representing the zodiac signs or months) and 9 (representing the nine planets), symbolizing the entire cosmic order.

It's important to note that the significance of 108 may vary across different cultures and spiritual traditions. The number holds deep symbolism and is often considered auspicious, representing unity, cosmic harmony, and the divine presence.

Associations between planets and food:

While there are some traditional associations between planets and certain types of food in astrology, it's important to note that these associations may vary depending on different astrological traditions and individual interpretations. Here are some general associations between planets and food:

1. Sun: Sun is associated with vitality, energy, and strength. It is often linked to foods that are warming, energizing, and nourishing. Foods that are rich in vitamin D, such as citrus fruits, yellow vegetables, and grains, are sometimes associated with the Sun.

2. Moon: Moon is associated with emotions, comfort, and nourishment. It is often linked to foods that are cooling, soothing, and hydrating. Foods that are high in water content, such as cucumbers, melons, and leafy greens, are sometimes associated with the Moon.

3. Mars: Mars is associated with energy, passion, and assertiveness. It is often linked to foods that are spicy, stimulating, and energizing. Foods with strong flavors and heat, such as chili peppers, ginger, and garlic, are sometimes associated with Mars.

4. Mercury: Mercury is associated with communication, intellect, and agility. It is often linked to foods that are quick, light, and brain-boosting. Foods that are rich in Omega-3 fatty acids, such as fish, nuts, and seeds, are sometimes associated with Mercury.

5. Jupiter: Jupiter is associated with expansion, abundance, and wisdom. It is often linked to foods that are generous, nourishing, and flavorful. Foods that are rich in nutrients and promote overall well-being, such as whole grains, fruits, and nuts, are sometimes associated with Jupiter.

6. Venus: Venus is associated with love, beauty, and pleasure. It is often linked to foods that are indulgent, aesthetically pleasing, and luxurious. Foods that are sweet, rich, and visually appealing, such as chocolates, desserts, and gourmet dishes, are sometimes associated with Venus.

7. Saturn: Saturn is associated with discipline, structure, and simplicity. It is often linked to foods that are grounding, nutritious, and promote longevity. Foods that are high in fiber, protein, and antioxidants, such as whole grains, legumes, and vegetables, are sometimes associated with Saturn.

It's important to remember that these associations are symbolic in nature and should not be seen as strict dietary guidelines. Dietary choices should be based on individual preferences, nutritional needs, and ethical considerations.

Association of planets with Vata, Pitta and Kapha:

In Ayurveda, the traditional system of medicine in India, the three doshas - Vata, Pitta, and Kapha - are considered fundamental energies that influence the physical, mental, and emotional aspects of a person. While the doshas are primarily associated with the elements (Vata with Air and Ether, Pitta with Fire and Water, Kapha with Earth and Water), they can also be loosely associated with the planets. Here are some general associations:

1. Vata:

   - Planet: Mercury

   - Characteristics: Cold, dry, light, subtle, quick, mobile

   - Foods: Warm, grounding, nourishing foods to balance Vata, such as cooked grains, root vegetables, soups, stews, warm spices, ghee, and herbal teas.

2. Pitta:

   - Planet: Sun

   - Characteristics: Hot, intense, sharp, focused, transformative

   - Foods: Cooling, hydrating, and calming foods to balance Pitta, such as sweet fruits, leafy greens, cucumbers, coconut water, yogurt, and cooling herbs like coriander and mint.

3. Kapha:

- Planet: Moon
- Characteristics: Heavy, slow, steady, stable, cold, moist
- Foods: Warm, light, and stimulating foods to balance Kapha, such as spicy herbs and spices, light grains, legumes, bitter greens, cruciferous vegetables, and warming herbal teas.

It's important to note that these associations are not rigid rules, and individual constitutions may vary. Ayurveda emphasizes the balance of the doshas within each person, and diet and lifestyle choices should be made accordingly, considering one's unique constitution and imbalances. Consulting with an Ayurvedic practitioner can provide personalized guidance on diet and lifestyle for balancing the doshas.

Associations between planets and architecture:

In astrology, there is a connection between planets and various aspects of life, including architecture. While the primary focus of astrology is on individuals and their birth charts, certain planetary energies can be associated with architectural styles and preferences. Here are some associations between planets and architecture:

1. Sun: The Sun represents vitality, power, and self-expression. In architecture, it is associated with grand, bold designs, impressive structures, and buildings that make a statement. Sun-inspired architecture often

features large windows, open spaces, and dramatic elements.

2. Moon: The Moon represents emotions, intuition, and nurturing. Moon-inspired architecture tends to focus on comfort, coziness, and a sense of familiarity. It may incorporate soft, flowing lines, natural materials, and spaces that evoke a sense of emotional well-being.

3. Mercury: Mercury represents communication, intellect, and adaptability. In architecture, Mercury's influence can be seen in modern, innovative designs that incorporate technology and efficient use of space. It may involve open floor plans, flexible layouts, and designs that facilitate communication and intellectual engagement.

4. Venus: Venus represents beauty, harmony, and aesthetics. Venus-inspired architecture emphasizes elegance, balance, and visual appeal. It often incorporates artistic elements, attention to detail, and a sense of grace and refinement.

5. Mars: Mars represents energy, action, and assertiveness. Mars-inspired architecture may include bold, dynamic designs, structures with strong lines and angles, and buildings that exude a sense of strength and power.

6. Jupiter: Jupiter represents expansion, abundance, and higher knowledge. Jupiter-inspired architecture tends to be large-scale, with generous spaces and a focus on luxury and opulence. It may feature grand entrances,

high ceilings, and architectural details that convey a sense of abundance and prosperity.

7. Saturn: Saturn represents discipline, structure, and tradition. Saturn-inspired architecture often involves solid, enduring designs, with a focus on functionality and practicality. It may emphasize stability, durability, and architectural elements that stand the test of time.

These associations provide a general idea of how planetary energies can be reflected in architectural styles. However, it's important to note that individual birth charts and other astrological factors can influence personal preferences and the specific manifestation of these influences in architectural choices.

The associations between planets and chemical elements:

In astrology, there is a symbolic association between planets and chemical elements based on their characteristics and energies. Here are the associations between planets and chemical elements:

1. Sun: The Sun is associated with the element of Gold (Au). It represents power, vitality, and leadership.

2. Moon: The Moon is associated with the element of Silver (Ag). It represents emotions, intuition, and reflection.

3. Mercury: Mercury is associated with the element of Mercury (Hg). It represents communication, intellect, and adaptability.

4. Venus: Venus is associated with the element of Copper (Cu). It represents love, beauty, and harmony.

5. Mars: Mars is associated with the element of Iron (Fe). It represents energy, passion, and action.

6. Jupiter: Jupiter is associated with the element of Tin (Sn). It represents expansion, growth, and wisdom.

7. Saturn: Saturn is associated with the element of Lead (Pb). It represents structure, discipline, and responsibility.

8. Uranus: Uranus is associated with the element of Uranium (U). It represents innovation, revolution, and unpredictability.

9. Neptune: Neptune is associated with the element of Neptune (Np). It represents spirituality, imagination, and illusion.

10. Pluto: Pluto is associated with the element of Plutonium (Pu). It represents transformation, power, and intensity.

It's important to note that these associations are symbolic and metaphorical, connecting the qualities of the planets with the characteristics of the chemical elements.

Associations between planets and Kundalini chakras:

In Kundalini Yoga and certain spiritual traditions, there is an association between the planets and the seven main chakras, which are energy centers in the body. Here are the associations between planets and Kundalini chakras:

1. Saturn: Saturn is associated with the Root Chakra (Muladhara). It represents stability, grounding, and a sense of security.

2. Jupiter: Jupiter is associated with the Sacral Chakra (Svadhisthana). It represents creativity, abundance, and expansion of consciousness.

3. Mars: Mars is associated with the Solar Plexus Chakra (Manipura). It represents personal power, will, and courage.

4. Venus: Venus is associated with the Heart Chakra (Anahata). It represents love, compassion, and harmonious relationships.

5. Mercury: Mercury is associated with the Throat Chakra (Vishuddha). It represents communication, self-expression, and clarity of thought.

6. Moon: The Moon is associated with the Third Eye Chakra (Ajna). It represents intuition, inner wisdom, and psychic abilities.

7. Sun: The Sun is associated with the Crown Chakra (Sahasrara). It represents spiritual connection, higher consciousness, and enlightenment.

It's important to note that these associations serve as a guide and can vary in different spiritual traditions and practices. The purpose is to align and balance the energies of the planets and chakras to promote overall well-being and spiritual growth.

Associations between planets and birds:

In astrology, there are traditional associations between planets and birds based on their symbolism and qualities. Here are some common associations between planets and birds:

1. Sun: The association of the Sun is often linked to the Eagle, as it represents strength, power, and leadership.

2. Moon: The association of the Moon is often linked to the Owl, as it symbolizes wisdom, intuition, and the mysteries of the night.

3. Mars: The association of Mars is often linked to the Falcon, as it represents courage, action, and a strong predatory instinct.

4. Mercury: The association of Mercury is often linked to the Parrot, as it symbolizes intelligence, communication, and adaptability.

5. Jupiter: The association of Jupiter is often linked to the Peacock, as it represents abundance, expansion, and spiritual wisdom.

6. Venus: The association of Venus is often linked to the Dove, as it symbolizes love, harmony, and peacefulness.

7. Saturn: The association of Saturn is often linked to the Crow, as it represents wisdom, discipline, and transformation.

8. Rahu (North Node): The association of Rahu is often linked to the Vulture or Serpent, as it represents desires, obsessions, and hidden forces.

9. Ketu (South Node): The association of Ketu is often linked to the Owl or Serpent, as it symbolizes spirituality, intuition, and mystical experiences.

It's important to note that these associations can vary in different cultures and traditions. They are symbolic representations that highlight certain qualities or characteristics associated with each planet.

16. Conclusion:

In concluding this astrology book, we embark on a journey of self-discovery and cosmic exploration. We have delved into the intricate tapestry of the stars, deciphered the language of the planets, and unraveled the secrets of the zodiac signs. Throughout this journey, we have witnessed the profound influence of celestial bodies on our lives and gained insights into the mysteries of the universe.

Astrology is not merely a tool for prediction, but a profound system that offers guidance, self-awareness, and a deeper understanding of our place in the cosmos. It invites us to connect with the rhythms of the universe, to embrace our unique planetary configurations, and to harness the energies that surround us.

Through the pages of this book, we have explored the significance of each planet, the power of the zodiac signs, and the interplay of cosmic forces. We have uncovered the associations between planets and various aspects of life, from colors and gemstones to plants and body parts. We have witnessed the intricate dance of planets in our birth charts and learned how they shape our personalities, relationships, and life events.

Astrology is a powerful tool that empowers us to make informed decisions, navigate life's challenges, and tap into our inherent potentials. It offers a roadmap for self-discovery and a deeper connection with the universe. By embracing astrology, we open ourselves to the possibilities of growth, transformation, and alignment with the cosmic energies that surround us.

As we reach the end of this book, let us remember that astrology is a lifelong journey of exploration and learning. It invites us to continuously deepen our understanding, refine our interpretations, and adapt to the ever-changing celestial patterns. May this book serve as a foundation for your astrological journey, guiding you towards self-awareness, enlightenment, and a greater connection with the cosmos.

May the stars continue to illuminate your path and may astrology be a source of inspiration, guidance, and empowerment in your life's journey.

With heartfelt gratitude and cosmic blessings,

Shivnath Shinde.

Astrologer.

Gmail: shivnathshinde.official@gmail.com

17. References :

1. For "Bhrigu Samhita" by T.M. Rao:
   - In-text citation: According to T.M. Rao's "Bhrigu Samhita" (April 2008),...
   - Bibliography/Reference entry: Rao, T.M. (2008. Bhrigu Samhita. Publisher.
3. For YouTube videos by Amit Kudwal:
   - In-text citation: In a YouTube video by Amit Kudwal (2020),
   - Bibliography/Reference entry: Kudwal, Amit.[https://www.youtube.com/channel/UCnGiZp6hVmJhtpPYZcS509Q]. YouTube.

"Please Rate This Book On Amazon To Help Others"

The End

Made in the USA
Coppell, TX
08 April 2025